Feeling Jewish

Feeling Jewish

(a Book for Just About Anyone)

DEVORAH BAUM

Yale UNIVERSITY PRESS

New Haven and London

Published with assistance from the foundation established in memory of
Philip Hamilton McMillan of the Class of 1894, Yale College.

Yale University Press books may be purchased in quantity for educational,
business, or promotional use. For information, please e-mail sales.press@
yale.edu (U.S. office) or sales@yaleup.co.uk (U.K. office).

Set in Janson Roman type by IDS Infotech, Ltd.
Printed in the United States of America.

Library of Congress Control Number: 2016958619
ISBN 978-0-300-21244-0 (hardcover : alk. paper)

A catalogue record for this book is available from the British Library.

This paper meets the requirements of ANSI/NISO Z39.48-1992
(Permanence of Paper).

10 9 8 7 6 5 4 3 2 1

For Shirley and Geoffrey, my parents

From the outside, you've always looked like an insider.

—MATTHEW ALUN RAY, *In the Absence of Human Beauty*

Contents

Contents

Feeling Jewish

Introduction

How Are You?

If we truly *knew* which emotions we should have, we would no
longer feel like having any.

—REI TERADA, *Feeling in Theory*

There's a joke Jews sometimes like to tell about the moment when
two non-Jews, Tom and Dick, bump into each other in the street:

TOM: How are you?
DICK: Fine, thanks.

Ha! Just imagine *not* being Jewish! "Fine, thanks!" What a blast!

What the joke's really about, of course, is Jewish fantasies of how
social relations between gentiles must surely be. So breezy. So easy.
Straightforward questions always answered positively, identities
forever stable, no one even suspecting it might be otherwise. No
one, that is, except the teller of a joke hinting at just such a suspicion . . . what if Tom and Dick *are* in fact hiding something? Does
Tom *really* want to know how Dick is feeling? And does Dick really

I

feel "fine," or is "fine" his way of not sharing how he feels, or possibly his way of not having to feel anything at all? "How are you?" "Fine. No feelings here." As if feelings, properly felt, threatened to undermine one's outward assurances, opening up an unwanted interrogation of the self.

Yet no one in their right mind genuinely expects the question to be taken literally. "The exchange, 'How are you?'—'Fine,'" writes Stephen Frosh, "is a sophisticated social interaction, in which the first speaker expresses some fleeting recognition of the status of the other person as a human being, and the second speaker thanks them for this, indicates that the message has been understood, shows awareness of the social conventions that make interactions of this kind possible and proceeds with business."[1] Affable but professional, that's how we keep things running smoothly. So while the question raises the possibility that there *might* be some other answer than the one habitually received, everyone knows that there's only one answer you're supposed to give. Someone who fails to understand that, who takes the question seriously every time it's asked or uses the question as an opportunity for introspection, is a social irritant—either an outsider who has not yet learned the rules of civil discourse, or else shockingly self-involved.

I mention this somewhat shamefully knowing I'm exactly the type of person to go to pieces when faced with "how are you?" *I'm* a social irritant. So what is it about the most everyday of interactions that flusters me? It's not as though I don't know the script. Do I suspect that "fine" won't be deemed credible in my case? That no one will believe me? That the person asking the question already knows the answer better than I do? Or maybe it's that *I* don't deem "fine" a credible response. Fine, thanks? In *this* world? You have to be kidding.

If it's hard to give an honest account of one's own feelings, then it goes, or should go, without saying that no one can claim with any certainty to know what another person feels. Feelings seem an insurmountable border between ourselves and others. Although it's equally true that our feelings are precisely what we can and do seek to share with others. Or even if we would rather not share, our feelings have a tendency to escape us. Feelings give us away, endlessly troubling the boundary between our private and public lives.

Since at least Aristotle's day, however, it has been more customary to think of emotion as personal property; as that which not only belongs to but constitutes subjects as subjects.[2] On this account, my feelings are mine and mine alone. As such, whenever I feel unsure of myself, or uncertain what to think, I need only check the pulse of my feelings to regain a sense of self-possession and composure. My feelings, seen this way, are a measure of myself. They authenticate me by telling me who I am, what I believe, and where I stand.

Such a view of emotion lends epistemological import to feelings. Feelings, it advises, are not to be ignored. Given how intimately embodied our feelings are, it's easy to understand why such an idea of them should have taken hold. But do our feelings really offer us such self-assurance as the classical view implies? If so, then why do so many people seem to work so hard to avoid their feelings? And why is it that feelings are so often experienced ambivalently as those divisive and unsettling currents within our lives that can make us seem less rather than more knowable, or even strangers to ourselves? It's in opposition to the classical view of emotion, therefore, that Rei Terada has claimed that "we would have no emotions if we *were* subjects."[3] Not only, that is, do our emotions fail to guarantee our existence as unified selves, but they create a disturbance in us, a sense of instability. It is in this sense too that our feelings may fairly be described as *moving*—even if we don't always appreciate where it is they move us to.

Ugly Feelings

Certain people appear more readily moved than others. Such sensitivity has historically been accorded both positive and negative values. The eighteenth-century "age of sensibility," for example, and its progression into the nineteenth-century era of romanticism, was a time when feelings were said to be so stirring, so terrifyingly *sublime*, as to get out of hand—yet this was also a period that yielded tropes and figures of "fine feeling," whereby man's capacity for sentiment was considered proof and validation of his superiority over, among other things, the rise of the machines.

But being moved has not always been considered sublime, and not always considered fine—or not, at least, fine for everyone. In *Ugly Feelings* Sianne Ngai describes a different age of sensibility, an age neither beautiful nor sublime, but more, in a word, *machinic*: that of the "fully 'administered world' of late modernity."[4] Her focus within this period is on the affects most commonly associated with women and racially or ethnically marginalized groups who, at a time of intensified and bureaucratized self-monitoring and self-management, have often been characterized as "excessively emotional."[5] Hence while, as the cliché has long held, men are meant to be motivated by their heads and women by their hearts, women are supposed to be *so* in thrall to their feelings that their feelings are imagined to be particularly prone to getting nasty. Meanwhile, the racialized subject has consistently been stereotyped as one whose emotions can overtake so suddenly as to render the subject dangerously disordered and out of control.[6] Fine feelings thus turn ugly when the state of being moved implies not the subject's *own* agency but that of some external agent or puppet master pulling the strings—a grievous breach, therefore, to the conceit of emotional self-possession.

Feeling Odd

One of the first to give voice to the feelings permeating the fully "administered world" was Franz Kafka. When reading Kafka one confronts what it is to feel ashamed, guilty, self-hating, anxious, neurotic, paranoid, sexually hung up. One also confronts what it is to feel strange, feel funny, feel alienated from what Kafka may well have imagined to be natural feelings. Indeed, what Kafka seems to have felt most keenly was his own grotesque creatureliness in a prewar Europe whose rules, values, and norms were so prescriptive that feeling "natural" implied the natural confidence and propriety one might feel if one were correspondingly sure of one's identity, one's historical rootedness, one's position in the family and in society: the natural feelings of deference to one's father, of love for one's mother or wife, the natural feeling of wanting to become a parent oneself—these were the affective relations that Kafka consistently condemned himself for failing *instinctively* to feel.

Of course, what Kafka felt about himself was in many respects what European nations in the first half of the twentieth century were prone to feel about Jews more generally, the most notorious representation of which comes down to us from later Nazi ideology. Jews, according to this worldview, were characterized as unnatural creatures, out of touch with their feelings, hybrid, parasitic, incapable of originality or creative genius, corrosive of both the physical body and the body politic, and contaminating of natural cultures, peoples, and languages. Since modern nation-states were increasingly being envisaged in racial and ethnic terms, those who belonged were said to belong by natural ties of blood and soil and to possess a native sensibility for beauty and art that was the original and spontaneous source of national music, theater, and literature, and the purity of the national language. Fine feelings indeed.

In its nationalist incarnation as well, this rather romantic figure of the feeling subject, perfectly balanced between mind and body and living in harmonious relation to both nature and culture, relied on its opposition to the Jew as a kind of grotesque perversion of the ideal type: the Jew was one whose feelings were unreal, unnatural, mimetic, copied, fake. Indeed, the Jew was not so much a figure of feeling as one of emotion: exaggerated, melodramatic, and over the top. If a "feeling person" was someone whose sense of self was so authentic, so instinctive, that she need never behave untowardly, the emotional personality was unpredictable, consistently intruded on by an anxiety about how the other regards him, and thus mediated always by a terrible sense of self-consciousness circuiting the possibility of simple or natural feeling.

Such, it might be said, is the situation of a diasporic people who are unsure of their place in the world—people who are persistently mobile, looking all the time over their shoulder, and jostling for position. Yet such feelings too, it can be argued, along with the situations that engender them, have become ever more common within the era of globalization, when everyone feels more uprooted, unsettled, insecure about group identity and forms of belonging—and hence more anxious, guilty, self-loathing, nostalgic, paranoid.[7] Jews, as one popular saying has it, "are just like everyone else, only more so." And by the same token we can say that the modern European sensibility so often associated with Kafka and with Jews generally was at the vanguard of the still unfolding affective conditions of our own era.

Modern Jews have frequently been represented as having feelings in ways instructive for reflecting on how all kinds of people are living and feeling now. Thus while I've called this book *Feeling Jewish*, I don't wish to claim this is a feeling or series of feelings felt by all, or even most, Jews, any more than I would wish to claim that these feelings are somehow exclusive to Jews. As Kafka put it so memorably in his diary—"What have I in common with Jews? I have hardly anything in common with myself and should stand very quietly in the corner, content that I can breathe"—a diary entry that admits of a feeling that, paradoxically, I'll go on to consider a stereotypically "Jewish feeling."[8] You don't *have* to be Jewish to feel you have nothing in common with Jews, but being Jewish helps.

A Problem Shared

That having nothing in common with others may be precisely what one has in common with others is a neat paradox which also raises the question as to whether one can share that which was never one's own in the first place—in Kafka's case, a sense of himself. Feelings partake of the same slippery logic. For if my feeling is, per the classical view, that which is mine and mine alone, then how can something so essentially private ever be shared with another? Yet if my feeling is precisely that which dispossesses me of myself and so something I can never rightfully lay claim to, then how can I presume to share that, either?

It is no doubt because feelings are just such a tricky terrain to navigate that we have so many contextual conventions for the civil discourse on how to handle them. The idea that feelings can be shared, for instance, and perhaps, to an extent, always already *are* shared, is part of their contaminating danger as well as their allure. When it comes to talking about feelings, the polite and impolite, politic and impolitic, are tremendously difficult to tell apart. Thus while it may be deemed problematic to tell someone "I know how you feel," because, quite simply, you don't, we also hear in the statement "I know how you feel" an invitation to feel less alone in the world, more understood. "I know how you feel" holds out the promise of community, always at the risk of condescension.

A literary critical furor erupted around Sylvia Plath's poem "Daddy," for example, because of its inclusion of the lines "I began to talk like a Jew. / I think I may well be a Jew."[9] Many critics decried Plath's explicit identification with the suffering of Holocaust victims as a way of expressing her own family drama, not to mention that assuming a "Jewish" identity for Plath seemed to be completely bound up with her personal feelings of powerlessness and abject victimhood. But while some judged Plath for treading on the sensitivities of Jewish feelings—not by rejecting those feelings, but by appropriating them as her own—others thought her work enlarged the overall sense of sympathy and understanding of Jews within their historical experiences. What's more, the tropes of the Holocaust, say Plath's defenders, have become a literary convention. To imagine that feelings don't circulate, break loose from their original context, and infect others is to misunderstand them altogether.

Not that the Holocaust should be considered the sole origin of "Jewish feelings."[10] It's telling, for instance, that Holocaust survivor and author Aharon Appelfeld first read Kafka *after* the war, yet it was Kafka who seemed to best understand and give expression to Appelfeld's own feelings in the wake of the Holocaust, notwithstanding that Kafka had died long before.[11] Encountering Kafka at the time he did thus helped Appelfeld recognize how our feelings may be much less distinctly our own, or less bound to our own experiences, than we're often inclined to believe.

In this respect, too, one could consider a claim made by Edward Said in one of his last interviews, with a journalist for the Israeli newspaper *Ha'aretz*: "I'm the last Jewish intellectual. You don't know anyone else. All your other Jewish intellectuals are now suburban squires. . . . So I'm the last one. The only true follower of Adorno. Let me put it this way: I'm a Jewish-Palestinian."[12] Said's statement is an ironic and intentionally provocative one. But it's a statement that also, in its twistiness, makes a painful appeal to Jewish feelings, or rather, seeks to remind Jews of what perhaps ought to be their feelings: *you* of all people should know how *we*

(Palestinians) feel. The implication here is that Jewish feelings, so intimately related to their unique historical experiences, have migrated to another group. Hence the rhetoric of Said's statement implicitly contains and laments a forlorn wish: that those subjected to certain feelings will naturally carry forward that sensitivity to others afflicted in similar ways. Yet the tragic irony of the Palestinians, he writes elsewhere, is to have been rendered "exiles by the proverbial people of exile."[13] For if Jews as a group—if *any* group—become too sure of what and how they feel, and if what they feel is that they are powerless, or victims, then the elasticity of feelings must have hardened into a fixed identity, making it difficult for those thus sensitized to recognize themselves in any other role, such as that of potential victimizers. Feelings can be misleading.

Feelings often do block movement, action, or even sympathy. A number of the feelings examined in this book—feelings such as self-hatred, envy, guilt, and paranoia—are generally experienced by those subject to them as negative rather than positive, blocking rather than motivating emotions. Yet in the nebulous arena of feelings, and given the way in which one's feelings so often contaminate and mirror the feelings of even hostile others, identities are always at least potentially open, portable, and liable to change or transformation.[14] So even when our feelings are what most seem to hold us back, they may still be the best means available of moving us forward.

Any feeling that takes us out of our comfort zone has the potential to help forge new forms of recognition and community. We might think here of Lenny Bruce's notorious "Jewish and Goyish" comedy sketch, for example, in which Jewish identity has less to do with a shared ancestry or common dogma than with those things Bruce feels are relatable. So "If you live in New York or any other big city, you are Jewish. It doesn't matter even if you're Catholic; if you live in New York, you're Jewish. If you live in Butte, Montana, you're going to be Goyish even if you're Jewish." Or later: "Negroes are all Jews. Italians are all Jews. Irishmen who have rejected their religion are Jews. Mouths are very Jewish. And bosoms. Baton-twirling is very Goyish."[15]

Bruce's joke presupposes certain assumptions on the part of its audience, namely that they know and recognize the concepts "Jewish and Goyish" in the manner he deploys them. What Bruce was suggesting to his New York audience was that these terms are not the exclusive vocabulary of Jews, but they belong, potentially, to everyone—New Yorkers especially. And the joke also explicitly picks up on the term "Jew-*ish*" as a word that seems to imply a sufficiently indistinct category that just about anyone can be Jew-ish, so you're Jewish if you live in a certain kind of place, mix with a certain kind of people, listen to a certain kind of music, and eat a certain kind of food—though this food is no longer prescribed by religious dietary laws; it now has to do with something a lot less easy to pin down: instinct, identification, taste, or the rejection of taste.

By laughing, implicitly, at those humorless "insiders" who play by the rules, Bruce's joke seems to take the side of minority, outsiderness, and difference. You could say it's on the defensive. Yet in giving his audience the benefit of the doubt by presuming that it is "in" on the joke, he also tenders an invitation to join the outsiders' club. Like all jokes, then, his creates, in the very telling, its own community and rules of belonging. So if you "get" Bruce's sketch, if you find it funny, then you must be Jewish. If you don't get it, you must be Goyish. When Zadie Smith begins her novel *The Autograph Man* by quoting the sketch in full, it's because she *gets* it. She *is*, in Bruce's terms, Jew-*ish*.

Universal Mercurianism
Here's how historian Yuri Slezkine begins his book *The Jewish Century:*

The Modern Age is the Jewish Age, and the twentieth century, in particular, is the Jewish Century. Modernization is about everyone becoming urban, mobile, literate, articulate, intellectually intricate, physically fastidious, and occupationally flexible. . . . It is about transforming peasants and princes into merchants and priests, replacing inherited privilege with acquired prestige, and dismantling social estates for the benefits of individuals, nuclear families, and book-reading tribes (nations). Modernization, in other words, is about everyone becoming Jewish.

And no one "is better at being Jewish than the Jews themselves. In the age of capital, they are the most experienced entrepreneurs; in the age of alienation, they are the most experienced exiles; and in the age of expertise they are the most proficient professionals."[16]

Jews became the most "model moderns" by "being exemplary ancients" (1). The skills, that is, that have since become more or less mandatory in a globalized economy were once the preserve of specific groups of internal strangers ("service nomads" [12]) commonly found among traditional agrarian and pastoral societies. These were groups that would provide human resources to native populations and expertise in foreign affairs. Slezkine terms these internal stranger groups "Mercurians," after the messenger god Mercury, who lived, like his followers, by "wit, craft, and art" (8). Their Apollonian hosts, on the other hand, were generally warriors, herders of animals, and tillers of soil. "The difference between Apollonians and Mercurians is the all-important difference between those who grow food and those who create concepts and artefacts" (24). Mercurians are history's middlemen par excellence, the advance guard of today's middle classes whose proficiency in "urban arts amid rural labors" rendered them the quintessential moderns. But while the world has always included such groups, says Slezkine,

"The Age of Universal Mercurianism became Jewish because it began in Europe" (39). Jews were Europe's foremost Mercurians.

It is against this backdrop that one can grasp why Nationalism was to be the principal religion of the Modern Age. Reacting to emerging conditions of globalized rootlessness and cosmopolitanism, nationalism provided a cover story of blood and soil and offered a nostalgic and romantic vision of the old community as having been magically preserved as an eternal principle.[17] Since Jews did not belong to the new nations in these terms, however, they became, despite their modern adeptness, modernity's victims: "All modernity is about 'nakedness' covered by modern nationalism. The Jews—tragically—had become emperors with no clothes" (350).

Hence the story of twentieth-century Jews is a story of "one Hell and three Promised Lands" (104). The Hell was Europe. The three promised lands were Russia (communism), America (capitalism), and Israel (nationalism). As Slezkine tells it, the underpinning philosophies aiding and abetting each of these political promises were also the modern Jewish innovations of Marxism (Russia), Freudianism (America), and Zionism (Israel). In all three cases the Promised Land promised to answer the Jewish question by effectively dissolving Jewishness—including the case of what was at that time a predominantly secular form of Zionism as a means of national normalization—as an antimodern hangover. Yet by the end of the twentieth century, this repudiated Jewishness had returned to Jews in all three Promised Lands.[18]

Freud and His Discontents

The story Slezkine tells is primarily that of the "Jewish Century" in Russia and how it came to be that the revolutionary dream that had at first buoyed Jews with its promise of emancipation was ultimately to turn against them. By contrast, it's in the new world of

America that modern Jews have had their most unencumbered success as the most experienced of Mercurians: "Mid-twentieth-century America was a country of universal nakedness because America's commitment to capitalism seemed boundless and because the American nationality was, by European standards, chimerical" (350). Thus while Jews in Russia were eventually to turn away from the socialism that had once again made aliens of them, in America, Jews in the 1940s and 1950s were largely moving away from Marxism and toward liberalism as they ascended the socioeconomic ladder. It's on this basis, suggests Slezkine, that, for American Jews in particular, Freudianism's "strictly individual" path to salvation proved the more attractive self-cure: "Freudianism aspired to being the religion of modern capitalism as much as Marxism aspired to being the religion of anticapitalism. . . . The pursuit of individual happiness—like the maintenance of a decent society—turned out to be a matter of managing imperfection, of imposing fragile checks and balances on ineradicable internal pressures" (319). Freudianism, in other words, as the therapeutic handmaiden to the fully administered world of late modernity, showed modern people how to handle their feelings as an ongoing part of their self-administration.

Since the pursuit of happiness in America is something of a patriotic act, to perform its duties well, psychotherapy had to become a means of positive thinking—a development about as far removed from Freud's original psychoanalysis "as Castro's Cuba is from Marx's *Das Kapital*" (321). It's a point that's also been made by the sociologist Eva Illouz. In wide-ranging remarks disparaging the American self-help industry, Illouz takes care to note that Freud himself was among the first to denounce the possibility of the self-made recovery. Yet as part of her broader investigation into what she terms "emotional capitalism," Illouz has also sought to explore and explain how therapy became "the lingua franca of the new service class in most countries with advanced capitalist economies." In such economies, she observes, therapeutic discourse as a means of self-monitoring and self-management ("especially for members of the middle class and perhaps even more especially for women") means that within certain social circles it is no longer wrong—*even* for men—to be in touch with one's "feminine side"; indeed, being reflexive and emotionally open is now widely considered a public good.[19] But there is a "but." *But,* only insofar as this introspection is put at the service of greater industry, productivity, and a critique aimed always at the individual's history of trauma and its self-overcoming, never at the institutions within which the individual resides.

Such criticisms of Freud's legacy in America are of course pertinent, although I'd question the implicit assumption that by becoming self-reflexive one is somehow shirking one's responsibility to tough-minded social or institutional critique. While much of the culture and literature I cover in this book is American, for example, and while psychoanalysis informs my approach throughout, psychoanalysis as an inspiration for self-help and positive thinking is not the perspective I adhere to. Rather, the Freudian legacy I'm interested in is as much concerned with group as with individual psychology, and it seems right too to note that, despite the assimilation of some forms of therapeutic discourse by capitalist economics, Freud has always been and continues to be of equal interest to anti-capitalists. This can be seen in the profound engagement with Freudian and post-Freudian (especially Lacanian) ideas one can find in the work of Slavoj Žižek, for instance, among numerous others.

That said, it's not my project here to advance a particular political agenda. I want to talk instead about how the feelings that seem so often to divide us may also be a means of uniting us: on opposing sides of the same battlefield our feelings about each other may be precisely what we share. And especially modern feelings. For though the promise of emancipation was to widen participation so that those on the margins could move toward the center, isn't it the reverse that has actually occurred? Today everyone—*even* Tom and Dick—appears inclined to feel if not existentially threatened, then at the very least marginalized.

The proliferation of these "Jewish" feelings, then, can be observed not only in those from the marginal positions of race, migration, gender, class, or sexuality, whose trajectories might be said to structurally resemble the Jewish one, but to entire segments of the Western populace. And these same unsettling feelings can equally be said to afflict late capitalism's "winners" as well as losers—which, in America especially, Jews have certainly been. For however central the pursuit of happiness may be to the prevailing American ideology, "neurasthenia," as Sander Gilman has put it, "the American disease, the disease of modern life, is also the disease of the Jews, modern people incarnate."[20] (This too was a point Freud was among the first to make when he extended Charcot's diagnosis of the marginal, underclass, and outcast figures in the Salpêtrière hospital for hysterics in Paris to the most affluent and middle-class representatives of Freud's own Viennese society.)[21]

My interpretation of feelings is accordingly *not* guided by the notion of self-help or the pursuit of happiness. The Freud who will aid my analyses is rather a thinker for whom feelings and their ambivalences are never wholly good or bad, right or wrong, just or unjust, or ever just one thing. Feelings invariably contain and threaten to become their own opposites: thus love is a form of hate, lust is a form of disgust, desire a form of fear, passivity has something of aggression in it, and vice versa. Viewed this way, feelings are unreliable, often seem entirely inappropriate, and are frequently if not always conflicted. As such, they're a destabilizing element for any interpreter, for to admit feelings is by necessity to acknowledge uncertainty, and probably a painful uncertainty, which may well be why we so often defend ourselves against feelings, although it's for this reason too that our feelings can create change, create an opening, be or become radical.

To the degree, therefore, that one's "feeling" can be described, as it is in much psychoanalytic theory, as destabilizing of one's identity, it shares a certain kinship with the "Jewishness" whose identity has proven equally unstable.[22] Both "feeling" and "Jewishness" can even be regarded as complementary forces dually assaulting the classical idea of the self as a unified subject. Nor, on that account, is it such a strain to suppose that Freud's ideas *about* feelings may well have been rooted in his own conflicted feelings as a Jew.[23] Indeed, it's by drawing on the influence of Freud's own Jewish background that Adam Phillips has recently suggested that the picture of the human that Freudian psychoanalysis gives us is quintessentially that of the immigrant.[24] With Freud, that is to say, it is the exception or outsider who becomes the rule.

Getting Personal

If it was personal for Freud, it's personal for me too.

I have been concerned with Jewish feelings—with *feeling Jewish*—for as long as I can remember. This is something I share with a number of my Jewish friends, and it has been observed by other Jewish and non-Jewish friends with a certain degree of puzzlement if not concern: why is it that how I feel in all kinds of situations is so often bound up with how I feel about myself as a Jew? My feelings often seem inseparable from my Jewish "identity," and Jews frequently get together, as do other minorities and subcultures, from avant-garde poets to metal-heads to, say, "women," to obsessively chronicle and analyze the ways in which their distinctive identifications have affected how they experience the world. It's why the famous stereotype of the neurotic Jew who goes into therapy to share feelings he has sought to keep hidden in his daily life is so inextricably linked to our sense of how his Jewishness has been somehow active in his behaviors, in his responses, in his thinking, and in pretty much everything.

The American comedian and star of *Curb Your Enthusiasm* Larry David once stated: "Religion doesn't play any part in my life in terms of how I live my life. But I don't think I've ever gone through a day in my life without hearing someone say the word 'Jew' or saying it myself."[25] David's comment recalls remarks Kafka once made in his famous "Letter to My Father," detailing the way in which his Jewishness, despite being emptied of any discernible religious content or meaning, continued to lay an irresistible claim on him. In the case of my own life, religion does continue to play a part (however modest), and, as I've written at length elsewhere, I do not concede that secular culture is ever quite as secular as it likes to believe.[26] All the same, by offering for the most part readings of various works of modern fiction, I *am* here taking up the sense of a Jewishness not bound to any religious or cultural definition. I do so because I share David's inference that a word whose meaning is felt to be unstable or uncertain remains strangely in contention in such a way that it exerts a powerful hold over those who, however loosely, feel themselves identified by it.

Of course, hearing someone say the word "Jew" aloud almost every day, as Larry David does, might be construed as a particularly American occurrence. It's not, for example, a word you hear so often stated publicly in the England where I live. In Philip Roth's novel *Deception*, which is set in England and features a protagonist who just happens to be a writer called Philip Roth, this difference becomes a theme. As the author-protagonist complains at one point to his mistress, "In England, whenever I'm in a public place, a restaurant, a party, the theatre, and someone happens to mention the word 'Jew,' I notice that the voice always drops just a little."

"Jew" in England is a word to be whispered beneath one's breath, as if one were alluding to someone's bad smell—it's how Brits "all say 'Jew,'" he adds, "Jews included."[27]

Obviously, Roth's observation isn't true of everyone in England, but it's pretty much exactly how I utter the word in public: quietly, in order not to be heard saying something so, well, uncouth. I should confess too that whenever I've been asked the name of the book I've been writing—the book you're reading—I nearly always fudge or muffle my answer. Can I really say "Feeling Jewish" out loud? Oh, the irony: that "feeling Jewish," for me at least, should be so neatly exposed by the way I feel about saying those very words.

So, rather worryingly, it does look as though, in some quite visceral sense, feeling Jewish is a source of shame for me. Yet just how far I can trust this seemingly instinctive response on my part is also a question I'm asking *about* feelings. Is the feeling of shame I have here associated to my Jewishness really mine; if not, whose shame might I be expressing? Indeed, is my shame really shame at all, or might I be feeling something else that merely calls itself shame?[28] As I hope this book will make clear, I certainly don't think that I or anyone else *should* feel ashamed of feeling Jewish; hence, both despite and because of my feelings on the matter, I've gone ahead and written it.

Still, like it or not, in the England of Roth's *Deception* "Jew" is one of those words (and, let's be clear, there are many others—"black," "Muslim," "gay," take your pick—words, one might say, that seem to carry their own trigger warnings) that is no sooner uttered aloud than it seems to leave a faint trace of embarrassment on the faces of everyone within range, as if they felt unfairly tested by its appearance, or as if one lived in a climate whose rules of civility demanded that it would be better or more polite not to utter it at all. It's for this reason that the Philip Roth character claims that he finally decides to leave England and return to America—because, he tells his mistress, he's missing "Jews." "We've got some of them in England, you know," she reminds him. "Jews with force, I'm talking about," he replies, "Jews with appetite. Jews without shame."[29]

But one man's Jew is always another man's self-hating Jew, and if the English Jew appears as a self-hater to the American Jew, then it's the American Jew who appears—most famously in Roth's own *Portnoy's Complaint*—as a self-hater to the Israeli Jew.[30] If Jews in America *are* "without shame," then, this must be a relatively recent innovation:

> Jackie Mason used to get laughs simply by saying the word *Jew*. At times his entire act seemed to consist of little more than opening his mouth and pronouncing that one syllable, over and over, until the gentiles in the audience were looking at each other in confusion, while the Jews rolled around on the floor gagging hysterically.
>
> The hysteria came from the fact that Mason was proclaiming aloud, and with pride, a matter commonly viewed as an embarrassment. And even if he was overcompensating, that was part of the joke, for this mixture of vanity and shame was central to the business of being a Jew in America at the time.[31]

These are the words of the Jewish-American director Henry Bean, whose film *The Believer* explores Jewish self-hatred in the United States, and who remains unconvinced that America has altogether moved on from that earlier state of Jewish hysteria, even if, as always with hysteria, the symptoms may have adapted and altered their form.[32]

In the United States the existence of "secondary loyalties is a consistent part of the political arrangement," remarks Slezkine in seeking an explanation as to why Jews should have enjoyed such a golden age there.[33] But if an American's identity is generally hyphenated (Jewish-American, African-American, Irish-American, Arab-American), that does not necessarily render the still *secondary* loyalty any freer or more resolved. Is there such a great difference between a word that convention dictates should be whispered and a word that convention dictates should be proclaimed out loud? If you overlook my Jewishness, you don't really see me; but if, for you, my Jewishness defines me, you don't see me either. Ditto for blackness. Ditto for Asianness. Et cetera. In terms of political recognition it's precisely this damned-if-you-do-or-don't scenario that has all along been a problem for the discourse of human rights.[34]

Bodies of Words

There is at least one unspeakable word that retains the power to scandalize in the America of today. Not the J-word but the N-word. This is the subject of American author David Bradley's provocative essay "A Eulogy for Nigger," in which he examines what further racism might be entrenched by silencing rather than recovering or redressing the repressed history within any form of terminology, including a racist one.

The occasion for Bradley's essay was a symbolic ceremony held in Detroit in 2007 by the National Association for the Advancement of Colored People, which, with crowds of onlookers cheering on, "put to rest a long-standing expression of racism by holding a public burial for the N-word." Reading about this ceremony in an Associated Press report, Bradley remarks that "word of Nigger's burial shocked me. I hadn't known Nigger was even sick"—not when all his "vital signs" were still there: mass unemployment, vastly lower median income, and greater likelihood of arrest, conviction, stop and search, and being shot to death "for black—excuse me, African Americans." What makes Bradley especially irate with the "Colored People" who buried "Nigger," however, is not only that they didn't even bother holding a wake, but that they rejoiced at the funeral and even dared to dis the deceased. In recompense for this lack of respect, Bradley claims, he wrote his own eulogy for someone who was, he says, his best "mentor," who was always the life and soul of the party, and who was "quite a comedian"—he even wrote half of Richard Pryor's jokes.[35]

In rhetorically charged prose laced with irony, Bradley's essay exposes how a racist ideology and language forge a split within the psyche of the victim or derogated group such that the racism gets internalized within the individual or group as a form of self-abuse, self-censorship, and self-loathing. It's a feeling and dynamic that I also explore by showing how, as with the contradictions involved in the N-word's public burial, every attempt to escape self-hatred seems to wind up reinforcing it. So it's instructive to consider how Bradley learned to respond to the negative feelings aroused by negative words—by moving from his schoolboy "cringing at the sound of Nigger's name" toward a later appreciation of what "Nigger" had taught him. What he'd taught him was one lesson above all: that no matter where he might find himself, even when studying "in the Ivory League," the euphemisms he'd never cease to hear echoing around and about him were words and phrases that Nigger best knew how to understand. "By the time I'd completed my coursework, I'd realized Nigger was ineradicable."[36]

The conclusion that "Nigger was ineradicable" means, of course, that there can be no burying him. But this conclusion does not deny the possibility of giving new meanings and new values to his much maligned name. The same goes here. In what follows it's not my aim to bury negative words or negative feelings. I wish, rather, to revisit them with the possible intention of changing the meaning of these words and feelings. Feelings and words, after all, are alike in precisely this respect: they're equally capable of change (as, too, are bodies).

Indeed, such an affective relationship to language—as something strange, equivocal, open, undetermined—is arguably what gives literature the quality we tend to call "literary." And something similar is true of psychoanalysis (or the psychoanalysis in which I have an investment): it aims not to provide the patient with a new vocabulary that buries the old (which would be as impossible as its attempt would be damaging), but to alter the meaning of the vocabulary the patient arrives with, such that the patient can find new ways to retell, reimagine, and thus reexperience his or her own story.

So while there remains a classical view of emotion that, in order to preserve some sense of the subject's authentic or true feelings, might like to seal off what the body is believed to feel on its own from the external influence of words and names, I have no intention of appealing to any form of feeling imagined to take place outside language. I distinguish instead between the (bodily) emotion that comes first and the feeling that subsequently unfolds into consciousness. If "feeling is emotion plus words," Frosh proposes, "it is also the place at which this polarity collapses."[37] Feeling, then, may be perceived as the arena where bodies and words are so closely bound up as to become inseparable. Insofar as we share a language, we also share the feelings that being subject to language arouses and invites. So it is that, since all are affected by language, I take literature as my primary material. Literature is situated here as the place where feelings can be most richly shared as felt and felt as shared.

What's with All the Negativity?

The fact that throughout my life I've filtered so many of my personal feelings and experiences through my sense of Jewishness doesn't mean, of course, that I'm a representative Jew or that any other Jew would necessarily feel or experience things in the same way as I do. No matter how widespread the malaise or ecstasy we may be experiencing, our personal feelings and the reasons we're feeling them are always rooted in the highly specific conditions of our individual lives (hence the unconscious opportunism attending moments of mass hysteria, when the tensions assailing an individual's private plights can be blended into the general mood). Thus, while I acknowledge my own involvement here, what I'll mostly be analyzing are theoretical debates alongside various examples of fiction, film, and memoir written by others. Nor is the notion of Jewishness I'm pursuing within these sources something fixed. It's one, rather, that I allow to develop in its various forms so as to become gradually encased in a network of associations. As such, "Jewishness" often gets melded with other perspectives and texts in which I find similar ideas and themes. The reader should not be too surprised to note, for instance, that there are long stretches in what follows where Jews and Jewishness as specific terms seem to disappear from view. Indeed, the fact that I both couple and uncouple "feelings" and "Jewishness" directly relates to what I'm suggesting about these terms. For "feeling," as I understand it, is "Jewish" only insofar as it induces experiences of dispossession over which Jewishness can, of course, claim no monopoly. But even though the term "Jewish" does at times slip out of sight, it's always there in the background, and always also returns to the foreground to show how and why so many aspects of modern Jewish experience have been, can be, and indeed *are* shared.

Of course, it's hard not to notice how many of the feelings famously associated with Jews—self-hatred, guilt, hysteria, nervousness, paranoia, mother love (even mother love, as we'll see, has been painted unappealingly in recent decades)—so often sound negative.[38] So are these just anti-Semitic stereotypes? Possibly. But if so it remains to be seen why so many Jews have attested to their experiences in such broadly negative terms. Why have large numbers of Jews come to feel in these ways? Why are they so often accused of feeling in these ways? And why are such feelings increasingly common to us all at a time when countless people are feeling themselves uncomfortably exposed to the unsettling effects of a hyper-connected but ever more insecure world? Hyper-connected but insecure . . . could anything *be* more Jewish? Hence what I also want to understand by both admitting and anatomizing these difficult feelings is why they should have persisted even at times and in places of relative safety when Jews appear not only to have been accepted but to have achieved high levels of success.

Needless (I hope) to say, there are equally all manner of positive feelings associated with Jews and Jewish history, from joy and pleasure to fellow feeling, holiness, humility, and pride, none of which I'm immune to in my own life.[39] Though just as I don't consider negatives to be necessarily negative, nor do I consider positives to be entirely positive.[40] And I'm mindful here too of Ngai's excellent point that "there is a sense in which ugly feelings can be described as conducive to producing ironic distance in a way that the grander and more prestigious passions, or even the moral emotions associated with sentimental literature, do not."[41] The less prestigious the passion, in other words, the more critically valuable it may turn out to be. So in questioning the negativity of the feelings I've chosen to focus on, I aim to question as well the negativity so often attributed to the character of those who have been stereotypically marked by these feelings.

But whether they're coded as positive or negative, *all* feelings, I want to say, properly felt, can ultimately be ways of reexperiencing oneself as strange, odd, ambivalent, out of place, and thus, in a certain sense, funny. As such, I conclude this introduction with another joke, this one about the moment when two Jews, Shmuley and Heschel, bump into each other in the street:

SHMULEY: Heschel, we've been chatting for ten minutes and you still haven't asked me how I am.

HESCHEL: Sorry, Shmuley. How *are* you?

SHMULEY: Don't ask.

"How *are* you?" "Don't ask." This works much better for me as a general rule—the civil discourse of the future, perhaps? Though put like that, of course, how can one not ask? So in what follows I really *am* asking.

ONE

Self-Hatred

From a bad case of internalized anti-Semitism I'm slowly
recovering.
—WAYNE KOESTENBAUM, *Humiliation*

Self-hatred can arise when the face you see in the mirror isn't the
one you want, when the body you wash in the bath isn't the kind
you imagine others want, when you seem to have the wrong accent,
the wrong name, the wrong parents. What you lack is the power of
self-determination: your personhood has been determined *im*personally by forces beyond your control. And so, given that who you
are or appear to be isn't *really* you, you may well decide to alter
these things, whether through marriage, name change, surgery, or
any of the various measures people resort to in order to disassociate
themselves from family, history, body, roots. You reinvent yourself,
becoming the person you would much rather be, the person you
feel you are. But is this new self really you? Not according to the

voice that whispers constantly inside your head: "What if the old me resurfaces? What if my mask slips?"

Socializing

Since self-hatred, according to Sander Gilman, typically afflicts outsiders, it can be most fruitfully be analyzed within a social context: "Self-hatred results from outsiders' acceptance of the mirage of themselves generated by their reference group—that group in society which they see as defining them—as reality."[1] Groups or identities cast as "other" (always the lower-ranked term in a system of hierarchical binaries) internalize the social order's dominant system of values and then accordingly judge themselves – unfavorably. Within the purview of the West, for example, self-hatred might be expected to particularly afflict women, the dark-skinned, the disabled, the poor, homosexuals, Jews, Muslims, immigrants, and so forth. To cope with this negative social positioning, the implicated "other" often unconsciously splits her identity into good and bad versions. So, for instance, in order to align herself with the privileged or "reference" group, the self-hating person may well support the general thesis about the negative characteristics pertaining to her group identity. She may even be the first to declaim and decry such characteristics. And there is, as we know, no shortage of women willing to slut-shame or otherwise police female sexuality. Those deprived of social power often imagine they can attain a sense of the agency they feel they lack by lording it over rejected parts of themselves. As such, it belongs to the logic of self-hatred to replicate social hierarchies, whether directly by means of actual self-denigration and self-harm, or indirectly by attacking others in the group, much as the school bully acts out on the perceived weaklings in the playground the blows he receives without redress at home.

Or, to put this slightly differently, there is no "at home" for the self-hater. To hate oneself is to have no "safe space" to return to, no comfortable way of withdrawing from the world into the shelter of a private sphere. But if this is, as I aim to show, how more and more of us are feeling in an unsettled, ever-changing, and globalized world—a world in which just about every identity, club, or community has started to paint itself as dispossessed, persecuted, misunderstood, outsider—then it's a malaise that sits uneasily alongside another ubiquitous demand of our day: that everyone take charge of positively curating, publicizing, and marketing their own identities, no matter how "outsider" those identities might feel or even be.

No place says this better than the teen bedroom. What may once have been a sanctuary away from the watchful world is today the site of open windows onto a social scene whose appetite for interrogation—present yourself! show yourself! account for yourself!—apparently has no limit. And now that taunts can be remotely accessed, most school bullying doesn't take place in the playground any longer either, and so would seem, in effect, to have morphed into a kind of masochistic self-bullying. Parents are often perplexed as to why any young person should allow himself to be stalked in this way . . . "Why let yourself be so exposed? You may not be able to evade your bully in the schoolyard, but surely you can refuse to engage with him online?" Yet such arguments can only fall on deaf ears when a failure to participate in social media is akin, for the average school kid, to not existing at all. But while it surprises precisely no one to learn that the positive representations of the online self belie the less-than-confident reality of the offline self, the complaint we're more accustomed to hearing from disapproving elders is that the internet has spawned a generation of narcissists perpetually engaged in their own publicity campaigns. This, however, as we'll see, is a critique that begins to sound a little hollow when one considers that the era of the selfie might just as plausibly stem from earlier generations' trumpeting of the individual's right to be self-determining in almost wholly progressive terms.

Safe Spaces

Stranger by the Lake (2013) is a French thriller that subtly alerts us to the ways in which the self who is supposed today to stand "out and proud" may be just another disguise for the self who remains closeted and ashamed. Set on a gay nudist beach and cruising spot, the film, which appears at first glance to feature a liberated group of unselfconsciously naked men, unfolds on a scene populated by men who, notwithstanding their nakedness, are all in subtly different ways hiding the truth of their desires from one another and themselves, and so succumbing, even on this circumscribed strip of beach, to shades of homosexual self-loathing. One man, for example, claims he's there because he's primarily interested in women and men are just a diversion. Another claims he's looking for the women who he's sure are about to turn up (though there's patently no sign of them). Yet another claims he's happily married to his husband and disgusted by the activities of the other gay men on the beach. Another says he just wants to watch, not participate. And so on. In each case the man is splitting off the homosexual side of his identity in order to denigrate even as he indulges it, in much the same way as the beach to which they have come is likewise cut off, hidden away from the rest of a world that seems to sanction only what it doesn't have to see.

Ultimately *Stranger by the Lake* is a genre film about a serial killer, but the "stranger" in question is not a homophobic murderer attacking a vulnerable community from the outside but one of the beach regulars who kills the men he has sex with, thus taking to a logical extreme the self-hatred all the other characters exhibit by varying degrees. It's a self-hatred whose denial in what might otherwise be viewed as a utopian spot of open sexual and social relations is precisely what renders everyone at the beach acutely exposed to the danger the killer represents. This point is especially dramatized by the protagonist, an attractive young man who could have anyone he wants but is inexplicably drawn to take the killer as his lover even after secretly witnessing one of his murders.

And couldn't one describe the internet in strikingly similar terms? The internet is for many just such a utopian "safe space" in which to become the self one dreams of being, the self one feels compelled to deny or dissimulate in one's everyday life. And a space where not only are all desires legitimized and catered to, but all may find a like-minded community of people with whom to share, people who will understand, while those who don't want to don't have to visit those sites—they don't have to even *see* them. Yet just as the film's depiction of graphic sex scenes can be interpreted as a sort of ruse that powerfully undercuts the way this very openness leaves the men at risk—because in all that nakedness they can no longer see what it is they are hiding—so too the internet has proven to be not only a garden of earthly delights but a stalking ground for those whose vivid lives online (whether as fans, gamers, role-players, information sharers, and so on) can sometimes lead them to forget that the very avatars with whom they're sharing their most intimate secrets are completely unknown to them, untraceable as strangers.

Sexual emancipation's false promise is also a theme of Michel Foucault's seminal *History of Sexuality*. Foucault saw modernity as the time when sexual identity became, first and foremost, a way of categorizing people. The putatively liberal or permissive society, he suggested, actually works to extend social and political control by reducing all subjects to sexual types. This is the era, for instance, when you're free to be gay or straight just so long as you *are* either gay or straight: your sexuality now stands for everything anyone needs to know about you. But while all manner of professionals, from doctors and clergy to novelists and lawyers, contribute to this modern discourse on sex, it is above all the psychoanalyst whom Foucault charges as bearing the responsibility for its mystification. Since Freud, Foucault cautions, sexuality has been regarded as a dark hinterland of the self, a secret about you that not even you know—and a secret that it requires an expert to bring to light, precisely in order to "liberate" you.

I agree with Foucault that the most regular misuse of psychoanalysis is as he diagnosed it: the use of shrinkery to lay categorical claims to self-knowledge. But if Foucault was correct in claiming that modern sexuality cancels out its own proffered freedoms by imprisoning the modern subject within her sexual identity, his own effort to demystify sexuality by means of historicization is hardly immune from the same wish to "free" sex or make of sex something uncomplicated, untroubled, and self-evident. What I'm defending, conversely, is a much less "knowing" psychoanalysis—a psychoanalysis that does not aspire to the unveiling of sexual secrets in order to parade them in public, but understands human sexuality as a secret we'll always have insofar as it's one we'll never quite possess.[2] The stranger who stalks the lakeside community from within can in this sense be compared to the stranger within that psychoanalysis dubs the unconscious: that most intimate of strangers, who can never quite be known, domesticated, or made safe, but who becomes all the more threatening when one's fleshy intimacy is flaunted in such a way that one's resident strangeness is denied.

Politics, then, whether conservative or progressive, seems the wrong place to look for a solution to the perennial problem of human strangeness. For though we may be living at a time when "knowing oneself" sounds like the virtue of true wisdom, the waywardness of human drives and desires will never cease to shame and unsettle the person whose real secret may be not that she desires a forbidden fruit so much as that she knows nothing of her own desires.

Wants

Knowing nothing of one's own desire does, however, bear a political significance. It does so not least because this ignorance has historically been ascribed to *her* rather than *him*. The question of "what woman wants," after all, which famously belongs to the early history of psychoanalysis, is a question that implicates man as the person who must be unfailingly decisive since, presumably, he knows exactly what it is that *he* wants. A familiar theme. One can find a similar idea, for example, in the existentialist philosophy of Jean-Paul Sartre, where one encounters "the example of a woman who has consented to go out with a particular man for the first time" but whose response to his sexual advances, both verbal and physical, is to flee present reality for the realm of the intellect, for by escaping to the cerebral she can then behave as though he has not just taken a physical hold of her hand. This action is precisely what, for Sartre, constitutes "bad faith." Woman's problem, he says, is that "she does not quite know what she wants. She is profoundly aware of the desire which she inspires, but the desire cruel and naked would humiliate and horrify her."[3] So if only this woman would cease her self-conscious questioning of what it is the Other wants of her and simply be as men are—"cruel and naked"— then that, surely, would liberate her from the horror and humiliation that dog her days.

But do any of us really know what it is we want? Or isn't to want something, by very definition, not to know it? In which case cruelty would be just another cover story to hide the problematic fact that, in the arena of desire, there is no unadorned nakedness, whether one is talking about the oneiric nudity we see in *Stranger by the Lake* or the unabashed bareness of the male locker room at my local swimming pool: while the women's changing rooms have doors on the showers and curtains on the cubicles, neither of these is present in the men's changing rooms, as if to underscore this idea that, when it comes to showing what you're about, men have nothing and women everything to hide. (Though these rules are reversed when watching is sanctioned: thus in film ratings female genitalia are permitted to be seen by younger viewers in a way that men's genitals are not, legally entrenching the idea that what females lack—nothing to be seen here!—men have plenty to boast about.)

So if you can never say for certain what it is that you lack or want, then, since no political transformation can reasonably be expected to relieve the subject of his or her self-doubt, it might be better to dream of a political state that would be able to admit of a subject who has such doubts. This, though, may be a lesson we have yet to learn, as it's always with the best of intentions that progressive politics can sometimes wind up reinforcing the harms it exists to alleviate. Whenever, for example, we "reclaim" a previously denigrated identity in order to positivize it, we risk forgetting that somewhere buried inside every one of us remains an amorphous and protean infant self whose inchoate, inarticulate demands have never gone away, but who may well risk being further silenced by our heroic struggles at self-determination.

Matrophobia

Our positivity trips us up most when it turns a blind eye to our own internal contradictions. Nowhere is this more clearly the case than in the movement for women's liberation. Here, for example, is Adrienne Rich describing one of the great bugbears of feminism as "the fear not of one's mother or of motherhood but of *becoming one's mother.* Thousands of daughters see their mothers as having taught a compromise and self-hatred they are struggling to win free of, the one through whom the restrictions and degradations of a female existence were perforce transmitted."[4]

Feminism's wish to retrieve from a patriarchal history the silenced voice of the mother—her hidden feelings, her lost opportunities, her unsuspected desires—frequently goes hand in hand with a rejection of everything the mother stands for: all she has taught, her entire worldview. It's for such reasons that successive waves of feminism have contradicted without canceling each other out, indicating a capacity to carry and sustain opposing views that has brought real dynamism to the women's movement. And yet the question remains: how do you "win free" of a history of "compromise and self-hatred"? For not only have feminist "daughters" had to consistently negotiate how to reject their mothers' lessons without compounding the problem by hating their mothers *for* those lessons, they've also had to be vigilant lest their alternatives impose on women *new* norms and values—new reasons, that is, for women to hate themselves.

Aye, there's the rub, as many a woman in heels so high they give her blisters will tell you: rather than preventing the self-harm she undertakes on account of her subordination to a patriarchal code that has made hurting heels irresistible for her, she remains attached to her footwear but now also hates herself for failing by the standards of the feminism that would liberate her from those heels. And even the proudly feminist woman who does resist the demands made on her to look or act in an acceptably "feminine" way may find it hard to square her politics with the secret fantasy life in which she desires precisely those objects or persons whom she does not deem a public good. Like her sister in heels, the positive self-image she's projecting is really, she suspects, only a cosmetic one, which hides, as we all hide, the stranger within.

Ultimately, then, while women may have been induced by historical processes of social othering to hate themselves *as* women, they ask too much of their own emancipation movement if they imagine it will free them from every last vestige of their self-hatred. To do so, in fact, would be to join their oppressor in scapegoating their own sex by imagining that it is this alone that could account for the whole of their self-loathing. In a bid to move the goalposts, therefore, what I want to suggest we look forward to in the feminist future is something else: a woman who will still find reasons to hate herself, though not any longer *because* she's a woman.

Jewish Self-Hatred

We can find an analogous expression of the same idea in Woody Allen's 1997 film *Deconstructing Harry:*

DORIS: Burt is right about you. You're a self-hating Jew.
HARRY: Hey, I may hate myself, but not because I'm Jewish.

It's true, of course: you don't *have* to be Jewish to hate yourself, but self-hatred is a condition Jews often seem so remarkably well-versed in that, while Harry may be right to distinguish between his self-hatred and his Jewishness, it could still be the case that his Jewishness is what has inspired the subtlety of his response.

Type self-hatred into Amazon and a number of Jewish book titles instantly come up. Jews are famous for it. Accusations of self-hatred get hurled between different members of the Jewish community with the kind of ease with which teenage siblings trade insults at home. But what exactly constitutes a self-hating Jew is less clear. In the period immediately after World War II, for example, when Jewish sensitivities were at their most raw, the charge of self-hatred was usually leveled at Jewish novelists whose portrayals of Jews were deemed unflattering. Today, on the other hand, the term seems to have taken on a more overtly political meaning, and certainly one can be sure that it's never far away when there's a discussion of Israel going on. But no matter how hot-tempered and immoderate its appearance in public exchanges, Jewish self-hatred remains, like Jewishness itself, remarkably tricky to pin down. It's not uncommon, for instance, for those on opposing sides of the same argument to accuse each other of self-hatred. So while these days those most accustomed to being labeled self-hating Jews are generally Jews who are publicly critical of Israel or Zionism, there was once a time when it was Jewish *Zionists* who had the reputation for self-hatred on account of their putative contempt for the nonnational diasporic Jew.

When one Jew accuses another of self-hatred, then, more often than not, it's an attempt to silence or delegitimize the political views the target espouses. As such, those who find themselves accused frequently feel they've been backed into a corner out of which all they can do is deny the accusation. This is a great shame, it seems to me, not only in that it ignores what any discussion of feelings has the potential to open up between antagonists, but because it risks reinforcing the problem by turning self-hatred into such an odious insult that it is always what the *other* guy feels.

Yet few Jews can be strangers to the affliction with which they tend to castigate their Jewish opponents. An experience that many Jews will find familiar, for example, is that of getting together with "like-minded" Jewish friends and giving vent to their collective self-hatred in a frenzied, gleeful burst of uncensored caterwauling: "Uch, did you *see* those Jews? I can't stand them! How embarrassing! Aren't they the worst! Honestly, they make my skin crawl!" This is a more or less "knowing" expression of the anxiety surrounding one's identity, which quasi-consciously splits off the rhetorical "good" Jew from the "bad" in order to collectively scorn the latter.

In an essay introducing the screenplay for his film about Jewish self-hatred, *The Believer,* the director Henry Bean confesses to having personally indulged in the "sheer visceral pleasure of hatred" of this kind. "I got off," he says, "on anti-Semitism."[5] Meanwhile, the Jewish writer and perpetual "pilgrim" Gideon Lewis-Kraus has entertainingly described having joined up with a Hasidic sect on its annual pilgrimage to the tomb of their leader in the Ukraine, then finding himself utterly repelled at the thought of anyone mistaking him for a member of this group. He was reminded of a joke: a

Jewish woman sits on a plane next to a Hasid and berates him for his backward, primitive views, his misogyny, and so on. The man tells her he's Amish. The woman is suddenly charmed and simpers about the way he's preserved his traditional culture.[6] It's charming, in other words, when what one deems "primitive" is a tourist attraction, but it quickly becomes threatening when it appears as part of oneself. The Jewish joke is a case in point. While Lewis-Kraus's is arguably a joke *about* self-hatred, many Jewish jokes are forms of it. "I do not know," writes Freud, "whether there are many other instances of a people making fun to such a degree of its own character."[7] Freud interprets this efflorescence of self-deprecatory humor among Jews as being generally prompted by some unconscious wish on the part of the joker to distinguish himself from the other members of his community—and often enough, in his examples, the butt of the joke is one of the poorer and less assimilated *Ostjuden* (eastern Jews).

Exchanging such jokes, impersonating or even becoming the anti-Semite one fears among Jewish friends, is one thing. Quite another is when this badmouthing of Jews on the part of other Jews ("ugh, those Jews") escapes into the open to be witnessed by non-Jews, who are often left bewildered and uncomfortable, unsure how to respond to what would certainly count as hate speech were it uttered by anyone else. And, certainly, it *is* discomfiting when you're being relied on to prove to the self-hating subject that you do not group her together with the disavowed members of her community—not least because the anti-Semitic worldview she is projecting must have been implicitly ascribed to you as well.

Most Jews I've spoken to about this claim to have experienced both situations—sometimes they're the self-hating Jew humiliated by association, sometimes they've felt themselves the target of other self-hating Jews. That's certainly been the case for me. I am often the Jew who publicly disassociates herself from the group, scorning other Jews for being too conspicuous, too cliquey, too vulgar, too much the stereotype—too all-around Jewish. But just as often I sense that I may be carrying the stigma of not having renounced all the "tribal" affiliations already "transcended" by the more assimilated members of my community: I *still* keep kosher, I *still* observe the High Holy Days, even to myself I sometimes seem to have too many Jewish friends, so many that it looks suspicious— I too am too Jewish! Like a stray symptom that has wandered upsettingly out of the unconscious into an otherwise impeccably modern, cosmopolitan setting, I feel myself in these moments as the return of the repressed.

It's a commonplace that those accused of self-hatred by other members of their own community are loathed with a particular ferocity reserved only for the insider-outsiders, the Uncle Toms, the coconuts, the Log Cabin Republicans, the court Jews or kapos. Yet this special level of hatred directed toward self-haters may itself be counted as a form of self-hatred: hatred intensified by identification. We see this, for instance, in the pugnacious reaction of "macho" Jews, such as the playwright David Mamet, who identifies the psychology of self-loathing with the figure of the "wicked son" who features in the Passover ceremony. In the Passover Haggadah the wicked son is the kid who seeks to exclude himself from the rest of his Jewish family by mocking them for their rituals and remembrances.[8] Updating the concept, Mamet has written a polemical book, *The Wicked Son*, to castigate Jewish people who not only deliberately lose all signs of tribal belonging but make an overt show of how slight their regard is for those who retain such attachments.[9] It isn't clear, though, how Mamet can point the finger without succumbing to the very pathology he wishes to ascribe elsewhere. Isn't he too, by casting a significant proportion of the Jewish population as wicked sons, also guilty of splitting his identity into good and bad versions?

Self-hatred, that is to say, is never more obvious than when it strives to escape itself, as when Jews counsel each other to behave "perfectly" in order to solve their problems (tell that to the person with OCD, anorexia, or any other perfectionist disorder). If, on the other hand, accusing others of self-hatred is often enough a projection—a manifestation of one's own disavowed self-hatred—then being accused of self-hatred is equally likely to stimulate feelings of aggression and antipathy toward one's accusers, and precisely insofar as they represent a collective identity: "Damn those persecutory Jews for calling me a self-hater! *I'm* the real victim here—of the Jews!" The foundations are thus laid for an internecine conflict the moment the self-hating slur raises its ugly head. When Bean first nervously screened *The Believer* to an audience in Israel, he was amazed at first by how well it was received there, but he soon learned that its themes were unobjectionable precisely because they were so familiar. The war with the Arabs, the audience assured him, is what best protects Israeli Jews from internal conflicts over the identity of the Jewish state—a state in which the religious and secular hate each other, Ashkenazis and Sephardis hate each other, the right and left hate each other, and on it goes.

The Origins of Jewish Self-Hatred

If, in the medieval world, the doubt that could not be admitted was doubt in God, "bad faith" in the modern world assails the one who doubts himself. Yet self-doubt could also be said to distinguish a historical moment that saw the position of the self becoming ever more tenuous: suddenly it was the case that a modern person could no longer necessarily expect his own status to resemble that of his parents. Little wonder, then, that the question of belonging was to become so integral to the concept of modern statehood. Nor, indeed, is it any accident that the so-called "Jewish question," which hovered so menacingly over Jewish modernity, first arose during the period when Europe was forming its nation states.

The "Jewish question" was primarily one of categorization. To what category belonged the postemancipation Jew? Were the Jews still a religion? Or were they a race? Or a nation? Or a culture? Were they Asiatic or European? Were they ancients or moderns? The lack of a unified response to this question suggested some strange ambivalence at the heart of Jewish identity, an ambivalence that put Jews in danger at a time of increasing nationalistic fervor. As Nietzsche was to put it, scathingly, when describing the "morality of truthfulness in the herd": "You shall be knowable, express your inner nature by clear and constant signs—otherwise you are dangerous. . . . We despise the secret and unrecognizable."[10] But a doubtful identity not only stimulates the predictable hatred of the herd for the stranger, it also provokes *self*-hatred in a world where knowing who one is and what one stands for is the key to social success.

Few expressed modern doubts and their discontents better than did Franz Kafka. And it was Kafka, too, who connected the void within himself to the void he detected at the heart of his Jewish inheritance. In his "Letter to My Father" Kafka describes his Jewishness as at once entirely meaningless and completely unassailable, just as, in his famous parable "Before the Law," man remains powerless before a law that retains its authority over him despite the absence of any particular prescription. Yet Kafka was too sensitive to allow this delineation of the modern Jewish predicament to tempt him into the unreflective Jewish self-hatred to which so many of his coreligionists succumbed. Thus while the fantasy Kafka once described of stuffing all Jews, including himself, into the drawer of the laundry chest and "suffocating" them could well be interpreted (and often has been) as a critical case of Jewish self-hatred, "maybe," as Paul Reitter suggests, "Kafka's line, which occurs in a letter to Milena Jesenská, is a provocation meant to elicit a revealing response from his non-Jewish married lover."[11] To read the line that way is to understand it instead as the kind of rhetorical expression of self-doubt that lovers typically voice in order to gain each other's reassurance: self-doubt floated in flirtation.

Reitter's strikes me as an inspired reading of this difficult sentence from the Kafka archive, not least because it sets up such a suggestive parallel between modern Jewish and modern romantic experiences, both of which entail turning toward an all-powerful Other with the projected power to "please tell me who I am."

In *On the Origins of Jewish Self-Hatred*, Reitter describes "a modern crisis of nervous self-alienation and existential inauthenticity" concerning Jewish thinkers in fin-de-siècle Germany and Austria. For these thinkers "Jewish self-disaffection could, and did, serve as a kind of metaphor for the more general malaise." The two thinkers to popularize the term "Jewish self-hatred" were the German-Jewish philosopher Theodor Lessing and the Austrian-Jewish journalist and essayist Anton Kuh, both of whom, Reitter believes, have been subject to a great deal of misreading and misunderstanding. Kuh, in particular, placed Jewish self-hatred in its modern context as a response to assimilation. For Jewish self-hatred to come about, he theorized, "a recalcitrant boy had to be born" to assimilated Jewish parents, the "knowing child" of "their curse" who counsels "rejection of the father."[12] Cursed with a father who appears less as a standard bearer of tradition and the moral law than as a charlatan whose values can change with the passing fashions,[13] the child of assimilation seeks a radical solution to the problem of his existential humiliation. Jewish self-hatred is that solution.

It's striking how much Kuh's diagnosis of the problem, if not his manner of resolving it, anticipates Sartre's later presentation of the existential inauthenticity he perceived as marking assimilating western Jews in particular. In Sartre's well-meaning if problematic polemic of 1945, *Anti-Semite and Jew*, the inauthentic Jew is said to have allowed the anti-Semite to decide who and what he is.[14] It is this lack of self-determination on his part that curses the inauthentic Jew to the life of a showman who, over the course of incessant theatrical performances, could at any time forget one of his lines—as in the classic joke in which a Jew in a posh restaurant is doing a great job of "passing" until asked, "What would Sir like for his entrée?" "Oh, anything, as long as it's *treif*" (not kosher).

Yet not all modern Jews chose to simply pass or dissolve their pasts through assimilation. Many sought instead to decisively transform their identities and destinies by means of conversion, whether to another religion (for example, Christianity), philosophy (communism), or political ideology (Zionism). But insofar as their more positive attempts at rebirth were also inspired by the same wish to escape the stigmatism of their Jewishness, these would-be ex-Jews soon found that, try as they might, they could never quite overcome the shadow cast by their origins.

To truly overcome one's self-hatred, "the ideal state," counsels Gilman, "is never to have been the Other, a state that cannot be achieved."[15] We can observe this in the way the accusation of Jewish self-hatred seems to continually reappear in connection with all the conventional options for modern Jews. Thus while many Jews chose to convert to Christianity, it was Nietzsche, Christianity's greatest modern critic, who would picture the Christian creed as being at root the expression of the apostle Paul's Jewish self-hatred.

Or in the case of communism, the ideology that attracted so many Jews from the mid-nineteenth century onward for its promise of bringing an end to the old tribalisms by creating a universal brotherhood of mankind, Reds and Jews were from the outset continually identified with each other in anticommunist rhetoric.

And though Marx was a particularly ungenerous critic of Jews and Judaism, an identity from which he made every attempt to distance himself, his Jewish roots remain one of the first things most people still know and remember about him today—as was also the case in his own time.

Other Jews hoped entrepreneurial capitalism, with its promise of the free circulation of capital and social mobility, could emancipate them from the prison of the past, but who if not the Jew and the European history assigned to Jews as moneylenders is more readily identified with finance and capital? And who, if not the Jew, fears the witch hunt that always ensues when capitalism has its periodic "crises"?

For others there was nationalism, or in the Jewish case Zionism—self-determination on a national scale—but if these days it is Jewish anti-Zionists who most regularly get labeled self-haters for their denigration of Israel, when Zionism first took shape as a modern ideology, it was generally, as we've noted, the Zionists who felt the force of the accusation as Jews contemptuous of their nonnational (nonmacho) diasporic standing.

And even the discourse most alive to these contradictions, Freudian psychoanalysis, has not been immune to Jewish self-loathing. "Don't you think," Freud once mused in a letter to a Jewish colleague, "that self-hatred like [Theodor Lessing's] is an exquisite Jewish phenomenon?"[16] It's a question posed as if with professional detachment in the manner of a scientific speculation, yet Jewish self-hatred was an exquisite phenomenon that Freud also seems to have known personally, from the inside.

Psychoanalysis and Jewish Self-Hatred

In a private letter to Karl Abraham on the subject of Jung's anti-Semitism, Freud once proffered the following: "My opinion is that we must as Jews if we want to cooperate with other people, develop

44

a little masochism and be prepared to endure a little injustice."[17] Jewish masochism, for Freud, was the price to be paid for spreading the new gospel of a psychoanalysis, whose future he believed only Jung could be trusted to secure as the non-Jewish public face of the movement. It was masochism, then, that doubled up as a sort of world-weary Jewish realism—and realism for Freud (or acceptance of the reality principle) always has an element of the heroic in it. That said, Jewish masochism was also something Freud had inherited from a father whom he viewed as unheroic precisely on account of his failure to stand up to the anti-Semitic slights and barbs hurled his way. In fact, Freud subsequently claimed to have found the spectacle of his father's passivity so humiliating that he was determined, his letter to Abraham notwithstanding, never to resemble his father in his own later years.

So, was Freud a self-hater? As noted, Kuh contends that the sensitive Jewish child born to assimilating parents is at pains to reject a father whose implicit lessons in compromise and self-hatred remind one of Adrienne Rich's representation of the similar problems mothers pose for feminists. One could even say that Kuh's conceptualization of the Jewish father in modernity precisely parallels Rich's conceptualization of the mother within patriarchy, both of whom seem to bequeath to those children who would take them as role models a legacy of weakness and abjectness. What these children reject is their respective parent's lack of power, and particularly the power to be self-determining (rejections entirely at odds with those of the anti-Semite and misogynist, who, conversely, tends to see the Jew or the mother as all *too* powerful).

If Jewish self-hatred is a reaction to a weak father, this contrasts usefully with the sense usually given to self-hatred within psychoanalysis, which tends, in most cases, to ascribe the term to the subject's internalization of an oppressive father figure via the superego. That process is described by Freud as "a portion of one's ego, which sets itself over against the rest of the ego as superego, and which now, in the form of 'conscience,' is ready to put into action against the ego the same harsh aggressiveness that the ego would have liked to have satisfied upon other, extraneous individuals."[18] In this situation self-hatred is thought to ensue when the child sees herself, not her oppressive parent, as the truly bad one. This also has the benefit of allowing her to retain a sense of her own agency, for by imagining that her badness is entirely a question of her own behavior, she need not then admit of a bad parent— which would likewise mean admitting of a terrifying, hostile world over which she has no control. Consequently, the self-hatred derived from a strong superego might be conceived of as a defense against another kind of self-hatred: the kind that occurs when someone has been forced to confront his or her complete lack of self-determination.

A father, of course, can be simultaneously weak and oppressive. Indeed, it's precisely when the child detects weakness in the father, however oppressive he may otherwise be, that we encounter the conditions for what Kuh considers to be the characteristically Jewish form of self-hatred. This might make sense of a case like that of Kafka, for instance, whose father appears as something of a rough brute next to whom the author felt himself to be correspondingly weak and pathetic, but whom, as Kafka's famous "Letter" attests, he also felt able to brutally criticize as someone that, for all his bluster, was radically *not* in charge of his own destiny.

And in a different way this too addresses the basis of Freud's own remembered humiliation before a father who failed to stand up for himself as a Jew when taunted with anti-Semitism; a father he vowed then never to resemble. Thus Freud, in his effort to move away from the Jewish self-loathing he was so quick to detect in others by means of his own reality principle to "accept who you are,"[19] nonetheless betrayed his contempt for the emasculated, skulking Jew who could *not* accept himself: the Jew, that is, whose acceptance of his own weakness admitted a rather different reality principle—that exhibited by his father's masochism—from the one more often advocated by Freud.

Even Freud's prescription for Jewish self-acceptance, in other words, becomes, on closer inspection, a way of contemptuously describing the majority of Jews as those who do not stand up for themselves. Hence, as with Mamet, accepting one's Jewishness is ultimately a way to reject one's Jewishness, as once again the very principle by which one strives to overcome one's self-hatred becomes a further expression of the same malaise. Thus while it may be the case that, as Adam Phillips has urged, we're "at our most stupid in our self-hatred," it's a remark made with the accustomed irony of someone well aware how such comments can risk exacerbating the disorder at the very point of diagnosing it.[20] Though this leaves us in a sticky spot: if self-hatred is the hatred aroused by nothing less than self-hatred, what, then, is its cure?

Amy Levy

"Cohen of Trinity," a remarkable short story from the end of the nineteenth century, sheds significant light on the cryptic character of modern self-hatred. Written by the British poet and novelist Amy Levy, the story was published shortly after Levy had gained great literary success with *Ruben Sachs*. This comic and not altogether flattering novel of Anglo-Jewish manners was considered a betrayal by editors of the U.K. Jewish community's newspaper, *The Jewish Chronicle*, who accused its author of fouling her own nest. That real-world controversy is worth noting because in her subsequent short story Levy has the eponymous Cohen, a Jewish student at Trinity College Cambridge who went on to achieve major literary success following the publication of *his* first novel, commit suicide. This raises the question, posed by the narrator in the first paragraph, as to why he should take his life "now, when his book was in everyone's hands, his name on everyone's lips; when that recognition for which he had longed was so completely his; that success for which he had thirsted was poured out for him in so generous a draft—to turn away, to vanish without a word of explanation (he was so fond of explaining himself) is the very last thing one would have expected of him."[21]

Not long after this short story was published Levy, the second Jewish woman to go to Cambridge University, herself took her own life. Like Cohen too, Levy vanished without a word of explanation, although her story does perhaps possess something of the enigmatic qualities of a suicide note. Sometime before his own suicide, for instance, the story's narrator tells us that Cohen had "often declared a taste for suicide to be among the characteristics of his versatile race" (478), and while Cohen's reported speech is certainly no "explanation" for his subsequent actions, we *can*, I think, trace within it the outline of a Jewish character hating himself (or his fellow Jews) for hating himself (or his fellow Jews).

The question as to why both Levy and her fictional Cohen took their own lives at a high point in their careers might be extended to all modern Jews who had successfully gained political and cultural recognition, making "names" for themselves and getting admitted into the upper echelons of British society and its elite institutions, and yet whose feeling of nonbelonging had endured. This sense of Jewish alienation permeates Levy's story. Hence, though the picture we get of Cohen displays plenty of stock stereotyping—Cohen's "full, prominent lips, full, prominent eyes, and the curved beak of the nose" (479)—the narrative point of view on the story's bewildering subject comes from a non-Jewish contemporary of Cohen's at Cambridge who plainly regards his Jewish colleague as a kind of puzzle in need of deciphering. It's this use of an unreliable narrator that problematizes any facile charge of authorial self-hatred, given that our perspective on Cohen is patently that of someone whose vision of the outsider has been obscured by his own sense of entitlement.

In the eyes of our narrator, Cohen's is an over the top personality. He's always courting attention, always surrounded by an audience willing to laugh at his self-deprecatory shtick. He's also, we're told, "melodramatic, self-conscious," ways of being and acting that can seem terribly affected, for who can really trust someone so eager to be liked, wanted, let in? Isn't such a person obviously an imposter? Yet Cohen still possesses a certain magnetism despite or possibly because of the fact that he at all times seems to imagine himself from the other's point of view—so much so that one begins to suspect that this external perspective on himself (that of the "reference group" in Gilman's terms) may be the only one he has access to.

But isn't that the idea here? For while there is an ongoing debate as to whether Amy Levy was a self-hating Jewish writer, a close reading of her story indicates why such a question misses the point. Self-hating she may well have been, but what her work brings into the field of representation is a sense of the social conditions that make self-hatred the closest thing to having a self at all. It is, in other words, only by hating who I am that I can index the feeling that who I am taken for isn't really me. Self-hatred, in this case, is the affective response of a self protesting its own absence. Cohen is thus a portrait of a character who perhaps feels (and we can guess this despite the partial view we have of him from our uncomprehending narrator) that he cannot, no matter how conspicuous or celebrated he becomes, ever become what he really aspires to be: self-determining.

Of course, in the highly class-conscious and clubbable world to which Cohen never quite belongs, this is true of everyone, but it appears especially true of Jews, who, as our narrator has asserted, are a quintessentially "versatile race." Note again that use of "versatile." What counts as characteristically Jewish, in other words, is whatever a Jew does. Nothing, for a Jew, is unstereotypical. Hence, though Cohen is a charismatic and creative personality who has sought to become his own man by distinguishing himself, in his writing, from his family, his history, and his race . . . his novel, described by the narrator as "wholly unclassifiable" (483), is, no less than its author, mistakable in every way but one: to be unclassifiable is still to be, classifiably, Jewish.

Philip Roth

In another time and another place, America after World War II, we meet another group of writers—Bernard Malamud, Saul Bellow, Philip Roth—all struggling with the classification of their identities and their works as Jewish. All three contested the notion that they should be considered Jewish-American writers, preferring to be seen as American writers who just happened also to be Jewish. Bellow, for instance, suspected that the gesture of grouping them together was a ruse to render them marginal figures and thus distinguish between their works and those belonging to a "properly" American canon. Malamud, somewhat gnomically, rejected the classification in more sensational terms by claiming that "all men are Jews."[22] Roth, however, though a generation younger than Malamud and Bellow, conceded that something along these lines may well have united them. All three, he said, were engaged in "imagining Jews *being* imagined, by themselves and by others."[23]

Roth's description of the Jewish-American writer's imagination reminds us of the point of view of Amy Levy. Unable simply to assume their identities as a given, Jews as a minority group within society cannot seem to conceive of themselves without an awareness of how they may be seen or represented by others. Since to be preoccupied with how one is seen will necessarily affect one's behavior, however, this is precisely, for Sartre, what imbues the modern Jewish experience with such existential inauthenticity. For to imagine how one appears in the eyes of others is to try to change how one appears, both in the eyes of others and in one's own eyes: a particularly insoluble problem for writers, since to be creative surely requires a free imagination, not one forever second-guessing the reader.

The Jew, snarled that notorious anti-Semite Richard Wagner, "can only mimic and mock—not truly make a poem of his words, an artwork of his doings."[24] Both Levy and her alter ego Cohen seem to have accepted this damning account of their own identities: both felt incapable of true art, and both felt they excelled at mimicking and mocking. To read Roth, on the other hand, including his always plentiful mimicry and mockery, is to gain a new confidence that the Jew's alienated point of view can bestow a unique imagination in and of itself.

Dogged by the accusation of Jewish self-hatred from the beginning of his career, Roth made this charge a recurrent theme in his work. Perhaps the most famous example appears at the end of his 1969 classic *Portnoy's Complaint*, in which Alexander Portnoy goes to Israel and finds himself labeled a Jewish self-hater by an Israeli woman for whom he can muster no erection. Engaging her criticism, Portnoy wonders whether or not self-hating Jews aren't perhaps the best or only real kind—a notion underscored by the fact that the section of the book set in Israel is subtitled "Exile," implying that the true Jew, like the self-hater, is someone who can never expect to feel at home anywhere. (And isn't Israel, too, another example of a "safe space" that has turned out to be anything but?)

Roth, remarks critic James Wood, "has shown that postmodern artifice and American realism are not incompatible, but actually feed each other."[25] It's an observation that helps to explain why it is that, though the typical Rothian protagonist is, like the subject of any unraveling postmodernist fiction, notoriously mercurial and impossible to pin down, the intensely personal or even quasi-autobiographical atmosphere of Roth's writings has meant that his readers seldom feel they're straying, with Roth, into the literary unfathomable. Yet in Roth there is no self-knowledge to be had. Everyone is undone, both by the slipperiness of the text and especially by the tormenting and tantalizing presence of the libido.

What psychoanalysis calls the superego is sometimes also referred to as the "antilibidinal ego." It's that part of the ego that borrows from cruel authority figures "a sense of power—if only over the self—and fills it with self-hatred." Yet this is a self-hatred that, for some, seems worth suffering because the sense of power "serves a crucial defensive function to hold that self together."[26] Like the narcissist, then, the self-hater prefers the certainty of the self to the uncertainty of life. Roth seems to prefer things the other way around in his novels, however, which is not, of course, to imply that he is immune to either narcissism or self-hatred. Rather, it suggests that his means of escaping the self-hatred supplied by the superego (qua internal spokesperson for the punitive parent) is with recourse to another self-hatred—the kind that afflicts the "self" forced to confront its own lack of unity once the patriarchal law that might have shored it up has been found wanting. This, in fin-de-siècle Europe, was the classic form taken by Jewish self-hatred. Though of the American postmodern-realist Philip Roth it might be more pertinent to remark, as Woody Allen's Harry does in *Deconstructing Harry*, that while he hates himself it is not, any longer, because he's Jewish—even if it's his being Jewish that has allowed him so many creative insights into his self-hatred.

Literature and Self-Hatred

Roth is not alone in turning to literature as a means of freeing the self from its unwanted determinations. We see this same theme in the memoir of a Russian-Jewish writer and immigrant to the United States, Gary Shteyngart. *Little Failure* includes a reference to Shteyngart's not-un-Kafkaesque father warning his son at the outset of his publishing career, "Just don't write like a self-hating Jew," although later on Shteyngart suggests that without the animating spirit of self-hatred he would never have been inspired to write at all.[27] The writer Wayne Koestenbaum agrees. "I don't like confident literature," he declares, "or literature that seems immune to self-incrimination; literature should bear witness to the fact that the writer was humiliated by the very process of writing the work. . . . Language isn't transcendent. Every sentence, however stuffed and upholstered with confident maturity, attests to that earlier, infant time when we couldn't master words."[28]

The literature Koestenbaum likes sees the text less as a site of authority than as an expression of its absence. Note the analogy here to that form of Jewish self-hatred we've already described which rides on a parallel rejection of the father—his authority, his confident maturity, his claim to transcendence through mastery of words. Such a rejection leads to a weakening of the Oedipal law and a raising of the status and influence of the mother within the patriarchal family. It's a dynamic that seems more than merely metaphorical for those writers whose creative agency depends on their ability to detect a lack or weakness in the Father/Word—a lack that then allows them to wrest an all too fragile or failing "authority" from disapproving parents who, in the case of Kafka and Shteyngart, really do exist outside the text (and there is no doubt that Roth likewise encountered more than his fair share of censoring Jewish elders).

But if this has been a common motif of the immigrant or assimilating Jewish family, it has also become a hallmark of the modern bourgeois family generally, whose insecurity, fragmentation, and perennial efforts at conservation might be said to resemble that of the modern text. So it is for perhaps the most celebrated contemporary life writer, Karl Ove Knausgård, whose painstaking narration of his fairly mundane, middle-class, suburban life in Norway is beset by painful memories of the humiliated bravado of an intimidating, authoritarian father. Though he could appear a standard bearer of the canonical tradition (white, male, straight, European) handed down by divine right between the generations, Knausgård, like Shteyngart and Koestenbaum, also attests to the profound feelings of shame, anxiety, and self-hatred that got him writing in the first place.

The modern Jewish diasporic experience of economic, social, and geographic mobility thus seems to have deepened and widened, and in such conditions, regardless of whether this mobility is achieved or denied, self-hatred abounds. In Zadie Smith's novel *NW*, for example, we encounter the kind of fitful toxic atmosphere of a metropolitan world in which few people make it up the ladder of success and those who do feel lost, fake, inauthentic fictions, even to themselves. The most adept in social mobility in the novel is a young black woman, Keisha, whose given name she rejects as too ethnic, rebranding herself Natalie, but only in order to reassign to herself, on certain self-selected occasions, her forsaken African identity: "She picked an outfit. Glittering sandals and hoop earrings and bangles and a long ochre skirt and a brown vest and hair in a giant Afro puff held off her face by means of one leg of a black pair of tights, cut off and knotted at the back of her head. She felt African in this outfit, although nothing she wore came from Africa except perhaps the earrings and bangles, conceptually."[29]

Natalie is, even to herself, a conceptual African: her identity put on and taken off like a costume, as if it really could be. But if her costume feels hollow, a carapace, and not even really African, it still has the power to lay a claim on her: a claim as absolute and unassailable as it is alien, like the "Law" in Kafka's famous parable, whose authority remains in force even in the absence of any determinate meaning.

Amy Levy's fiction reveals the false promise of a new world order in which Jews were to be admitted so long as they left their Jewishness behind. The world of Smith's *NW*, by contrast, shows us the same problem in reverse—now multicultural identities are to be worn, shown, fetishized, and celebrated, but, as Foucault was to say of sexual identities, the liberty to be who "you really are" turns out to encode yet further fixings, imprisonments, alienations. It's more than a hundred years since "Cohen of Trinity," but Smith's characters feel no less self-hatred than do Levy's.

Of modern Jews Kafka wrote, "With their posterior legs they were still glued to their father's Jewishness, and with their waving anterior legs they found no new ground."[30] To which remark Smith, in a remarkable essay on Kafka, responds: "Alienation from oneself, the conflicted assimilation of migrants, losing one place without gaining another. . . . This feels like Kafka in the genuine clothes of an existential prophet. . . . For there is a sense in which Kafka's Jewish question ('What have I in common with Jews?') has become everybody's question, Jewish alienation the template for all our doubts. What is Muslimness? What is femaleness? What is Polishness? What is Englishness? These days we all find our anterior legs flailing before us. We're all insects, all *Ungeziefer*, now."[31]

Jewish alienation the template for all our doubts. It's what Bernard Malamud meant when he said "all men are Jews." Not that all men are the same—rather that all men are strangers, lost, uprooted, wandering around a world that would feel permanently hostile and unwelcoming were we to fail to recognize that what we share is precisely this: the feeling that we all differ. None of us fit in. None of us belong. The world feels unnatural for everyone, now.

Getting over Oneself

If the text—and especially the conspicuous strangeness of the literary text—is where things we thought we knew begin to unravel, where identities are loosened and the narrative self finds itself continually undone, this too is the sense that was given to overcoming by Nietzsche: the self that forms, deforms, and reforms in writing is always, for Nietzsche, the hated self whose fixity is precisely what one must indeed hate to free up another, freer self. Nietzsche sought to envision a self whose freedom it would be never to stabilize into anything so furnished as an identity. And if he was ultimately able to get over the self-hatred he explicitly felt for his own national collective identity—his German identity—he had, instructively, to first overcome another hatred, or rather his hatred for the Other: his own anti-Semitism.

As Sarah Kofman has lucidly shown, in ceasing to hate Jews, Nietzsche instead began to admire Jews precisely for their "sublime self-hatred," whose emancipatory potential for himself he recognized, seeing in Jewish self-hatred a means of overcoming the limiting problem of the self *tout court.*[32] It is with reference to Nietzsche too that Reitter's book recommends Jewish self-hatred, done well, as potentially a good thing.[33] Indeed, for Kuh and Lessing, Jewish self-hatred "was a heading that stood at once for a very big problem and its world-saving solution."[34] And while Kuh conceded that Jewish self-hatred isn't the easiest path for Jews to follow, he saw it as preferable to both assimilation and Zionism, both of which, he argued, "would lead Jews further into the disaster of nationalism." It's in this sense that Jewish self-hatred, properly executed, rather than betraying Jews, can be reinterpreted as a way of restoring faith in the Jewish messianic project. Self-hatred accedes to this "messianic" promise when it keeps open the possibility of a future whose express purpose is not to repeat the past. This it achieves when it neither advances a particular ideal of the subject nor proposes a particular political program but, rather, reflects who and what, in any given generation, is unaccounted for by the culture and politics of the historical moment.

Groucho Marx put it more simply, however, when he said that he didn't wish to belong to a club that would have him as a member. Surely the pithiest account we have of how so many Jews have come to experience their own identities, Groucho's is a statement of self-hatred at its purest. Yet Groucho's quip at least breathes some air and lightness into an impossible situation by suggesting a kind of confidence within and about the unrelentingness of one's self-doubt. Because isn't it the self that has become assured of its own position, comfortable, at home with itself, certain that it knows who it is, who it wants to be, and to which club it belongs, precisely the one we should really be asking questions of? For what you have there is not the "authentic" self—no, *that* is the imposter!

TWO

Envy

Each man envies, the strong openly, the weak in secret.
—SCHEHERAZADE, *One Thousand and One Nights*

It's miserable to succumb to envy. Who can admit to such an ignoble thing? Envy is the passion that dare not speak its name. You can confess your guilt, be righteous in your anger, romantic in your fears, unapologetic in your lusts, comic in your paranoia, and you can even take pride, as God does, in your jealousy. To be jealous, after all, is to feel yourself entitled. It's the prerogative of the father to jealously lay claim over the body of the mother, forcing his son to transfer affections elsewhere. But neither God nor man wants to appear so petty as to be envious. If jealousy is a potent, manly emotion, then envy suffers by comparison from some deficiency, some lack. The envious person has nothing to lay claim to. The feeling, says Nietzsche, is fundamentally one of impotence—the sense that one lacks both power and potential: a life without possibilities.

The envious feel blocked, bereft in a world of goods belonging to others. Indeed, for the envious person, who never fails to feel left out, belonging itself seems a good belonging to others. So in envying belongings, what the envious really envy is belonging. "It is certain," writes Chaucer, "that envy is the worst sin that is; for all other sins are sins only against one virtue, whereas envy is against all virtue and against all goodness."[1] And in Milton's *Paradise Lost* we get Satan, who, "pale with envy," seeks to damage God by damaging what belongs to God: all the goods and goodness of creation. Creativeness, says Melanie Klein, is "the deepest cause for envy" (202). One finds plenty of it, therefore, in what I do— criticism—a public discourse officially sanctioning the critic's right to take down the creative works of others. Some criticism has no other goal than that of damaging its objects.[2]

The Worst Sin That Is

Klein imagines the envious personality as one whose feelings of personal failure lead him to attack vindictively whichever values he sees on display. He experiences in another's success a kind of persecution that can be obstructed only by "spoiling" the other rather than by achieving anything for himself. Envy is, in other words, a feeling about one's social standing, about how one compares with others. Yet it's a feeling that, for Klein, takes root in infancy, beginning with the infant's relation to the primary object, the "breast that has frustrated him" (180). The idea baffles at first. If envy is a social disorder, isn't an envious infant something of a contradiction in terms? But when my own baby went through an early phase of biting me, I wondered whether he was indeed a Kleinian infant discovering that he is not omnipotent but dependent on others—and especially his mother—for the goods that may or may not come his way. Klein's envy is a response to this basic fact of life: that one *depends* on others. To live at all is to live socially.

And so envy is the hatred and resentment we are bound to sometimes feel for those whom we cannot but love.

Envy becomes excessive for Klein when it tries to defend against this position of ambivalence by splitting off the idealized from the devouring breast. In such a world, full of impossible monsters and ideals, persecutory anxiety permeates. The envious person feels constantly under attack. We get a similar idea from Kierkegaard, for whom "Envy is concealed admiration." "Admiration is happy self-abandon," he says. "Envy is unhappy self-assertion."[3] What he's splitting is the difference between admiring a good object and admiring an idealized one. While the good object can *inspire* creativity, the idealized one can only inhibit it as the sneaking thought creeps in: if such an object or person exists, then what's the point of me?

Klein's essay is called "Envy and Gratitude," two feelings that cancel each other out. Gratitude acknowledges your dependency on others in a positive sense. A grateful relation to the bountiful breast sustains "hope, trust and belief in goodness," which becomes "an impetus towards creativeness" (202). Envy, though, is a state of chronic ingratitude. The envious person cannot be placated. Nothing you do for him will make him any less envious. On the contrary: another's generosity only deepens the envier's sense that the giver possesses all the gifts. "A particular cause of envy," says Klein, "is the relative absence of it in others" (203). How enviable the person who feels no envy!

As someone who has, for as long as I can remember, lived in fear of envy's evil eye, I am genuinely scared by the thought that the envious cannot be appeased. In its ability to spread fear and insecurity, envy seems a sort of accomplice of terror. Yet envy's hatred is not "open and violent," writes Kant, but "secret and disguised."[4] It delights in the downfall of others—especially family, friends, and neighbors—but mostly indulges in reaction rather than action.

The envious tend to commit what the philosopher Max Scheler calls "crimes of spite": trolling under a pseudonym online, for example, or gossiping, or secretly identifying with those real-world actors who sow the seeds of chaos and destruction.[5]

Envy's preferred anonymity means we rarely know how much or how little it operates in our lives. How many things or opportunities have been blocked or lost to us on account of another's envy? And how much has our own envy blocked or harmed others? I'm seldom shy of admitting negative feelings—guilt, anxiety, fear, disgust, depression—but am I, have I been, fully cognizant of my envy? In my imagination I always seem at risk of other people's envy. And even when thinking theoretically about envy, I consistently find myself envisaging other people as providing better examples of the envious personality than I consider myself to be, as if envy were too unbearable for me to feel, even hypothetically.

The psychoanalyst, of course, will always suspect that what the subject fails to know about herself, what she works hardest to deny, and what she cannot even allow herself to imagine, may well have some significant purchase on her. And yes, shamefully, in doing this work I have come across ample evidence of my own envy. I say "shamefully" because one of the chief reasons why envy hides, both from others and from itself, is the condemnation it frequently provokes. If envy is our most Satanic trait, our deadliest sin, whose only agenda is vanquishing the good, then it's hardly surprising if we repress it. So at this point it may be worth my stating three things:

- First, the moralizing discourse that condemns envy needs itself to be examined for its concealment of the envious motive. As we'll see, it was precisely this mask of morality worn by envy that Nietzsche identified and called *ressentiment*.

- Second, if what envy envies above all is a kind of creativity or expressiveness, then expressing envy may be a means of locating the blocked creative potential residing *within* envy. An expression of envy is then already not, in the strictest sense, envy.
- Hence, third, envy isn't all bad. It can be put to good use.

The Age of Envy

One can find, especially in North America, a capitalization upon envy in the rhetoric of advertisers that promise products whose purchase will incite the feeling. Advertisers always seem to know us better than we know ourselves, for as much as we may fear and seek to deflect the envy of others, don't we also crave their envy, so that we might believe ourselves to be not the envious but the enviable? The only thing worse than being envied, as Oscar Wilde nearly said, is not being envied.

But being envied is no picnic either. In his sociological study of 1966, Helmut Schoeck contends that both envy and the fear of envy are universal, confined to no particular society, political system, or historical epoch. Yet the period after World War II can be called "the age of envy," he says, because envy then moves out of the shadows and attempts "public self-justification."[6] Envy's public self-justification refers not to the rich American consumer looking to incite envy, however, but to those who find themselves consumed *by* envy. Those, for example, whose social identities—as constructed along the lines of class, race, gender—can be mobilized (for example, via civil rights) in such a way as to legitimate envy as the inevitable outcome of social inequality.

So the admission of envy into the political lexicon can be said to have advanced the program of democracy. Yet an expanded democratic field does not make envy go away. Far from it. Even in antiquity Aristotle recognized that envy is felt most keenly by those whose social positions resemble each other, where the differences between them are relatively small. Thus the effect of making, even if only in theory, all men—and eventually all creeds, women, and races—equal citizens is that more and more people can enviously compare themselves with those with whom they previously dared not imagine any comparison. So envy has a distinct role in making and spreading democracy, and democracy has a distinct role in making and spreading envy. Envy and democracy are joined at the hip! The absolute moral abhorrence most people feel toward envy is rather curious in light of this fact: that envy is the "only antagonistic emotion perceived as having inequality as its object."[7] Might our criticism of envy, then, also imply an attack on our concept of justice?

Ressentiment

Certainly for Nietzsche the association between envy and such social ideals as equality was not only unpalatable but deeply suspect. His concept of the "slave revolt in morality," which he traces back to the Hebrew Bible, is what happens when values are reversed. Unable to do anything else, the slave renders strength a kind of weakness and weakness a kind of strength—and it's under the yoke of just such a dubious morality that those naturally endowed with superior gifts are required to disavow the noble features that distinguish them on account of how those who lack these virtues have been made to *feel*. Thus the slave revolt raises no one but, rather, draws everyone down to the level of slaves.

Yet this slave revolt in morality is not, for Nietzsche, so terrible in the Hebrew slaves themselves, who are at least motivated by a real will to power.[8] Ressentiment's reversal of values becomes truly toxic only when the slaves' envy passes unnoticed into what purports to be its negation—Christian love—whose idealization turns all men into slaves. Christian love, for Nietzsche, is what false-consciousness looks like, though Scheler, a Nietzschean-Christian, disagrees that ressentiment is at root an ancient religious phenomenon, perceiving it, rather, as the invention of the secular and democratic era. Not in Christian love but in the deliberately depersonalizing tenor of humanitarian love—a love "directed at the *species*"—does Scheler detect the infiltration of a "glimmering *hatred* against the positive higher values."[9]

The implicit elitism within Nietzsche's repudiation of modern morality gave his philosophy some unlovely political bedfellows, to say the least, and it remains a tragic irony that the greatest critic of the herd instinct should have been so attractive to the instinctive herd. But if one reads Nietzsche as a psychological rather than a political thinker, one can find in his work a handy way of diagnosing one's own ressentiment. Whenever we console ourselves, for instance, with the thought that while so-and-so has more power, status, or success than we do, we are much purer (or, alternatively: happier) than they are—*we* haven't sold out—that would be our envy talking.

Like Nietzsche, Freud sought to remind us of the envy animating our most brotherly love. In his essay on "Group Psychology" he presents the overcoming of sibling rivalry as the basis of social life. The envious child sees that his parents love his sibling just as much as they do him and comes thereby to understand how his envy only leads to self-harm. So he presses instead for equality: there must be no favoritism! His self-cure is to identify with the sibling whom he had previously taken as a rival on the basis of their shared love for the same parent. The idea that hatred becomes love through identification is therefore key to Freud's concept of the group as a reaction-formation: the group is a collective identity that members achieve by phantasmatically projecting themselves into one another's place.

"Social justice," writes Freud with marked irony, "means that we deny ourselves many things so that others may have to do without them as well."[10] To illustrate his point he refers to the biblical parable of Solomon's justice in which the Israelite king must rule over a case brought before him by two women who have shared a home, each with a baby. One night, one of these women rolls over in her sleep and accidentally kills her child. Bereft, she swaps her dead baby for the other's living one. In the morning the other woman sees what has been done and brings the case to Solomon, who must decide which of these women is the true mother. The king calls for his sword and says he'll cut the child in two so that each woman can be treated fairly to half a baby. Terrified, the baby's true mother insists the child be given to the other woman, who for her part accepts the ruling of a half portion each. Hence Solomon divines who the true mother is—she who will give up her claim to preserve the life—and returns the child to her.

Solomon, observes John Forrester, is a sort of "master dialectician" *avant la lettre* (14). He says one thing, and the very opposite of what he says (the truth he is after) comes out. So our paradigmatic story of justice is first of all a story about the wise judgment of a subtle king. But it is also a story about the love of a true mother, who will sacrifice anything, including her motherhood, for her child. She too, says Forrester, has a sort of dialectical part to play, for by renouncing her claim to her child, she ultimately regains her child. However, it takes another wise man (an updated Jewish patriarch), Sigmund Freud, to notice the part played by the third actor and true protagonist of the story. As Freud puts it, "If one woman's child is dead, the other shall not have a live one either. The bereaved woman is recognised by this wish" (quoted 15). It is, after all, hardly remarkable to find the true mother saying that she'd rather have no child than half a child—any "*ordinary* human being" would reject the notion of cutting a child in half (16). So the wisdom of Solomon for Freud is that he discovers not who the true mother is, but who the bereaved mother is, by revealing to us, as Freud also reveals to us, her compulsion to repeat her crime. Yet we who are less subtle and less wise seem to turn quickly away from her suffering by choosing instead to identify with the goodies—fatherly wisdom and motherly love—thus repressing the role played by envy in our story of justice.

"We have been duped," suggests Forrester, "by the structure of the parable," as slippery and enigmatic a source as any dream or joke (15). What, after all, is our excuse for assuming a malign interpretation of the bereaved woman's feelings in favor of the parable's other protagonists? Might it be that we neglect to think too much about her claim because we come to this story already envisaging ourselves as the champions of justice (albeit, in the search for justice for the true mother, the bereaved mother's lack of justice gets conveniently forgotten)? And mightn't it also be the case that we denigrate her claim because we deem it too obvious to bother with? Unlike the king and the true mother, whose words are assumed indirect, subtle, and thus worthy of interpretation, her words get taken literally, as if no additional effort were needed in order to understand her, or as if her wish to cause harm to others were only to be expected of someone *like* her. But isn't this rather a strange conclusion to draw, given that she is the one in the story whose persona and statement (that she'd happily accept *half* a baby) might just as plausibly be regarded as the *most* difficult to understand?

Later in the chapter we'll see why the bereaved woman's rhetoric may be less murderous in intent than a literal reading of it would have us believe. Yet even at this stage one can note how her claim presents an interesting parallel to that of the other actors. For she too says one thing while meaning the opposite. She says she wants the living child, but plainly she wants her housemate to have, as she has, a dead child. And while she makes this claim in a court of justice, it hardly needs pointing out that she is in no way just herself in seeking to avenge her own loss by hurting another who has done her no injury, whose only crime is that of still having what she has not. Yet, suggests Freud, our most cherished notions of "social justice" spring from just such an envy that would aim to equalize by denying "ourselves many things so that others may have to do without them as well."

The Politics of Envy

Make no mistake, Frantz Fanon tells us, the "colonised man is an envious man" who every day dreams of being in the place of the colonialist: in his house, in his bed, with his wife.[11] Nor will he rest until things between them have been equalized. His envy thus attests to all he has been dispossessed of, not only materially but spiritually, for in his dreams of having what his oppressor has he reveals how his very *dreams* have been colonized. He wants what he does not want to want. He wants what he hates, much as the Kleinian infant hates and envies what he cannot help but love. So while, for Fanon, envy's demand for equality begins the process of decolonization, ultimately, in wishing to equalize, the colonized man is still in thrall to a slave mentality, for he hasn't been able to want something different from that which his "master" has shown him. To do so he must free not only his body and land but his creative vision for another kind of world and a different future for humanity. This, for Fanon, is the real meaning of decolonization: it means wanting something else.

Feminism has arguably had a harder time thinking creatively about the envy within its ranks. For unlike the colonized man's legitimate claim to have had his own property torn out from under him, the feminist has sought to resist the notion that she lacks anything, that her sex is in any way deficient. So she hasn't taken kindly to the notion of "penis envy," or to Freud's suggestion that, in order to get over her envy, the woman needs to transform her wish for a penis into a baby. Yet such ideas have taken hold and might well impinge on how we view, for example, the battle over a baby in the court of Solomon. For it isn't hard to imagine that scene as a displacement activity on the part of the women, whose envy for the sovereign with his big sword has been turned upon each other, while he, for his part, dangles the sword over the baby and rewards only the woman who promises to give up the child while damning her who demands her equal share.

Women, it would seem, have long since been regarded as peculiarly susceptible to envy. Woman, Scheler tells us, is "the weaker and therefore the more vindictive sex," hence the "strong feminine tendency to indulge in detractive gossip."[12] Unlike the open and honest conflicts fought between men, conflicts between women are often seen as underhand, catty, *dis*honest. And this reputation for catfighting has been a problem even for the disagreements that take place between feminists who are often wary of bringing their own movement into disrepute when they're most passionately engaging with it.

So what if, rather than simply rejecting the role played by envy in female homosocial relations, one can reinterpret its significance in a way that helps to release the critical potential of envy *for* feminism? That has been done brilliantly by Sianne Ngai, who begins by looking again at how Freud genders his analysis of envy. To recap: sibling rivalry, as the form taken by an envy that includes boys, has the capacity to establish norms that can lead to social group formation and systems of justice. This is possible because the envious boy phantasmatically projects himself into his brother's place. "Thus social feeling," says Freud, "is based upon the reversal of what was first a hostile feeling into . . . an identification."[13] But Ngai is interested in why Freud's examples of exclusively female envy do not involve this same phantasmatic or imaginative dimension. This, too, is something Forrester observes regarding the difference between Freud's treatment of penis envy and "envy in general": the former, applying only to females, skips "the subsequent reaction-formation: the identification with the other child and the clamorous demand for equality."[14] Similarly, Ngai's examination of Freud's use of female examples in "Group Psychology" reveals that female envy establishes no norms, values, or laws because the girl's identification is performative, acted out, even to the point of hysteria. She *emulates* her rival. Hence it is emulation that, for Freud, typifies the mode of female identification. So while the envious male identifies, the envious female copies. She may, for instance, develop a cough just like her mother, thus proving herself secondary with respect to a preexisting idea of how or who she should be. Unlike her male counterpart, then, the female can barely be said to exist in her own right at all. This, certainly, must be counted a source of her weakness. But mightn't it also be a key to her strength?

Copycats

To focus her discussion of envy between women, Ngai interprets the 1992 film *Single White Female*, a psychological thriller about an apartment shared by two women with similarly horrible consequences to the Bible's tale of two women living together. The "single white female" of the title is Allie, who owns the apartment and uses that description of herself when advertising her spare room. The room is subsequently rented out to another single white female, Hedy, who has no property of her own. The two women quickly become close friends. But the closeness that at first offers comfort just as quickly becomes a source of discomfort. What initially seems flattering when Hedy starts emulating Allie—in her dress, for example—soon enough seems flattening. When she not only borrows Allie's shoes but buys identical clothes and even has her hair cut and dyed in the same style, it becomes increasingly hard, especially for the men in the film, to tell the difference between them. Admiration becomes aggression. Imitation becomes mimicry. Hedy clearly envies Allie—we're aware of it, even if she isn't—but where will this envy lead her? Ultimately the action descends into murderousness, as the two women try to kill each other—Hedy tries to kill Allie first, but Allie in the end kills Hedy, thus restoring to herself the singularity she had originally advertised, along with her flat.

What makes possible this horrible end is the fact that Allie's single white female identity is so easily borrowed and copied. Allie, who works in fashion, has all the trappings of a successful woman: a model woman. What woman, one might ask, wouldn't want to emulate her? But what is she a model *of*, exactly? What primarily seems to single her out *is* her sense of fashion. So she's essentially a good model of being a good model, as if modelling were the ultimate goal for a woman. Women, says Ngai, are "excellent examples of excellent examples." And what defines the example is that it is not self-determining—it has no originality—because an example is always an example of something, some preexisting prototype that it exemplifies. So in emulating Allie, Hedy is, paradoxically, copying a copy, modeling herself on a model, as if femininity in its most ideal state were nothing but emulation. Femininity is "structured 'like' an example."[15]

What envy wants is to spoil things for the other. And what Hedy spoils by emulating Allie is, in the first place, Allie's singular identity. She exposes Allie to her own lack of self-sufficiency—her nonoriginality—which also has the effect of exposing Allie to her own aggression and murderousness toward the one who imitates her. It's in this way that envy, by working so hard to bring down others to its own level, reveals to the other her *own* envy.[16]

Single White Female is the work of a male director, Barbet Schroeder, and you could call it a sexist film in its stereotypical depiction of female friendship as a mask for hostility.[17] But Ngai does something creative with it. She takes on board the parallel between what Hedy is doing—desingularizing the other woman and creating a compound femaleness they can both share—and the feminist project of creating a sisterhood. She does it by going back to Klein's envious infant who has reacted to ambivalence with an idealization that then becomes persecutory. The feminist must likewise struggle with the fact that she has been acculturated into desiring a certain model of femininity that she sees as harmful to her. What her envy has enabled her to do is "transition from desire to antagonism."[18] And envy's pattern of emulation, as we'll see, is precisely the mechanism by means of which she *can* transition: away from admiration *toward* antagonism. This directly opposes Freud's view of emulation as the mode of feminine identification. Instead, the envy that emulates doesn't *identify* with the other but, more accurately, wishes to destroy, albeit unconsciously, by *means* of emulation, what it experiences as persecutory about the other: namely her idealization. In this sense we might say that the female envy in the film does not, per the normative group's psychology, want to overcome divisiveness by making two into one. Rather, Hedy wants to take the singular, the one, and break it into two.

Similarly, says Ngai, feminism is "internally divided or split, yet *held together* by this very split." What's important here is that the split subject no longer conforms to an existing model. Thus while a good example of a woman will always exemplify the ideal, a bad example of a woman—such as an envious woman—not only fails to uphold the ideal but even destabilizes it. By being a bad example, then, the bad woman undermines what may turn out to be the most disabling aspect of idealized femininity—including idealized feminism—which is the whole notion of a model woman. So the bad example of female solidarity we see in *Single White Female* turns out to be a surprisingly good example for feminism, for it shows us female subjects "as examples that do not properly exemplify, actively defining and redefining the category they would seem only to passively reflect."[19]

Now, what if we transport this idea to that paradigmatic scene of Jewish justice in the court of Solomon? The bereaved woman is recognized by her wish to divide the child. But why should we assume she means her words any more literally than Solomon, who, it is well known, never really intended to cut the baby in two? Indeed, what if, like that famously subtle king, she too is using her situation to make a larger point, a point about the suffering caused by ideals that we ourselves, no less than Solomon, are liable to have already judged and damned her by? To reinterpret her intervention that way requires a new understanding of her consent to divide the child. So what if we instead see the baby—who is, qua baby, always the figure of a future humanity—as representative of the split subject: a subject, that is, no longer constrained by some preexisting idealization of what it should be, but a subject whose very splitness leaves it open, free, full of creative possibilities (and thus symbolic of change, restitution, justice)? Whence, by blurring the dividing line between the true and the false mother and reintegrating this splitness into a *singular* subject, neither one thing nor another, the envious woman in fact attacks neither the other mother nor the child, but rather an *image* of mother and child whose idealization persecutes everyone. This, too, is what Klein tells us: that in order to overcome one's envy, one must learn to accept a reality in which good and bad are *not* split but coexist.

What the parable therefore offers us is the dialectical movement of a justice that can proceed from envy through wisdom to love, albeit only when we recover the voice of the bereaved woman to understand what may be motivating her. Nor is her side of the story the only feature of the parable that tends to get repressed in popular memory. Who remembers, for instance, that the two women who appear before Solomon are also prostitutes? Thus *even* the good woman, the self-sacrificing mother, is a bad example of idealized femininity, for in this oft repeated biblical story Madonna and Whore coexist in the same body. If that detail *has* dropped out of cultural memory, then it may be because our own relationship to the social order remains in the grip of an envy that prefers to see the world in stark binary terms—good and evil/black and white/ pure and impure—the ready hallmark of the type of thinking that so often renders its practitioners unjust. All is not lost, however, for *were* we to admit of the role played by envy in our highest ideals, then such an acknowledgment could have the potential to bring forth a justice—a social justice—of which even Nietzsche might approve.

Envying Jews

Nietzsche accused the Hebrew slaves in the Bible of inventing the ressentiment underpinning Judeo-Christian morality whose reversal of true values (strength, health, nobility) he believed to have been consecrated and universalized via the false consciousness of Christian love. The philosopher Scheler repudiated Nietzsche's attack on Christianity, redirecting his critique toward modern humanitarian movements. Though Scheler (himself the son of a Jewish mother) did agree there was such a thing as Jewish ressentiment, given "the discrepancy between the colossal national pride of 'the chosen people' and a contempt and discrimination which weighed on them for centuries like a destiny."[20]

According to Freud, the pride of Jewish people and the contempt they elicit are not unrelated. In "Group Psychology" he explains how the peer group can cohere only when no one stands out from the crowd—and when no child is favored by the parents over and above his siblings. His description of the group as a "reaction-formation" in that essay hints at a certain skepticism on Freud's part toward the social contract that binds the collective only by denying the special talents of individual members. Freud, after all, believed *himself* to be the favored "golden child" of his mother, so may well have detected a resemblance between his own situation as an esoteric interpreter of dreams and that of his biblical precursor, the dream interpreter Joseph, whose preferential treatment within his family (the emblem of which, significantly, was a fashion item— his showy, standout coat) led his brothers to plot against him. Indeed, that biblical story of sibling envy for the brother who doesn't play by the rules is one that Freud refers to in *Moses and Monotheism* (his final book, completed in exile from Nazism in England) in an effort to explain the hateful logic underpinning anti-Semitism.[21]

Freud's personal experience of the "contempt and discrimination" elicited by his Jewishness must surely have also influenced his view of the herd instinct and cult of the leader in "Group Psychology." Certainly, the position of Jews within the society where Freud grew up seemed to have less in common with the generalized and normatively male envy he believed could be overcome through group identification than with the female examples in that essay. The notion of the model woman we looked at above could, for example, be said to find her counterpart in the figure of the immigrant Jew hoping to prove himself a model citizen. Just as envy is envisaged as a typically feminine emotion, it may likewise be assumed a typically Jewish one: the imitative behavior of both these groups—each in its own way expected to emulate a preexisting ideal—underscores the structurally envious nature of their social relations. It's a secondary position, after all—that of dependence— whose consciousness, according to Klein, induces envy.

But isn't it equally possible that some corresponding envy actively sought to weaken and degrade both women and Jews by keeping them in second place? If excessive envy is, as Klein suggests, a pathological reaction to the discovery that one is unoriginal, secondary, late to the party—and thus dependent, inescapably, on another—then we might well interpret misogyny as a reaction to this first fact of life: that a powerful woman will have always preceded you. Whence, by the same token, Christian cultures have perhaps never quite been able to forgive Jews for Christianity's dependency on the Judaism that both preceded and engendered it.

Envy in Psychoanalysis

The role played by his Jewishness was not, Freud once said, unimportant to the genesis of his work. Still, he strenuously denied the charge that he was peddling a specifically "Jewish science." Relating his work to his background was evidently an ambivalent process for Freud, the ambivalence similar to that one can detect in a seeming inconstancy at the heart of Freud's ambitions *for* his work. For while believing, on the one hand, that universalizing is "a reaction-formation to the passion of envy," he was adamant, on the other, that his own ideas could and should be applied universally.[22] By his own definition, then, something of envy must surely animate psychoanalysis.

But just how much envy *is* there in psychoanalysis? If we recall Klein's description of the envious personality as intent on "spoiling" society's ideals, we can note that fewer discourses have taken greater delight in trashing the values of "civilization" than the one we've inherited from Freud. Yet one might also say that it's precisely this delight in its own iconoclasm that suggests psychoanalysis has neither been creatively blocked by "excessive envy" (Klein) nor allowed its envy to become the basis of degenerative ressentiment (Nietzsche). This too can be said of its clinical practice, which arguably becomes excessively envious only when it is deployed, passive aggressively, against the fragile ego without offering any new forms of life or creativity. Done well, on the other hand, psychoanalysis wages war on the ego only in order to destroy what may be inhibiting or blocking its capacity to love or work, create or enjoy.

Klein's response to Freud's identification of penis envy in girls was to identify an earlier source of envy in the infant—envy of the breast. But since, according to Klein, it is precisely the situation of dependence on the one who comes before you that awakens the infant's envy, her own reversal of the order of priority—putting envy of the breast ahead of envy of the penis—does, ironically, seem to conform to the envious pattern she herself describes. This notion is reinforced by her choice of "envy" as a way of describing the infant's "ambivalent" situation, since it is the repetition or emulation of this word that would seem, more than anything, to put her breast in direct competition with Freud's penis. Furthermore, the aggressive ambivalence that Klein claims the infant feels toward the mother also finds its own later reversal in the work of D. W. Winnicott, for whom "ambivalence" characterizes the mother's feelings toward her child.[23]

So envy *can* be plausibly viewed as an active principle in the development of psychoanalysis, structuring relations between both the sexes *and* the generations. For if envy is typically emulative, and a form of unconscious imitation that exposes at its limit the envy of the one envied, then these repetitions and reversals from Freud to Klein to Winnicott would seem to make a case for psychoanalysis as a discourse whose envious aggression has been turned into something constructive, critical, creative, dynamic. Envy can be good! Though in its wish for cultural respectability and universal recognition the envy within psychoanalysis can also become harmful, both toward itself and toward its subjects. Whenever, for example, psychoanalysis forsakes its position on the margins to gain admittance into the mainstream, it thereby "forgets" its own first insights into the endlessly unraveling presence of the unconscious stranger within, who might also be regarded, as Adam Phillips suggests in allusion to Freud's own formative experiences, as the immigrant within.

Trauma Envy

Eva Hoffman's *Lost in Translation*, a memoir of her youthful emigration with her family from Poland to Canada, offers a startlingly honest account of the affective life of the immigrant. Describing the excruciatingly painful uprooting from her mother tongue, and thus from her ability to express herself intimately or creatively, she writes that "linguistic dispossession," entails "the dispossession of one's self." And, she continues, "If all therapy is speaking therapy— a talking cure—then perhaps all neurosis is a speech dis-ease."[24] It is, she later surmises, a neurosis one can find at the heart of the North American immigrant experience, full of "anomie, loneliness, emotional repression, and excessive self-consciousness" (268).

Since a burden of envy is the lot of the immigrant, the immigrant must strive to acquire a vital new skill: "becoming immune to envy." This was Hoffman's own accomplishment: "With my new detachment, I can gaze at what my friends have as if they lived in a different world. . . . This way, I can be nice to my friends; I can smile pleasantly at their pleasures and sympathize with their problems of the good life. I can do so, because I've made myself untouchable. . . . There is something I can have though, with no cash or down payments, or being to the manor born: I can have internal goods" (136–137). These internal goods are achieved by withdrawing from the social world as the world of belonging via belongings. It's a movement that resembles Nietzsche's Zarathustra, whose temporary withdrawal from the world turns him into a superman, someone who has "finally succeeded in overcoming the envy within him."[25]

The word psychoanalysis uses to describe an experience that lacks a language, an experience of losing oneself or not being able to express one's own story, is "trauma." Trauma, explains Ruth Leys, is essentially "a problem of hypnotic imitation."[26] We might think again, for example, of Hedy's trancelike imitation of Allie. And this too may be traced within the typical immigrant experience of "the loss of a living connection" (107) to one's former self as one strives to assimilate by repeating and imitating alien words, alien laws, and alien codes of behavior, all of which are vital to learn if the immigrant is to adapt and survive in a new and unfamiliar environment.

So envy, it would seem, shares certain traits with trauma. The critic John Mowitt has pointed to the way in which both envy and trauma describe subjects who have been affected by their position of belatedness with respect to the person, object, or experience now deemed to be persecuting them.[27] Scheler characterizes ressentiment as "the repeated experiencing and reliving of a particular emotional response reaction against someone else. The continual reliving of the emotion sinks it more deeply into the center of the personality, but concomitantly removes it from the person's zone of action and expression."[28] Just as trauma is an experience that cannot quite experience itself, ressentiment is here envisaged as a feeling that cannot quite feel itself. Thus if it responds to this feeling by striving to level all people (the egalitarian principle beneath which both Nietzsche and Freud identify an envious animus), then that may be because, as Kierkegaard observes, leveling is a mathematical equation whose real intention is the avoidance of feelings.[29]

Perhaps this dissociation from the feelings it arouses can help to explain why even trauma, though not something anyone in her right mind *should* envy, nonetheless has its enviers and would-be levelers. Mowitt has even coined the term "trauma envy"—yet another reversal in the history of envy as a history of value reversals. Trauma envy, he says, took root in the critical and academic literature responding to the Holocaust, then soon after expanded into all areas of identity politics. Bound up with the envious relation to fluency in language that Hoffman's memoir describes, "trauma envy" refers to the mechanism whereby the unspeakable trauma that, by definition, cannot be represented has paradoxically become the only story that anyone has a right to tell. Hence, at a time when one's right to speak rests on the basis of one's "wounded attachment," and to speak with a moral weight that removes one's discourse from possible criticism, it appears to many that it is not the traumatized subject but the nontraumatized subject who has been silenced. Or to put it another way, since silencing is said to be the very essence of trauma, it is now the nontraumatized subject who effectively feels traumatized. One might think here, for instance, of the resentment often felt by the "angry white men" who sometimes claim that it is they who are the "real" victims of racism and sexism due to affirmative action, reverse discrimination, and so forth.[30]

Hoffman is once again the most sensitive explicator of this predicament. In *Lost in Translation* she tells of her emigration as the loss of a language and the consequent loss, however temporary, of herself. In a later work, *After Such Knowledge*, in a phrase analogous to Mowitt's "trauma envy," she refers to her own "significance envy," alluding to the affective state characteristic of children of Holocaust survivors like herself. Significance envy comes about when one's own story of suffering is not felt to be legitimate. It is not a story one feels one has the right or the sufficiently wounded attachment to tell. "How can you envy someone for having gone through hell?" Hoffman asks of herself in relation to her Holocaust survivor parents.[31] Yet envy them one might, for Hoffman's own life experiences are felt to have been overwhelmingly determined by a history (of the Holocaust) whose trauma she at the same time cannot quite lay claim to. If, in psychoanalytic parlance, trauma refers to a state of dissociation so that the subject is, in a certain sense, not present even when she *is* present, in Hoffman's case she *literally* wasn't present at the scene of the trauma whose shaping influence over her life story she nonetheless feels. Even her own *lack*, in other words, is not quite her own. So while the experience of envy she describes in *Lost in Translation* is envy for an intimate language, a language with which to express oneself, the "significance envy" she identifies in the later work is envy not for the language but for the "content" that might grant her permission to share her story as her own. "Content envy" may then be another term to describe this peculiar habit of resenting another for his wounded attachment, an attachment that not only affords him the right to tell his story but endows him with a story to tell. Seen this way, "content," no matter how traumatic, may get reimagined as a form of contentment. But what strange kind of a privilege is it if one is permitted to speak only from the vantage point of one's wound?

Translation Envy

American author Cynthia Ozick's 1969 short story "Envy; or Yiddish in America" was written at a time when the Holocaust was not yet a word on everyone's lips, and the figure of the Survivor was not yet the familiar icon s/he'd soon become. The legacy of the war was still in many ways a silent and silencing one.[32] However, Ozick's story examines a feature of this silencing rarely discussed in the various trauma studies since, studies that have largely focused on trauma's unrepresentability. Ozick looks at the loss of a common, not a personal, language. Her story imagines the effects on the remnants of a dying community of the more or less complete vanquishing of their mother tongue. Like the majority of European Jews, Yiddish, too, was murdered by Nazism.

The story is called "Envy" *or* "Yiddish in America," as if the position of the Old World (Yiddish) within the New World

(America) were quintessentially one of envy, a feeling aroused by age's proximity to youth. (It was Solomon's suggestion in the first place to cut that baby in half.) The envious protagonist in the story is indeed an old European Jewish man, an orphaned and childless Yiddish poet by the name of Edelshtein. Like the envious mother in the court of Solomon, he too is a man greatly bereaved— bereaved of his country, his family, his civilization, his language, his past, his present, his future. He is not, however, in the strict sense, a "survivor" of the Holocaust, having spent that era in New York. He is thus a version of the character of whom we have been speaking: someone who has suffered incomprehensible losses, but who cannot claim these experiences as his own. Edelshtein is self-hating, guilty, and grief-stricken. But even more than these burdens, what drives him to distraction is his envy.

Edelshtein has nothing but contempt for American culture, though, as we know, envy always craves what it despises, despising it all the more for having stimulated the craving. Thus Edelshtein finds himself irresistibly drawn to the America he hates: he wants its recognition and longs for its embrace. And since envy tends to focus on those whose social position most closely resembles the envier's own, Edelshtein particularly envies other American Jews, especially American Jewish writers. Among these he especially envies American Jewish writers in Yiddish, focusing the full fury of his envy on just one man, Ostrover, another old world Jew, but one who has somehow achieved the amazing, miraculous thing: translation. Ostrover has "made it" in America. He has successfully turned his Yiddish into a "modern" literature. He is the only Yiddish writer to have done so. No other writer in Yiddish is an international star. No one else requires translators.

As many of her readers will have been aware, Ozick's Ostrover is a barely disguised portrait of Isaac Bashevis Singer, and her story is really the story of the envy other Yiddish writers in America were known to have felt toward Singer's fame and acclaim. Singer, who was translated into many languages, even went on to win the 1978 Nobel Prize for literature, thus gaining international recognition for a marginal language, a language spoken and understood only by a marginal people. So in "Envy" Ozick ponders, via Edelshtein's relation to Ostrover, what it feels like when one's future, or the future of what means most, one's language, survives only on another man's tongue, not on one's own. Ostrover, after all, can speak and write in the knowledge that he will be listened to and read, whereas Edelshtein, if he cannot find a translator, can count on one hand his number of likely readers. He thus spends most of his time writing letters to publishers and editors in pursuit of a translator. To be translated is his only ambition: he wants to make sense in America. So when he meets Hannah, a young American girl who has learned to read Yiddish (so as to read Ostrover in the original), he is driven wild with desire for her—wild, that is, with the desire that *she* translate *him*. She refuses, coldly. He swings a punch at her. This girl is for Edelshtein a goddess of the future, and the future, he sees in her eyes, is utterly indifferent to his plight.

On the other hand, as much as Edelshtein longs to be translated, he also finds the thought of it unconscionable. So despite his persistent pleading with Hannah to translate him, he is equally compelled to warn her *against* translation. In the hands of the translators, he tells her, Yiddish is murdered again. How, then, can he allow himself to want what he does not want to want? How can he wish for personal recognition—survival, translation—when the majority of Yiddish speakers have died anonymous and unrecognized? As is envy's way, he does this by moralizing his ambition, by telling himself that his desire is not really to save or distinguish himself but to save his civilization, to speak not for the living but for the dead. And he manifests this same moralization in his criticism of the successful Ostrover, whom he accuses of using an impure Yiddish and of possessing a grotesque, pornographic, adulterer's imagination.

Ozick's Edelshtein is the remnant of a dying civilization gasping for life in a new world that has no wish to heed his story. American Jews instead "titter with shame" when they hear a word of Yiddish spoken aloud.[33] Raving, hysterical, and excessively envious, he is an antidote, *avant la lettre*, to the somber, saintly image of the survivor that was soon after to emerge and become the Holocaust's chief "representative." If the survivor, once formally recognized, was to become a taciturn presence whose silence was said to speak volumes, Edelshtein is a man whose language, in fragments, drives him over the edge. He is anything but taciturn and anything but polite. He is as pathetic, as grotesque and yet as vivid a character as those he so despises in Ostrover's fictions. Indeed, while Edelshtein's fate is that of a man blocked by his envy, unable to adapt, survive, translate, become modern, Ozick's own "Envy" is a very modern work of literature indeed: a literature whose content—the story of a language in crisis, a language broken and in pieces—is matched by a form, call it modernism, that makes a virtue of precisely those hesitancies and impasses as trailblazing literary qualities.

Ozick's story of a dying language, in other words, is told in a vibrant, living language that puts Ozick much closer to her Ostrover than to her Edelshtein. For she too shows us how the position of Yiddish in America, as one of envy, might become a means of creativity if only, like Ostrover, one is unafraid to let one's language adapt: if one allows one's language to be the language of the living and not the dead. Melanie Klein, as we said before, tells us that the envious aim to "spoil" things for the envied. Edelshtein tries to spoil things for Ostrover by endlessly criticizing his impure Yiddish: a criticism he wishes would silence his competitor. While by telling himself that he has safeguarded his *own* moral and linguistic purity, Edelshtein seeks to comfort himself—the essential gesture, for

Nietzsche, of ressentiment. Yet Ostrover also criticizes Edelshtein's writing, laughing at its sentimentalism, mocking its gravitas, its pretension to poetry. His criticism is harsh, but it's as constructive as it is brutal. Don't let Yiddish become a sacred language, he warns. When a language becomes too pure, too sacrosanct, it gets blocked, petrified, and thus falls foul of excessive envy.

Two key senses of "spoiling" in the English language are near opposites: to spoil by contaminating (thus treating badly), and to spoil by worshiping (thus treating too well). Edelshtein accuses Ostrover of spoiling Yiddish by treating it badly, with a lack of respect, with no thought of its history. Ostrover, on the other hand, accuses Edelshtein of spoiling Yiddish by treating it too well, according it too much respect—by idealizing it in such a way as to kill it off altogether. Spoiling a language is like spoiling a child. To spoil a child (so often the gesture of a guilty parent, and often enough a parent guilty about envying her child) is to deny the child the chance to have any awareness of his own lack, and thus of his own potential. In the French language, *envie* aligns envy and desire. So we might say that someone denied access to his own lack, desire, and envy can have no life, or no creative life. And the same can be said of a language. To spoil a child or a language, in other words, is to reduce creation to content, belonging to belongings. This is the mistake that envy, when excessive, always makes.

What is at stake in Ozick's "Envy" is survival—the survival of a people through their language—and it is Ostrover who, by adapting his language to the new world, not only survives but thrives. He does not, as Edelshtein enviously claims, forget Yiddish. Rather, he remembers what Yiddish always was: a language for a diasporic people; a language that could readily absorb foreign elements; a language that was never pure; and, more precisely, a language that was murdered in Europe by those who believed in national purity and its correlate, linguistic purity.

Yiddish, that is to say, has always drawn on the languages of the cultures in which it abides. It's a language that survived and proved crucial to diasporic survival by virtue of being adaptive to new people, new places, and new influences. So the accusation of adultery that other Yiddish writers hurl enviously at Ostrover turns out, paradoxically, to be the mark of his *fidelity* to a language whose continued survival as a living vernacular has, Ozick believes, been most powerfully expressed in the years since the war in the contribution made by Jewish authors to American English. In 1970, the year after publishing "Envy," Ozick declared that American English *is* the "New Yiddish."[34] By this she meant to draw attention to the way a once marginal, though necessarily international, language— a language of outsiders and immigrants—has found, in America, its way into the most globally spoken of contemporary languages.

If Ozick is right in calling American English the "New Yiddish," then this new Yiddish has not sought to abandon all its quirks and differences in a collective identity founded on the leveling of all members. Rather, to the extent that the new Yiddish *is* still Yiddish, it must have adapted itself to the new world in such a way as to have made of its native strangeness something intimate, creative, and constructively critical—qualities that Ozick's own story "Envy; or Yiddish in America" richly shows.[35] For despite the immensity of the losses it has suffered, if Yiddish is to speak once again and express itself familiarly in an international language *without* destroying that within it that remains fundamentally untranslatable, then it must communicate this untranslatability as something to be shared. Or to put this slightly differently, your own untranslatability, properly understood, may be both a source *of* envy and a solution *to* envy: for that which renders you excluded is what is, uniquely, yours—"yours," as in what you still have to give.

THREE

Guilt

Did you hear the one about Jewish Alzheimer's?
You forget everything but the guilt.

I feel guilty about everything. Already today I've felt guilty about having said the wrong thing to a friend. Then I felt guilty about avoiding that friend because of the wrong thing I'd said. Plus, I haven't called my mother yet today: guilty. And I really should have organized something special for my husband's birthday: guilty. I gave the wrong kind of food to my child: guilty. I've been cutting corners at work lately: guilty. I skipped breakfast: guilty. I snacked instead: double guilty. I'm taking up all this space in a world with not enough space in it: guilty, guilty, guilty. Just look at me now, for chrissakes, as I sit here "theorizing" in a well-heated house with a well-stocked fridge and clean running water, wearing cheaply available clothes made . . . I haven't checked where or by whom, but that information is just a click of a finger away, for in this place at this point in time I can hardly fail to be aware that, as the philosopher Emmanuel Levinas once put it, there are "somewhere in the world, wars and carnage, which result for these [my] advantages": guilty![1]

Nor am I feeling good about feeling bad. Not when sophisticated friends never fail to remind me how self-involved, self-aggrandizing, politically conservative, and morally stunted the guilty are. Poor me. Guilty about guilty! Filial guilt, fraternal guilt, spousal guilt, maternal guilt, peer guilt, work guilt, middle-class guilt, white guilt, liberal guilt, historical guilt, Jewish guilt: I'm guilty of them all.

Thankfully, there are those who say they can save me. According to Denise Duffield-Thomas, author of *Get Rich, Lucky Bitch!*, guilt is "one of the most common feelings women suffer." Guilty women, lured by guilt into obstructing their own paths to increased wealth, power, prestige, and happiness, just can't seem to take advantage of their advantages. "You might feel guilty," Duffield-Thomas writes, "for wanting more, or for spending money on yourself, or for taking time out of your busy family life to work on improving yourself. You might feel guilty that other people are poor, that your friend is jealous, that there are starving people in the world." Sure enough, I *do* feel guilty for those things. So it comes as something of a relief to hear that I can be helped. I can be self-helped! For that to happen what I must first understand is that (a) I'm worth it, and (b) none of these structures of global inequality predicated on historical injustices is my fault. My guilt, in other words, is a sign not of my guilt but of my innocence—even my victimhood. So it's only by forgiving myself for the wrongs for which I bear no direct responsibility that I can learn to release my "money blocks and live a first class life."[2]

Imagine that: a first-class life. By engaging the modern critique of guilt as our most fundamentally inhibiting emotion, insights that descend from psychoanalytic and feminist thinking are here transformed into the language of business motivation. The business model promises to expiate guilt by making—or unblocking—money. It's an idea that resonates especially in the German language, where guilt and debt are the same word, *schuld*. One thinks, for example, of Max Weber's thesis about the "spirit of capitalism" as conflating worldly with heavenly riches on the basis that what you accumulate in this world measures your spiritual state by showing your capacity for hard work, discipline, self-denial.

However, the "salvation anxiety" that Weber also detects within the Protestant work ethic departs from the self-help manual's promise to deliver the capitalist from her guilt. For Weber, in fact, the pursuit of profit not only fails to negate one's sense of guilt but actively exacerbates it—for in an economy that admonishes stagnation, there can be no rest for the wicked. So the guilt that blocks and inhibits us also propels us to work, work, work, to become relentlessly productive in the hope that we might, *by our good works*, rid ourselves of guilt. Guilt thus renders us both productive *and* unproductive, both workaholic *and* workphobic, which conflict may help to explain the extreme and even violent lengths to which people will sometimes go—whether by scapegoating others or sacrificing themselves—to extirpate what many consider their most unbearable emotion. For though the guilt in these cases isn't always conscious, there is, I'd argue, little we're more guilty of than the things we're prepared to do in order to dramatize our own innocence. To wit, what I'm wondering is whether our compulsion to be rid of our guilt is always necessarily the best course of action. I mean, is guilt really so bad as all that?

The Fall

We tend to blame religion for condemning man to life as a sinner. In the biblical story man's fall happens early: tempted by a knowledge that pits him against life, he is led by this forbidden fruit out of the Garden of Eden into an exile that has yet to end. His guilt is a constant nagging reminder that he has taken a wrong turn. Yet his guilt is also deceptive, as slippery and seductive as the serpent who led him astray. For if man has sinned by choosing knowledge over life, the guilt that punishes him *repeats* his crime: with all its finger-wagging and tenor of "I told you so," guilt too comes over as awfully "knowing"—and guilt too, it is often alleged, is antilife.

Guilt is antilife because it makes us weak (Nietzsche), neurotic (Freud), inauthentic (Sartre). It keeps us in thrall to that boring and repetitive voice inside our head that endlessly corrects, criticizes, censors, judges, and finds fault with us, but that brings us, says Adam Phillips, no news about ourselves.[3] In our feelings of guilt we seem already to have the measure of who it is we are and what it is we're capable of. If we were to meet our know-it-all superego at a party, Phillips speculates, we would probably assume that some terrible experience—some catastrophe or trauma—must have caused it to behave in such a haranguing way.

Trauma, for the psychoanalyst, names an experience so unsettling as to be inadmissible or inassimilable to full consciousness. A traumatic history can never be altogether fact-checked, though it might occasionally show itself in the form of some compulsive repetition of beliefs or behaviors, such as those that make up the limited vocabulary of the guilt-ridden self. *Feeling* guilty does not, for the psychoanalyst, bear any obvious correlation to *being* guilty in the eyes of the law. While "guilty as charged" brings full disclosure and finality to a narrative propelled by the wish to discover the culprit responsible for a *known* crime, the guilt we *feel* begins another kind of narrative, a different type of detective story altogether, one in which the confession often *precedes* the accusation of a crime whose particulars not even the guilty subject is sure of. For the detective-psychoanalyst, then, guilty feelings can be a means of opening up the very questions those feelings may well have been attempting to close down. So it is that the guilt we find blocking and repetitive can also, depending on how we approach it, get things moving.

Here, however, we stumble across a quandary that has contributed to making this the trickiest of feelings for me—even were I *not* so personally guilt afflicted—to think about and write about. Because *is* it really possible to divine the difference between our civilization's "discontent" at the guilt that inhibits and stops us from doing things and the guilt that might still have the power to move us? The answer to that question can only be moot. For though one may well envisage a procedure for deciding which is the "good" (motivating) and which the "bad" (paralyzing) variant of the emotion, one's judgment on the matter is unlikely to last for long before finding itself tested again by the numerous semantic, ethical, and political shifts that have come to characterize a modern history during which, as we'll see, a disorienting pendulum has been swinging repeatedly—and tellingly—between them.

On Survivor's Guilt

Though the "fall" is originally a biblical trope, forget, for a moment, religion. One can just as well recount a more recent and assuredly secular story of the fall of man. It's a "story" that's had countless narrators, though perhaps none finer or more emphatic than the German Jewish postwar critic Theodor Adorno. For Adorno, those who have survived the complete rupture that was "Auschwitz" are, at least insofar as they're still party to the same civilization that created the *conditions* for Auschwitz . . . guilty. Guilt, in other words, is our unassailable historical condition. It's our contract—that which we have contracted—as modern people. As such, says Adorno, we all have a shared responsibility "after Auschwitz" to be vigilant lest we collapse once more into the ways of thinking, believing, and behaving that brought down this guilty verdict upon us. And one of the chief measures we must take in order to enact this responsibility is to maintain a deep-rooted skepticism about the possibility of *anyone*'s forming *any* reasonable opinions or drawing *any* acceptable conclusions in the language and culture of a civilization so thoroughly implicated in the catastrophe that has befallen it. To make "sense" after Auschwitz is to risk complicity with its barbarism.

Adorno's own near sense-defying pronouncements on the epoch he named "after Auschwitz" are often cited, and not least because of the way in which they confront the absurdity of "going on when you can't go on."[4] However, what mostly strikes *me* about Adorno's guilty verdict is how it too regards our guilt as being fundamentally the fruit of our knowledge. Indeed, at a time of increased bureaucracy, surveillance, information technology, and managerialism, it's this perennial entanglement of guilt and knowledge that I'm primarily pursuing.

There is, though, another feature of Adorno's representation of guilt that I want to single out. We can find it expressed most starkly in his question "whether after Auschwitz you can go on living— especially whether one who escaped by accident, one who by rights should have been killed, may go on living. His mere survival calls for the coldness, the basic principle of bourgeois subjectivity, without which there could have been no Auschwitz; this is the drastic guilt of him who was spared."[5]

So although, for Adorno, the guilt of Auschwitz belongs to *all* of Western civilization, it's a guilt he assumed would be felt most keenly by "one who escaped by accident, one who by rights should have been killed"—the Jewish survivor of World War II. Adorno, in New York throughout the war, was probably attesting to his own sense of guilt. Yet his insight is one that we also get from psychologists who worked with concentration camp survivors after the war and found that "feelings of guilt accompanied by shame, self-condemnatory tendencies and self-accusations [are] experienced by the *victims* of the persecution, and apparently much less (if at all) by the perpetrators of it."[6] So what can it mean if victims feel guilty and perpetrators guilt-free? Are objective guilt and subjective guilt then completely at odds with each other?

Drawing on Freud's discussion of how the aggressive instincts against one's parents can become transformed into guilt reflexes, "survival guilt"—the expression is Anna Freud's—tended in the war's aftermath to be viewed as an affective response to the victim's identification with the aggressor. In a situation of existential threat the persecuted subject stands the best chance of survival by (unconsciously) identifying with the mindset of the persecutor. The logic this assumes is a painful and disturbing one. The survivor who may subsequently find it hard to forgive herself because others have died in her place (why am I still here when they are not?) may also feel guilty because of what she was forced to collude with for the sake of her own survival. This need not imply any incriminating *action* on her part; her guilt may simply be an unconscious registration of her historic preference that others suffer instead of her.

On this basis, then, it may be possible to think of survivor's guilt as a special case of the guilt we all of us bear when, aware or unaware, we're *glad* when others suffer rather than ourselves. That's obviously not a pleasant feeling, but nor is it a hard one to understand. Yet there remains, all the same, something deeply uncomfortable about accepting the self-ascription of guilt to traumatized survivors of the worst kinds of human atrocity. Shouldn't it be incumbent on us to seek to *save* the survivor from her guilt feelings, and thus establish, without smirch or quibble, her absolute innocence? If *anyone* is innocent, after all, then surely it's her . . .

According to the psychoanalytic writer Ruth Leys, the figure of the "survivor" came into being alongside just such a shift—from the postwar focus on the victim's feelings of guilt toward a subsequent insistence upon the victim's innocence. The shift is particularly clear within trauma studies, the discipline that arose in large part as a response to the war itself. Leys believes that this transformation—from the representation of the victim as beset by feelings of guilt to a redefinition of the victim as essentially innocent—has required the theorist to replace the term "guilt" with an alternative term: "shame." What differentiates guilt from shame is that "shame attaches to and sharpens the sense of what one is, whereas guilt attaches to what one does" (130). Unlike guilt, therefore, shame essentializes the subject. So whereas survivor's guilt had been regarded as a manifestation of the victim's unconscious identification with the aggressor, the refiguring of guilt as shame doesn't engage with the survivor's intentions, fantasies, or projections but draws instead on materialist accounts of the affects as the "built-in responses of the body" (184). By envisaging the survivor's feelings as automatic affects induced by specific triggers, the "survivor" can accordingly be imagined as "a new kind of material object, identity, or type of person" (68).[7] This new type of person, a sort of passive receptacle for the purely external forces of the trauma that has assailed her, may duly be counted as one of history's most "objective" witnesses.

By conceiving of trauma victims as the *objects* of history, then, trauma theorists, albeit with the best of motivations, may find themselves unconsciously *colluding* with the logic of those persecutory forces that first sought to deny the inner life of the victim. By taking seriously the survivor's own expressions of guilt, on the other hand, without converting that guilt, via shame, into innocence, the trauma victim may be recognized as someone still subject to her own drives and desires, however perverse or discomfiting we—who would like to save the victim from her guilt—may consider these to be.

Speaking in Moral Terms

Leys's thesis, broadly, is that the drive to exchange the survivor's guilt for innocence bespeaks, in the first place, a wish on the part of the survivor's spokesperson/interpreter to ease his conscience by laying claim to that innocence as his own; and, in the second place, a wish to render the survivor an objective witness to a traumatic history that might then be presumed known, understood, and thus laid to rest. But mightn't there also be a political motive for manufacturing innocence—or innocents—out of history? That is the view of John Mowitt, according to whom history's trauma victims have been co-opted by trauma theory into representing a moral discourse that works to silence all political dissent.

We discussed earlier how Nietzsche's *Genealogy of Morals* unmasks Judeo-Christian "slave morality" as a form of ressentiment—of the weak for the strong—that seeks to avenge itself by causing widespread guilt and psychological degeneration. And it's by drawing on this Nietzschean suspicion of moral rhetoric that Mowitt also identifies the risk he believes morality poses to politics. Politics, for Mowitt, is the arena where conflicts between people and ideas can be fairly and openly debated and tested against each other. Yet by positing a subject—the trauma victim—who is unable to account for either himself or his own experiences, trauma theory is assumed to address itself as if from the vantage point of a universal morality that stands beyond the reproaches of the partisan or merely political. As such, it's a discourse that could seriously undermine the democratic values of representation, compromise, and negotiation.

The Holocaust, for Mowitt, is a case in point. The Holocaust, in trauma theory, has often stood as a sort of byword for the idea of the unrepresentable. Yet by becoming a kind of ineffable or even sacred name, it's a term that is also open to the charge of having been instrumentalized in order to silence political opposition. Hence, whether it's invoked in the interests of Zionist ideology and the security of Israel ("never again") or in the interests of anti-Zionist ideology highlighting the plight of the Palestinians ("it's happening again"), the Holocaust is not so much silent as it is a referent that finds itself continually mobilized to ground the universal (moral) claims of opposing sides of the same (political) issues. (Nor are these the only issues so treated. In fact, so conventional has this argumentative move become that a popular online term has arisen to describe it—"Godwin's Law" is defined as the probability that the longer an online discussion continues, the more likely it is a Hitler comparison will be drawn into it.) Such observations can therefore only lend credence to the suspicion that those who elect to speak *in the name* of the Holocaust (or any other trauma) may be attempting to disguise their real interests and intentions, for here is a type of rhetoric that must be damaging for politics insofar as its leveraging of morality and historical memory renders hamstrung any chance of the negotiation and compromise that must surely be necessary for the most effective political solutions.

Yet the fact that the concept of the unrepresentable *can* be exploited to silence political opposition doesn't oblige us to jettison it altogether. Primo Levi's famous declaration, for example, that he could not be a reliable witness to his own experiences—the "true witnesses," he said, are the dead and murdered who cannot speak for themselves—is not a license for a particular group or party to claim the moral high ground. Rather, Levi's statement disputes *anyone's* claim to be able to speak in the name of the history he saw and experienced firsthand. Nor, indeed, is it *only* a cynical view of the slaves' morality that we can get from reading Nietzsche. His genealogy of morals is also a profound reflection on how and why it is that a moral discourse first appears among those who not only lack access to power but whose historical experiences have afforded no positive sense of group or personal identity such as they'd need for full participation in the democratic politics of representation. (The privilege of representing one's interests, after all, depends on knowing what one's interests are—and that, as it turns out, is quite another privilege altogether.)

So while it's the case that morality can be the rhetoric of hypocrites deploying a discourse of truth to better mask their will to power, it is simultaneously the case that morality can emerge in such a way as to unmask the real limitations of any given political or representational system. Adorno, for instance, who was so emphatic about Auschwitz's legacy of guilt for all, turned, as if instinctively, to a moral form of expression when announcing that a "new categorical imperative has been imposed by Hitler upon unfree mankind: to think and act in such a way that Auschwitz will not repeat itself and that nothing similar will happen. When we want to find reasons for it, this imperative is as refractory as the given one of Kant was once upon a time. Dealing discursively with it would be an outrage."[8]

To enunciate such a law is not to lay claim to its discovery or authorship. Analysis of the law, Adorno insists, has been foreclosed by the law itself. The law simply appears, as if from nowhere, and must be obeyed. And yet this law—"to think and act in such a way that Auschwitz will not repeat itself and that nothing similar will happen"—is already, as we noted of the biblical prohibition on knowledge, a kind of linguistic paradox whereby the law reveals itself, like that all-too-knowing pontificator/superego who goes on and on and on inside our head, as at once the repudiation and the repetition of the problem it describes. For the moment it has been necessary to *repeat* this law (*against* repetition), the law bears witness to the fact that we, who never fail to check our behavior within eyeshot of a policeman, all stand guilty before the law. To encounter the law *as* law, in other words, is to acknowledge both the law and the inevitability of its repeated transgression. Thus in telling ourselves "we must never" we also tell ourselves that we need the instruction only because, in one way or another, we always already have . . .

So it's precisely because law renders its subjects guilty rather than innocent that a critic like Adorno feels he has no alternative, after Auschwitz, but to move in this direction—to move, that is, from conceptual language—as a language that can abstract from all personal implication—to the strange and rather archaic language of moral commandment.[9] But if Adorno's postwar reflections on the inherent imperfection of the human condition seem to echo the biblical description of man as *fallen*, this need not be deemed unduly pessimistic. For while the vision here is of a man who is not ideal— far from it—and while human perfection remains impossible, there is always, for a fallen humanity, work to be done, changes and improvements to make . . . being wrong, in other words, isn't all bad—*if* you can bear it.

Being Right

So at what point did being wrong start to seem *un*bearable? When did having the wrong opinion or the wrong idea about something become so unconscionable, so utterly intolerable to the modern individual that being right began to assume a status not unlike that of a human right? Am *I* wrong in detecting such a trend? It's as if Adorno's critical injunction to doubt and question every positive assertion "after Auschwitz" has ultimately given way to a critical culture driven by the desire to achieve something else—an unerring quest for *correctness.*

In his controversial novel of 1971, *Mr. Sammler's Planet,* Saul Bellow imagines an elderly Jewish survivor of the Holocaust living out the remainder of his days in America. We first meet him in 1960s New York surveying "the books and papers of his West Side bedroom and suspect[ing] strongly that they were the wrong books, the wrong papers." "You had to be a crank," he reflects, "to insist on being right":

> Being right was largely a matter of explanations. Intellectual man had become an explaining creature. Fathers to children,

wives to husbands, lecturers to listeners, experts to laymen, colleagues to colleagues, doctors to patients, man to his own soul, explained. The roots of this, the causes of the other, the source of events, the history, the structure, the reasons why. For the most part, in one ear out the other. The soul wanted what it wanted. It had its own natural knowledge. It sat unhappily on superstructures of explanation, poor bird, not knowing which way to fly.[10]

Sammler's perception of the wrongheadedness of his own intellectual heritage is thus matched by a distinct discomfort regarding the intellectual fashions in vogue, and especially intellectual man's habit of "explaining" the world to himself.

Today, of course, we have the concept of "mansplaining." In her very funny essay on the subject, "Men Explain Things to Me," Rachel Solnit remarks that the "out-and-out confrontational confidence of the totally ignorant is, in my experience, gendered. Men explain things to me, and other women, whether or not they know what they're talking about. Some men."[11] A gesture of the strong over the weak, explanation is here regarded as a method for those with power to lord it over those whose point of view they have not only failed to take into account but failed to imagine altogether. Put differently, explanation is an excellent tool for not having to reckon with the problem of—in philosophical parlance—*other minds*.

But we can also hear something a little less confident and possibly even apologetic operating beneath the surface of whoever feels called upon to explain things. *Please, let me explain!* Mansplaining in this sense might appear less as a boast than as the resounding cry of a masculinity in crisis; a nervous masculinity eager to show its worth and shore up its own uncertain position with a wall of authoritative words. Likewise, the unease that Sammler feels about explanation as a mode of intellectual engagement intimates that such a discourse may be as vociferous as it is in order to cover something up—something that even the one intent on explaining things would prefer not to hear or know—something, that is to say, of our *guilt*.

There is, Sammler senses, something wrong with wanting all the time to be right. That's why he prefers to adopt a belief in the soul's "own natural knowledge"—as if this could anchor him in a morality somehow less troubled by the self-righteousness he identifies elsewhere: in philosophy, in politics, in critical theories of one kind or another.

Being Wrong

Despite winning the National Book Award, *Mr. Sammler's Planet* stirred up a strong strain of critical suspicion toward Bellow as an author whose reputation was suddenly in doubt, besmirched by the reactionary tendencies of his central character: racism, sexism, illiberalism, cynicism about the various movements of liberation. Sammler is, we would now say, politically incorrect. Still, the notion that an author and his protagonist are one and the same not only is obtuse from the point of view of literary studies, it also self-evidently reflects a misreading of a novel in which, over forty-eight hours in New York, an elderly Holocaust survivor is shown to still have plenty to learn. This is something we can infer early on when Sammler, on a bus, turns a racially dehumanizing gaze upon a character described only, here and throughout the novel, as a "black pickpocket." For what Sammler has yet to learn, shockingly in light of his personal experiences, concerns precisely this question of his own prejudices.

Yet one can't deny that Bellow's presentation of Sammler is a largely sympathetic one. Sammler is a man of discretion, civility, and insight, and it is these traits, as much as his prejudices, that seem to distinguish him from the younger intellectuals he encounters on the American scene at large. Published not long after the student protests of 1968, the novel explores the contrast and comparison between these two intellectual generations. Their difference appears, for example, in the mostly unspoken conflict between the taciturn Sammler and his vociferous American-born niece Margotte. Embodying the postwar intellectual youth culture from which her uncle feels himself completely alienated, Margotte is described as "boundlessly, achingly, hopelessly on the right side, the best side, of every big human question" (15). Certainly, she doesn't share her uncle's qualms about "superstructures of explanation"—not even when it comes to the Holocaust. "A mass society does not produce great criminals," she *explains.* "It's because of the division of labor all over society which broke up the whole idea of general responsibility" (11). Hers is thus a structural explanation that absolves the individual of any responsibility, any guilt. But everybody "knows what murder is," Sammler replies. "That is very old human knowledge." Only "intellectuals do not understand" (13–14).

But while what intellectuals fail to understand is arguably the central concern of this book, its protagonist, though profoundly troubled by the failings of the intellect, is no less subject to these failings himself. Sammler's professed belief in the moral truth that everybody "knows what murder is," for example, suggests not only that he cannot give up on the Enlightenment dream of universal knowledge, but that, in the realm of the intellect, he too may be, no less than Margotte, intent on occupying "the right side, the best side, of every big human question."

That said, Sammler also "knows what murder is" in reality. He is, after all, a man whose loved ones have been murdered, and he is a man who has himself murdered another man in order to save his own life. So it is not books or papers but *experience* that has shown him what murder is. What, then, has this experience taught him? Well, for one thing, that murder is not edifying. Sammler's war experiences have no more purified him of sin, error, or prejudice than they did the old Polish peasant who heroically risked his life to save Sammler's during the war, but whose subsequent letters included anti-Semitic sentiments. His savior, Sammler reflects, was "an ordinary human being [who] wanted again to be himself. Enough was enough. Didn't he have a right to be himself? To relax into the old prejudices?" (74).

Don't we have a *right*, in other words, to be wrong? For despite Sammler's many wrongs, what he may well have been right about is that rightness is not necessarily a matter, as Margotte seems to believe, of intellectual or political positioning. As if one could always be right, in advance, about everything. As if rightness were simply an issue of applying a more rigorous critique to decide where or on whose side to stand. This, indeed, was perhaps Bellow's larger point in presenting a thoughtful person reflecting on whether or not what one thinks has any real importance. Do our thoughts, he's asking, really justify us?

Many of my students are not unlike Margotte. *I'm* not unlike Margotte. When I teach "critical theory" to undergraduates, I tell myself that they're learning subversive reading practices, practices that demystify the workings of power. Yet there are times when I see these same critical tools as the means by which university students can better align themselves *with* power via cultural competence or political correctness.[12] Used thus, critical theory appears less invested in the unraveling of privilege than it is a further method of shoring it up—for what greater privilege is there, really, than that of having the right opinion about pretty much everything? (You need only witness the online scramble to adopt the most unassailable stance in the wake of each new global calamity.) Hence what my students fear, it would seem, is being wrong, or *saying* something wrong, perhaps because they sense how academic errors—getting something wrong—can quickly shade into moral ones: *being in* the wrong. So critical theory is attractive to such students, as I think it has partly been to me, because theories, as explanations that can never be *proven* wrong, seem to promise, for certain of their adherents, some sort of historical absolution.

What Sammler's experience has taught him, on the other hand, is that only in *theory* can one remain, like his niece, an innocent. How ironic, then, that it is he—a murderer!—who should become, precisely on account of his historical experiences, a sort of "symbolic character" for the young people he meets in America who seem to project on to him a kind of unimpeachable saintliness: the sanctity of the absolute victim. For if Sammler is a projection screen for the young people who imagine, with reference to him, that they can tell the difference between good and evil, left and right, right and wrong, Sammler's own experience of history has taught him otherwise. Who, after all, can tell who is right and who is wrong when an anti-Semitic peasant saved a Jewish life while the critical intellectuals of the academy coordinated with the Nazi regime?

What experience has *not* taught Sammler, therefore, is how to think. Though it *has* apparently taught him when action is required. We infer this in a scene near the end of the book, when Sammler impotently watches as the anonymous "black pickpocket" gets beaten to within an inch of his life, surrounded by a circle of spectators who, despite the elderly man's urgings that somebody with sufficient physical force *do* something to stop it, do not act at all. It is his Israeli son-in-law Eisen, another Holocaust survivor, who has, at Sammler's own prompting, intervened in a street fight involving the pickpocket and another young American. But Eisen goes too far, bringing down such blows on the poor man's skull that Sammler, horrified by the violence he seems to have unintentionally invited, screams, "What have I done! This is much worse! This is the worst thing yet" (241).[13] It's an extraordinary line. Bellow has placed a fictional Holocaust survivor on a New York street and had him call the "worst thing yet" something other than the Holocaust. The worst thing yet is to be the instigator and bystander of a crime against humanity that he has neither the power to prevent by himself nor the power to move others to prevent by taking appropriate action. As his words and cries fall on deaf ears, it seems clear that, in the new world no less than the old, Sammler is for the people around him not so much a person as an object or idea. Worse still, the idea they have of him, here as there, is wrong.

Eventually, therefore, it is the pickpocket with whom Sammler comes to sympathize most in this alien culture. What he "learns," as summarized by Stanley Crouch, is how to "summon the heroic feeling of compassion through the stern memories of his own shortcomings. The thick, red blood of the black pickpocket lying wounded and helpless in the street turns him into a man before Mr. Sammler, who feels again the butt of the Nazi rifle against his own head and knows that it partially blinded him to the humanity of others."[14]

If the young people in the novel have the wrong idea about the experienced Sammler—the idea of his innocence—those who reacted against the novel may well have fallen prey to the inverse idea about Bellow—replacing the notion of political innocence with one of political guilt. To claim, as I am here, that this idea is equally wrong, is not, of course, to suggest that Bellow is innocent rather than guilty. Rather, what I believe his novel is asking us to seriously reflect on is a political culture that considers a person guilty or innocent on the basis not of their actions, but the ideas they carry in their head. In this respect, therefore, we might agree that Bellow, *like* Sammler, may be wondering whether there isn't something wrong with wanting all the time to be right. For what, after all, are we to make of a politics in which all conflict and compromise seem abandoned in favor of that ideal state of purity known so often today as correctness?

Liberal Guilt

While Bellow's Margotte may have felt confident of her own political innocence, those who came after her seem to have felt something else. Liberal guilt, according to cultural critic Julie Ellison, took hold in America in the 1990s on the back of a post–Cold War fragmentation of the Left and a loss of faith in the utopian politics of collective action that had characterized that earlier generation of radicals.[15] The liberal who feels guilty has given up on the collective and recognizes herself to be acting out of self-interest. Her guilt is thus a sign of the gap between what she *feels* for the other's suffering and what she will actively *do* in order to alleviate it—which is not, as it turns out, a great deal.

As such, her guilt incites a great deal of hostility in others, and most especially in the person who feels himself to be the object of the liberal's guilt. This person (the designated victim) understands only too well how seldom the pity he elicits in the guilty liberal is likely to lead to any significant structural or political changes for him. Rather, the only "power" to be redirected his way is not political power but the moral or affective power to make those more fortunate than he is feel even more guilty about the privileges they are nonetheless not inclined to give up.

But just how in control of her feelings *is* the guilty liberal? Not very, thinks Ellison. Her guilt assails her unbidden, rendering her highly performative, exhibitionist, even hysterical.[16] In her guilt she experiences a "loss of control," though she remains conscious at all times of an audience before whom she feels that she must *show* how spectacularly sorry she is. Her guilt, then, is her way of "acting out," marking a disturbance in the liberal subject who does not know herself quite as well as her guilt would have her think.

The view of guilt as a blocking emotion corroborates the common critique of liberal guilt: that for all the suffering it enacts, it completely fails to motivate the guilty subject to effect meaningful political change. But what if the liberal's guilt, precisely because it is a blocking affect, affords the liberal respite from the very thing she may (unconsciously) feel even more guilty about: in a world that places such a premium on self-monitoring, self-presentation, and self-knowledge, the very lack of a fixed identity that might tell her who she is, what her responsibilities are, and where these come to an end?

If, indeed, anything can be said to characterize the notoriously woolly liberal, then guilt may well be it. Liberal guilt insinuates a certain class (middle), race (white), and geopolitical (first world) situation. As such, despite the genuine torment it brings to those who suffer it, the liberal's guilt might, paradoxically (and again, unconsciously), be felt as reassuring for someone whose real neurosis may be that she feels her identity to be so mobile, shifting, and uncertain that she can never quite be sure where she stands. If this *is* what chiefly concerns her, then one might envisage her guilt as that which seems to tell her who she is by virtue of who she is failing to be for others. Who is the liberal? She who suffers on account of those who suffer more than she! (I know whereof I speak.)

This may suggest why, in recent years, there has been mounting criticism of the liberal's sensibilities. To her critics, the liberal really *is* guilty. She's guilty of (a) secretly resenting victims for how *their* sufferings make *her* feel, (b) thus drawing attention away from *them* back toward *her;* (c) and even having the audacity to make an exhibition out of her self-lacerations, while (d) doing practically nothing to challenge the status quo. But however valid these criticisms, the language the stereotypical liberal uses to try to grasp and express her feelings should nonetheless be taken seriously. For even if the liberal's guilty attestations toward others *are* little more than a bandage to cover up another malaise, or another kind of guilt, insofar as she continues to imagine her emotion as, precisely, a "guilty" one, such professions still have the benefit of calling attention to the urgent nature of the ethical relation to others that guilt as guilt necessarily signifies.

Once again, therefore, in the case of liberal guilt, we can witness the double bind of a feeling so devilishly slippery that it repeats the problem to which it alludes in the very course of confessing it. For there clearly is a "false" sense of guilt that blocks rather than inspires action by turning guilt's inherently uncertain and open relation to others into an object of certainty and knowledge. Since that object, in a nutshell, is the self, this affective turn is one that also, as we saw in the case of the reinterpretation of survivor testimonies, works to mutate guilt into shame. Shame, indeed, could well be a more accurate appellation for what motivates the guilty liberal in her public and private self-condemnations. As such, the eruption of "liberal guilt" Ellison identifies post–Cold War may now find itself (as with postwar survivor's guilt) revised into the form of shame that can help to forge a new kind of innocence (though for those who have long suspected the liberal of hypocrisy, any such exculpatory move on her part can only count as further evidence against her).

Yet before considering (as I'm about to) this cultural shift toward shame in any more detail, shouldn't we perhaps already pause here to carry forward our earlier insights *into* survivor's guilt? Recall that Ruth Leys draws a distinction between the guilt that understands itself as active and thus responsible (a state of consciousness referring primarily, for Leys, to the subject's *intentions*) and the shame believed to be passive and thus powerless. The trauma victim, unlike the guilty liberal, has generally occupied a situation of abject powerlessness at the point of contracting his guilt. Yet *even* in this case, says Leys, to refuse to countenance his guilt as guilt is to do further damage to the victim by becoming complicit with the persecutory logic that has robbed him of all agency.

So wouldn't it be equally wise to show caution before denouncing the right of *any* subject inclined to speak in terms of her guilt? In the case of the liberal, for instance, regardless of whether we consider her own use of the term "guilt" to have been misapplied, doesn't the term at least retain the possibility of arousing the repressed memory of our indeterminate relation to and responsibility for others—the memory, that is, of what, arguably, is the *true* source of the guilt to which the self-avowedly guilty liberal continues, however obliquely, to attest?

Shame on You

But it's shame that's all the rage these days. There even seems, in the era of the internet, to have been a virtual renaissance of the medieval-sounding concept of "public shaming," as what appeared at first to be evidence of the internet's empowerment of the masses to create new forms of global connectivity that could inspire collective action for social change has just as often morphed into a kind of mob mentality whose purpose is the spread not so much of power as of powerlessness.

In *So You've Been Publicly Shamed*, journalist Jon Ronson investigates the devastating consequences when hundreds, thousands, even millions of strangers vilify you on social media. Looking at individual cases of people more sinned against than sinning—people who have lost their jobs, and in some cases their lives, because it's hard to survive, make friends, date, and find new employment in a world where a quick Google search informs the searcher that you are a liar/slut/racist/pervert—Ronson learned that the most shameful thing about being an "object of hate . . . isn't the hate. It's the object."[17]

The idea for his book was first seeded when Ronson sought revenge on a bunch of academics who had stolen his identity by creating a Twitter account in his name and posting inanities he found embarrassing. Their reasoning for refusing to take it down (is Jon Ronson himself any more real that their online version of him?) sounded typical of otherworldly academics who, as it turned out, are exactly the kind of people to incur the hatred and contempt of the web's angriest citizens. This was something Ronson was pleased to discover after he filmed himself confronting the three academics before uploading, with their permission, the video onto YouTube—a video that elicited reactions of ever more exaggerated hostility. The fake Jon Ronson Twitter account was subsequently taken down, a sweet revenge that made Ronson feel good at first, vindicated by the righteous indignation of anonymous strangers who agreed that he had been wronged, although he later started feeling a little queasy about the logic of repetition that had seen him shame his own shamers.

Ronson went on to find this same repetitive logic to be ubiquitous throughout his research into internet shaming. So, too, was the consistent binding of shame to some essential claim on the part of the shamer to a knowledge (of the shamed party) that seemed to willfully ignore or deny anything indeterminate: any question, doubt, or uncertainty.

Rendering words more literal than they can really be is therefore a key element of internet shaming. For if what marks the experience of shame is a sense of utter powerlessness, then this powerlessness is never more apparent than when we write or say something only to discover that our own words have been *taken the wrong way*, as happened to Justine Sacco, the public relations executive who tweeted a badly worded joke before boarding a plane to South Africa—"Going to Africa. Hope I don't get AIDS. Just kidding. I'm white!"—and discovered only upon landing that the top trending topic on Twitter was #hasjustinelandedyet. Over the course of the flight she had become the internet's public enemy number one. So she sought to *explain* herself. She genuinely *was* "just kidding." It wasn't racism but a joke *about* racism! She never intended for anyone to take her words literally! And she also apologized profusely for her error, telling the world how *ashamed* of herself she was for saying something so crass about a subject so serious. But the world wasn't listening, which is curious because, as Ronson remarks, "I hadn't needed to think about her tweet for more than a few seconds before I understood what she'd been trying to say. There must have been amongst her shamers a lot of people who chose to wilfully misunderstand it" (70).

If antiracism is a stance against the dehumanizing treatment of people as objects, then the online campaign against Justine Sacco was guilty of the same dehumanization. Sacco's accusers deem her punishable by public shaming not because she has *said* something racist, but because she essentially *is* a racist, with her social identity (female, blonde, attractive, white, American, well-off, employed, *guilty liberal*) regularly cited by way of evidence, and her joke merely bringing this underlying fact about her to the surface. So the essentializing gesture of antiracism becomes, in this instance, a quasi-repetition of the racism, just as Ronson himself, when taking revenge on his academic trolls, had found himself replicating the problem he was—or thought he was—attempting to resolve.

Repetition

Again and again, from the Bible to Freud to Adorno to Ronson, we find the same double bind of a guilt that seems always to repeat the wrong it admonishes at the moment of calling it out. And, as we've seen, it often does this by closing down the guilt that opens up the potential for change inscribed in the relation to the other with recourse to the shame that hermetically seals the self with an object lesson in its own powerlessness. But while this logic of repetition seems endemic, is it inevitable? Or if repetition *is* inevitable, then might it be possible to repeat in such a way that repetition could actually make a difference?

In *Diary of the Fall*, Brazilian author Michel Laub ponders whether one can ever quite avoid repeating the history from which one is endeavoring to escape. The novel begins: "My grandfather didn't talk about the past, which is not so very surprising given its nature."[18] His grandfather, we soon learn, was a Holocaust survivor. "I don't want to talk about [the past] either," our narrator continues.

> If there's one thing the world doesn't need it's to hear my thoughts on the subject. It's been dealt with in the cinema. It's been dealt with in books. Eyewitnesses have already recounted the story detail by detail, and there are sixty years of reports and essays and analyses, generations of historians and philosophers and artists who devoted their lives to adding footnotes to all that material in an effort to refresh yet again the world's views on the matter, the reflex reaction everyone has to the word *Auschwitz*, so not for a second would it occur to me to repeat those ideas if they were not, in some way, essential if I am to talk about my grandfather and, therefore, about my father and, therefore, about myself.

Though he'd rather not repeat what has already been repeated so many times, how, without exercising his right to repetition, can our narrator hope to change the script of his life? This change is something he proposes to do by means of life-writing, and what he would most dearly like to change is the degree to which his own life has been determined by his father and grandfather, each of whom is also the author of a diary with life-altering aims.

The narrator's grandfather wrote not a journal of his life as it actually was but a whitewashed version of his life as it should have been, as if Auschwitz had never happened. Words, for his grandfather, are erasers; their purpose: to deny. This he does behind the locked door of his study, the room in which he also takes his own life, his suicide becoming the "Auschwitz" of our narrator's father: the traumatic event in *his* life from which all else springs and the event he can barely bring himself to speak of or recall. Instead, the narrator's father reacts to his own father's silencing of Auschwitz by obsessively talking *about* Auschwitz. He raises the specter of Auschwitz in every conversation, making all of life a warning to his son about the dangers of anti-Semitism—this despite the fact that our narrator was born and lives after the war in a middle-class Jewish neighborhood in Brazil. The narrator's father is as determined to remember the history of the Holocaust as his own father was to forget it. Thus when he is diagnosed with Alzheimer's and his memory is put at risk, he starts writing his own life story: not, like his father's, his life as it should have been, but his life as it actually was.

In writing *his* diary, therefore, our narrator does not want to repeat the strategies of his grandfather and father, which strategies— repressive forgetting on the one hand and oppressive remembering on the other—both, in different ways, make of Auschwitz the only law, the only history, the only truth there really is. What distinguishes his diary, in fact, is its lack of any discernible strategy, an impression reinforced by the novel's lack of pagination. Admitting from the start how little of his life is known to him—including even when his own story begins—our narrator tells stories about himself, his father, and his grandfather that bleed into one another in such a way as to leave his readers without any reliable bearings that might tell them where they are or how far they've reached.

Falling, Falling, Falling

Diary of the Fall alludes to three falls, or three different kinds of fall, all three as related as the three memoirists are to one another. The

first and most literal fall in the book is that of our narrator's classmate when, on the boy's thirteenth birthday, his "friends" were
giving him celebratory bumps at his own party. Following a
prehatched plan, these boys deliberately let their classmate drop;
the prank nearly causes him to suffer lifelong paralysis, and leaves
him wearing a back brace. This fall is the narrator's "Auschwitz":
the traumatic story of origins that precipitates his own metaphorical fall. For the name of "Auschwitz" in this novel is the word for
the event in one's life that, because it cannot be borne, becomes the
key to everything. This everything is the name of one's guilty
secret: whatever it is that, on the basis of Auschwitz, or one's
personal Auschwitz, one believes one has the right to do, to say, to
believe. In the case of our narrator, Auschwitz provides him with
his single life-lesson: "the non-viability of human experience at all
times and in all places."

Examining his conscience later in life, our narrator feels that his
life began to fall apart at precisely the moment when he deliberately let his classmate fall. The aftereffects of that moment, as he
looks back upon it, include his turn to alcoholism at the age of four-
teen, a turn narrated later in the book, in the only section entitled
"The Fall." For if, as we've suggested, the moral law is that which
one breaks at the moment one attests to it, then no one, surely,
understands this repetition-compulsion better than the alcoholic
who swears to himself that he'll never drink again even as he's
uncorking the bottle. His alcoholism, our narrator subsequently
suspects, was his own attempt to forget his part in a traumatic
history by obliterating all memory of it, much as his grandfather
had done in another fashion before him.

But what made him let his friend fall? This is something he
ponders along with the motivations of his classmates in the privileged Jewish school in an upper-middle-class neighborhood in
Porto Alegre—kids with big houses and swimming pools. And what

he determines is that their cruel prank deliberately targeted the only non-Jewish scholarship kid in the class. They had persecuted this boy, all on the basis of the endless talk of anti-Semitism on the school's curriculum—a topic the author also heard rehearsed nonstop from his father at home.

After letting the boy fall, the narrator has a fight with his father, throwing a sharp object at his face that very nearly blinds him. The father, ceasing from that moment onward to talk to his son of Nazism, permits his son to switch schools along with the "friend" who fell. Both schoolboys then attend a non-Jewish school, where eventually the friend becomes the bully who leads his new peer group in explicitly anti-Semitic intimidation of our narrator. So it is that the cycle of repetition continues. Auschwitz continues. The fall continues.

Temptation

The third reference to falling in this book is in the form of a question:

> Is it possible to hate an Auschwitz survivor in the way my father did? Is it permissible to feel such pure hatred without at any moment falling into the temptation of moderating that feeling because of Auschwitz, without feeling guilty for placing one's own emotions above something like the memory of Auschwitz?

The temptation here is the temptation of guilt: to moderate one's feelings of pure hatred because of the guilt that has already attached itself to what one believes one already *knows*. Indeed the guilt *is* the belief that one already knows—that one already "knows" a history with the power to silence and overwhelm all objections, hesitancies, doubts, and indecisions, but whose real meaning has never been properly assimilated, recognized, or settled, and so in fact remains completely *un*known.

There's plenty of reason, of course, to feel guilty for hating a victim in the way the narrator's father seems to have hated his own Auschwitz-surviving suicidal father. But nor can one, in all honesty, simply love the source of one's misery: that person who makes you feel bad, whose suffering stimulates your own unequal suffering. Thus while we might well be tempted to feel guilty for hating someone who has suffered more than we can ever know or say, we risk committing a graver sin—maybe even an *actual* sin—by failing to acknowledge or *feel* our hatred toward him.[19] Why? Because the temptation to cover up one's hatred for the other who suffers is at the same time the temptation to determine the *meaning* of his suffering. So while our desire might be to bring an end to the influence of the past on the present, the effect of turning an open history into a settled score—an object of knowledge—is to close down not only the past but the future, making repetition in some guise inevitable.

Such a view shares much with the psychoanalytic conception of guilt as a blocked form of aggression or anger toward those we need and love. If, however, guilt is the feeling that typically blocks all other (buried, repressed, unconscious) feelings, that is not in itself a reason to block feelings of guilt. Feelings, after all, are what you must be prepared to feel if they are to move you, or if you are to feel something else. And guilt, as we said before, can both inhibit and get things going.

How so?

Well, for one thing, by responding to the superego's prohibition of aggressive and libidinal impulses toward others, feeling guilty also attests to the subject's own internal conflicts in *relation* to others. That is, it *admits* of others, unlike the shame whose self-debasement also has a narcissistic function: that of returning us to the stable image we would ideally like to have of ourselves. Yet as preferable as guilt, in its focus on human agency, might seem, it is, for those who would like to lay claim to objective knowledge and subjective innocence, precisely shame's putative powerlessness that seems to have turned it into a prized possession: a source of certainty in an uncertain world.[20] Though one need look no further than to the revival of public shaming via the internet to perceive the dead end to which such objectifications invariably lead.

In summary, then, the movement from guilt to shame in critical theory stemmed in part from an understandable wish not to blame the victim for her own suffering. Yet as we've seen, a risk is also entailed in seeking to "save" the victim from her guilt: the risk of depriving the victim of the very thing that might distinguish her from the objectifying aggression that has assailed her: a sense of her *own* intentions and wishes, however aggressive, perverse, or thwarted these might be. For this reason, then, it's vital to preserve the notion of "survivor's guilt" (and "liberal guilt") as that which could yet return to the survivor (or liberal) a power of agency such as must be absolutely necessary if she is to have a future that isn't bound, by the resolving or absolving of her guilt, to *repeat* ad infinitum the past.

What Each Man Knows

If religion often gets the blame for framing man as sinner, the secular effort to release man from his guilt hasn't offered much relief. The Italian philosopher Giorgio Agamben suggests that subjective innocence belongs to a bygone age, the age of the tragic hero.[21] Oedipus, for example, is someone whose objective guilt (parricide, incest) is matched by his subjective innocence—the subjective innocence of the man who acts *before* he knows. Whereas today, says Agamben, we can observe the opposing situation: modern man is objectively innocent (for he has not, like Oedipus, murdered with his own hands) yet subjectively guilty (he knows that his comforts and securities have been paid for by *someone, somewhere*, probably in blood).

Not all modern men are the same, of course. Reflecting on a childhood spent largely among Holocaust survivors, Lisa Appignanesi remarks, "I don't think anyone felt guilty about having made it through." "Maybe," she adds, "guilt is something one feels in situations of utter passivity, and these people had all acted."[22] A salutary reminder that there are always counterexamples. Yet Appignanesi's observation also chimes with Agamben's insofar as she too understands subjective guilt not as the telltale distinction between the victim and the perpetrator but as that which comes to distinguish between those who've been blocked from acting and those who *have* acted. Indeed, for Freud as well it's not so much the biblical Adam as an ultramodern Oedipus—an Oedipus whose unconscious desires have mostly *not* been acted on—who has bequeathed our civilization its most major "discontent": a subjective guilt that no wind of change yet has ever managed to sweep away. To wit, given that modernity has not only failed to obliterate but may even have exacerbated man's subjective guilt by falsely promising him an innocence bound to his historical and intellectual emancipation, the older religious assignation of man as a sinner—a fallen, abject, endlessly compromised, but also active, effective, and changeable creature—begins to look relatively comforting by comparison.

In this light, then, I return finally to *Mr. Sammler's Planet*, which ends with Sammler uttering a prayer for the soul of his recently deceased benefactor. His prayer eulogizes awkwardly with subclauses, parentheses, and semantic clarifications in a language on the brink of admitting its own defeat as Sammler finds himself explaining (yes, *explaining*) to God that his old friend "did meet the terms of his contract": "The terms which, in his inmost heart, each man knows. As I know mine. As all know. For that is the truth of it—that we all know, God, that we know, that we know, we know, we know."[23]

So the novel concludes much as it begins, with the repeated affirmation of the soul's own natural knowledge, "which, in his inmost heart, each man knows." But now, at the end of the book, what Sammler claims is known by "all" appears within the very form of discourse—prayer—to which man has traditionally turned, in hope and desperation, at the moment when knowledge has reached its limits. It thus ends with the strange invocation of a knowledge whose very context hollows out its own assurances. The verbal repetition—"we know, we know, we know"—makes the point. Our reliance upon repetition as the rubric of mastery is always at risk of repetition's own contradictory logic as both the means by which we display control and the compulsion that renders us *out* of control. Repetition, in other words, always risks *not* repeating itself. Hence Sammler's prayerful "we know, we know, we know" both repeats and departs from the knowledge it seeks to affirm. For whatever it is that Sammler still thinks he *knows*, by the end of the novel this knowledge has given way to a religious form of expression that seems to carry within it hope, rather than certainty, of a common morality. This morality is not, however, one that imposes itself on others as might a dogmatism; nor, despite its quality of injunction, is it one that permits, for the modern individual, *any* safe place to stand that could guarantee, in advance, her moral, cognitive, or political correctness.

FOUR

Over the Top

I don't know about hiding away, but I really only like to present
myself when I'm working on something—it's more my work
I like to present to the world rather than myself.
—KATE BUSH

None of us, surely, is immune to compulsion: that all-encompassing feeling of being driven by something, some force that seems to assail us from both without and within. For Jacques Lacan, what drives us is what we've been possessed by. In our drives and our repetitive compulsions we encounter, traumatically, a world without stability or security—what he called the Real. In this we're not unlike those ancient wayfarers of Greek mythology who find themselves impelled by sirens whose voices they know will imperil them but whose beauty they cannot resist. What the sirens sing, writes Renata Salecl, is a song whose past "has not yet been symbolized, it has not become a memory; such an unsymbolized past is traumatic for the listener, since it evokes something primordial, something between nature and culture that the subject does not want to remember."[1]

Stanley Cavell has made similar observations about the operatic voice of the soprano: "Men want and want not to hear the woman's voice; to know and not to know what and that she desires; to know and not to know what she knows about men's desires, for example, the extent to which theirs may be feminine, when hers may or may not be."[2] The (male) operagoer might in this sense be said to be playing at the loss of control signified by that now redundant medical term, hysteria. For is not the soprano a version of the hysteric? Someone, that is, whose voice seems to shatter the commonsense world, as if it were breaking through from another time, another place. Like the soprano, the hysteric threatens to infect her listener, to put him in the way of his own unmasterability, and like the soprano too, her voice seduces as much as disturbs. This may help to explain the peculiar ambivalence we can detect within a practice like Freud's. For it was he who, on the one hand, listened with genuine fascination to those voices, mostly female, frequently Jewish, that had tended to be censored or silenced, written off as mad, yet who, on the other hand, seems no sooner to have heard these voices than he returned them to the sphere of a patriarchal authority with the power to determine the significance of what the "hysteric" was trying to say. Just as the voices of the ancient sirens were said to endanger the men who approached them, it's perhaps for similar reasons that the hysteric's voice has for the most part been heeded only in the safety of the consulting room, where her listener can remain lashed to the mast of medical mastery. Though it's surely the operagoer who enjoys the ultimate state of luxury when he experiences the sublime shattering beauty of the soprano without ever losing confidence in his own position, for once the soprano sings her heart out, it is, as everyone knows, she and not her listener who must die.

Jane Eyre

If you are operatic, melodramatic, hysterical, you're over the top, you're too much, your feelings are running wild, you need to get hold of yourself, or someone needs to get hold of you. The late-nineteenth-century diagnosis of hysteria, which identified something intrinsically wrong with the female sex, is no longer in medical use, but we still retain this vernacular sense of the word "hysteria" as a kind of emotional frenzy or loss of control. We use the term especially to refer to a type of manic animal laughter—a laughter which seems to signify something more disturbing than mere amusement, and which may even have an element of the demonic within it. That maniacal laughter has taken me over a few times in recent years. When people first meet me, they often notice my nervous laughter—it's always there as a background noise, as if I'm constantly gasping for breath. However, on a few occasions, not all of them social, my laughter has moved from the background into the foreground. At these moments it loses any discernible connection to a source of amusement, and ends, invariably, in equally inexplicable tears. For those nearby me at the time there is something particularly unsettling about a laughter without mirth, a laughter so seemingly unanchored in a sense of the fun or the funny—not least because I have never known and still do not know what lies at the root of it.

Once this happened to me when I was rereading, for the sake of a course I was going to teach, that great feminine bildungsroman *Jane Eyre*. When Jane, working as a governess, hears the fugitive sound of a manic laughter and misrecognizes it as that of Mr. Rochester's maidservant—not suspecting its true origin with Bertha Mason, Rochester's first wife, hidden away in the attic—I succumbed to my own manic laughter. My husband was disturbed. He looked at the passage I was reading, but saw nothing to laugh about. This was Charlotte Brontë, after all—not a writer to provoke rolling in the aisles. Not Philip Roth.

Derived etymologically from the Attica region in ancient Greece, an "attic" is a place that lies over the top of the family home, a place where artifacts of the family's history can be stored so as to be neither forgotten nor remembered but postponed for a future reckoning. What the attic contains is what we deem surplus to our everyday requirements. What we place there is too much. Perhaps it's no accident, then, that over the top of the house of fiction, in the confined space of the attic, we also find the over-the-top figure of the hysteric, for, like the attic, the hysteric too is said to contain feelings and experiences that are too much for her. And she too embodies a hidden history that threatens at all times to spill out into the open, much as the attic threatens to cave in on those politely inhabiting the daylit rooms below.

In 1979 Sandra Gilbert and Susan Gubar published a foundational text of second-wave feminism, *The Madwoman in the Attic*, a text that focuses primarily on the nineteenth-century literary imagination of female writers: "We found what began to seem a distinctively female literary tradition. . . . Images of enclosure and escape, fantasies in which maddened doubles functioned as asocial surrogates for docile selves."[3] The book traces this trope of the female double all the way back to scripture (for example, to Lilith, who precedes Eve as Adam's first wife in midrashic and apocryphal texts), through fairy tales (the perpetual pairing of a good mother with an evil stepmother), to the modern novel, and consistently finds the figure of woman divided, whether internally or externally, between the monstrous and angelic, the hysterical and serene.

Above all, there is Jane Eyre. Plain Jane's spiritual progress toward the moment when she can utter her immortal line, "Reader, I married him," is in a sense a conventional bildungsroman narrative of the protagonist's maturation to the point of self-realization—the narrative in which becoming oneself, as in one self, is the goal.

In the case of Jane Eyre, however, there is also something exceptional in the drama of a female heroine on a quest for self-realization before entering a marriage based, according to her own demands, on a hard-won sexual equality.

Only late in the novel does Jane learn of the legal impediment to her marriage. It comes in the form of Rochester's surviving first wife, whose imprisonment in the attic Jane finally discovers when she sees a terrifying vision of a woman who seems half specter, half beast, pacing back and forth like a wild animal in a cage. As Gilbert and Gubar note, this scene is an echo of an earlier scene in the novel when the young Jane, confined as punishment to a red room and succumbing to delusions that push her close to the edge, herself paces the room like a constrained beast. Indeed, the authors claim that Rochester's first wife, a Jamaican Creole whose marriage brought not only herself but her significant property and wealth back to England, "is Jane's truest and darkest double: she is the angry aspect of the orphan child, the ferocious secret self Jane has been trying to repress."⁴ Unlike plain Jane, Bertha, her secret self, is sultry, seductive, and sensuous, and with that, monstrous. Ultimately, too, she is the *femme fatale* who burns down Thornfield, blinding Rochester and ending her own life, thus clearing the legal way for Jane to marry him on more equal terms (an equality in which the male potential for violence has been significantly neutered by blindness). It is, then, possible to give a persuasively psychological, if somewhat utopian, reading to the novel that identifies the hidden-away first wife as secretly enacting the repressed wishes of the second, whose triumphant emergence after the final conflagration enables her to self-realize as a unified individual only because she has at last been able to successfully integrate both these sides of herself into one ideal subject.

Yet such a protofeminist reading of the novel is problematic, for it colludes with the violence of the novel's own conclusion. Gayatri

Chakravorty Spivak raises the siren here when she warns that Jane's self-determination depends on treating Bertha as nothing more than a fantasy figure to be sacrificed as and when necessary: "In this fictive England, she [Bertha] must play out her role, act out the transformation of her 'self' into that fictive Other, set fire to the house and kill herself, so that Jane Eyre can become the feminist individualist heroine of British fiction. I must read this as an allegory of the general epistemic violence of imperialism, the construction of a self-immolating colonial subject for the glorification of the social mission of the colonizer."[5]

Hence it is to the Dominican writer Jean Rhys's retelling of the story of Rochester's first wife in her best-known novel, *Wide Sargasso Sea*, that Spivak turns for a rendering of the madwoman in the attic that "keeps Bertha's humanity, indeed her sanity as a critic of imperialism, intact."[6] In Rhys's book there is little doubt that Bertha has married for love and been taken for a ride. It is not, therefore, the innate bestiality of the Creole woman that ultimately prompts her violent reaction but rather the dissimulations of a colonial discourse that justifies its ill-gotten gains in the language of morality, religion, and law. As with the sirens in Greek mythology and the sopranos in opera, Bertha's voice cannot find a legitimate place in the world as it is; thus it is she, not Jane, who must surely die.

Like *The Madwoman in the Attic*, Catherine Clément's *Opera, or the Undoing of Women* was published in 1979. Its thesis, as summarized by Cavell, is that "opera is about the death of women, and about the singing of women, and can be seen to be about the fact that women die *because* they sing."[7] Opera, writes Clément, "comes to me from the womb. . . . They will tell you that hysteria is a sickness. . . . Do not believe it. Hysteria is woman's principal resource."[8] Her sentence, by daring to say something over the top, draws on what Salecl calls that "special form of happiness" felt by a person "when he or she is not at all concerned with the Other."[9] Lacan identified that type of enjoyment and called it *jouissance*.

Jouissance is the enjoyment of one's compulsion, one's drive, whatever it is within us that makes us excessive, over the top. It is "in the tonality of the voice," writes Salecl, "that we encounter *jouissance*—this is where the surplus enjoyment comes into being as something that eludes signification."[10] This voice, shorn of any binding relationship to content, is conceivably the voice we find in opera, where the rules of everyday communication are, as Cavell notes in a startling observation, breathtakingly reversed:

> People on the whole do not *literally* sing to one another, at least sane people on the whole do not, exactly. They do understandably sing to themselves, under certain circumstances—more understandably than if they are heard or seen speaking to themselves. We could almost take the blatant conventionality of opera as meant to call into question the conventions or conditions making civil discourse possible.[11]

Life as a Man

A third book published in 1979 bears no obvious relation to the feminist works of Clément or Gilbert and Gubar. In fact its author, Philip Roth, is more often taken to be a peddler of unreconstructed misogyny. This was a reputation that came early to Roth, especially following his 1969 paean to compulsive masturbation, *Portnoy's Complaint*. Yet it is also the case that Roth has many female fans and readers, and not, one would imagine, because they just can't help themselves as one might not be able to help oneself with a mad, bad, and dangerous-to-know guy like Rochester. You realize you shouldn't, of course, but you fall in love with Rochester. To read the monologue of Alexander Portnoy, on the other hand, is unlikely to inspire much ardor. Yet perhaps, all the same, it is possible to say of Roth that here is not an advocate for patriarchy, but an honest exposition of it. And perhaps, too, it is possible to identify a certain affinity between Roth's misogyny and those women, like myself, who find themselves irresistibly drawn to its siren's song.[12]

What, after all, animates the compulsion to repeat at the heart of so many of Alexander Portnoy's complaints as he lies on his back talking uninterrupted to his shrink, if not, as Deborah Shostak has observed, the split within his psyche between the "Jewboy" "(with all that word signifies to Jew and Gentile alike about aggression, appetite, and marginality) and the 'nice Jewish boy' (with all that epithet implies about repression, respectability, and social acceptance)"? It's a split that strikingly resembles the split between the angel and the monster in nineteenth-century women's writing. As Shostak puts it, Portnoy's acts of "obsessive masturbation and promiscuous sex paradoxically demonstrate not his wholeness but his altogether too feminizing hysteria."[13]

Certainly the legacy of this nineteenth-century association of women and Jewish men as hysterical creatures, diseased of mind and body and unassured in their sexual identities, would seem, in the perpetual intertwining of erotic and ethnic concerns that mark Roth's writing, to underpin that archetypal quest of the typical Rothian protagonist: to prove his manhood. The title of one of Roth's early works, *My Life as a Man*, could easily double as a title for an entire oeuvre in which masculinity seems to be what is at stake—always the goal, always the vision of what self-satisfaction might look like. Yet this ideal is ever an elusive one, endlessly threatened by the sexual power of women, and not least, of course, as we may recall from one of the best-known comic scenes in *Portnoy's Complaint*, the castrating figure of the (Jewish) mother. If masculinity is believed to precede and assure a Rothian man's autonomy, then, given the notorious difficulty of getting any reliable handle on the "self" in a work by Roth, masculinity is also continually compromised as an ideal state. For Roth, as Josh Cohen notes, "erotic, Jewish and literary life are all forms of . . . experiencing oneself as more than one self."[14] It's why, when reading Roth, there's a particular excitement and frustration in being unable to determine the line that divides fantasy from reality, fiction from fact, as if both were continually occurring at once.

Add to this that Roth draws conspicuously on his own life experiences *for* his fiction. *My Life as a Man*, for example, offers a fictional portrait of his destructive marriage to his "mad" first wife, a woman he later describes again in his nonfictional memoir *The Facts* as "my worst enemy ever" before announcing, "Reader, I married her"—which, as Hana Wirth-Nesher observes, makes "an ironic reference to Brontë that casts [his first wife] as the madwoman in the attic, and Roth as both a long-suffering Rochester and a moralistic Jane."[15] A literary allusion, then, that conjures up a double identification and a gender indeterminacy whose diagnostic meaning would point toward hysteria were it not for the "fact" that the subject he is emphatically *not* identifying with in this remark is the madwoman herself.

Unlike the future we're invited to imagine for Jane once wedded to Rochester, Roth's second marriage, to the actress Claire Bloom, did not end happily ever after. This was something Bloom knew to expect from the start, just as Odysseus and his men had been warned in advance against the sirens' seductions, for Roth's first gift to Bloom was, of all things, *My Life as a Man*! Reading it, she was both impressed and unnerved by the evidence it contained of someone with "a deep and irrepressible rage: anger at being trapped in marriage; fear of giving up autonomy; and a profound distrust of the sexual power of women. I noted the warning signals; but of course the situation would be different with me."[16] So she ignored the sirens. Indeed, Bloom's memoir, *Leaving a Doll's House*, goes into painstaking detail in recollecting the acrimony of their separation and the particular distress caused when Roth sought to reclaim whatever property they had shared in their marriage, but which he now insisted was wholly his own. This included a play he had written for Bloom to perform, based on David Plante's recollection of Jean Rhys in his memoir *Difficult Women*.

Plante had spent time with Rhys as her confidante and amanuensis in the latter part of her life, during the ill-fated composition of her stop-start autobiographic project. His portrait of her is of an alcoholic who used their every encounter to drink a lot of gin. Much married but now very alone, Rhys appears a woman in despair, isolated even from those who would attach themselves to her, including those critics who sought to hail her as an exemplary case for feminism and/or postcolonialism (both forms of criticism on which she cast aspersions). Anger at being trapped, even in a critical discourse, animates her complaints to the man who sits mostly listening to her like a shrink taking notes. Moreover, in a tragic echo of her own madwoman character, Plante's Rhys has locked herself into seclusion, playing to perfection the part of the knowingly "selfish" writer in a hermetically sealed solitude which she deems vital in order to be able to write freely; although by the time Plante meets her the writer's block that plagued Rhys her whole life has taken over almost completely. Certainly her description of the period she spent writing *Wide Sargasso Sea*—"I spent my time walking up and down the passage, afraid of the spiders and the mice, and all the people in the village. I think it was one of the worst times in my life"—can hardly fail to bring to mind the protagonist of that book.[17]

But if Rhys comes close to her own portrayal of Rochester's mad first wife, what then of Roth, whose second wife thought the play based on Rhys was written as a gift to her only to find Roth later reclaiming it in the midst of undergoing his own mental breakdown?

For though Roth, in *The Facts*, jests at a self-identification divided between Rochester and Jane, doesn't his play about Rhys suggest a still more profound identification with the much maligned figure of the first wife: the trapped, hysterical, femme fatale—the madwoman in the attic?

When collaborating on the adaptation of his Rhys recollections for the stage, Plante also wrote a portrait of Roth: the male author as difficult man. At one point, he muses, after Roth invites him to peruse his own study at leisure, "a curious self-consciousness came over me—not only that of a younger writer in the study of an older (not that much older) and renowned writer, but that of the younger writer having *read* in one of that renowned writer's novels a scene similar to the one in which the younger writer finds himself. Did Philip think of this when he put me in his study? What was odd was that I enjoyed this self-consciousness—enjoyed it without thinking I was being false, because the scene was already made real, made true, by its appearance in 'The Ghost Writer.' "[18]

Plante's self-assurance, autonomy, and sense of reality are thus curiously compromised in the company of Roth. Is he, he wonders, merely playing a part that Roth has himself scripted? Might he be a character within the author's own fiction? The Roth novel he finds himself in, the first of a series of novels about the Jewish-American author Nathan Zuckerman, is *The Ghost Writer*. Like *Madwoman in the Attic* and *Opera, or the Undoing of Women*, *The Ghost Writer* was published in 1979. At its conclusion, E. I. Lonoff, the elder writer in the novel, tells his young protégé that he looks forward to reading what Nathan will make of him in his writings. "You're not so nice and polite in your fiction," he said. "You're a different person."[19] Despite sensing his own reenactment of that novel, Plante apparently forgot about this scene, for when we read that Plante told Roth, "I'd like to do a portrait of you. You know I write about you in my diary. Why shouldn't I publish it?" Roth urges him on before adding, "You really are totally untrustworthy. You're worse than I am. It's true about you, you're not a nice boy at all." The older author thus imposes on the younger this quintessentially Rothian splitting of a subject, forcing us to ask, who is more real, the one we meet in life or the one we meet in the writing, the angel or the monster?

"Philip is a man completely devoid of femininity, of sexual ambiguity," Plante surmises, although once again he has been invited by Roth himself into this speculation: "You should call your portrait of me 'Straight Man.'" But what happens to that concept, "Straight Man," when it appears so evidently ironized between quotation marks, framed by another writer who is not himself a "straight man"? Certainly in reading Roth there is very little about sex that seems straight. Yet while works like *Portnoy* and *My Life as a Man* earned Roth a not inaccurate reputation for misogyny, it is the object of his masturbatory fantasies in *The Ghost Writer* that has the power to truly scandalize, for in that novel he goes so far as to sexualize the image and memory of not just any woman but a woman whose name and identity will always evoke a young girl; and not just any young girl: Anne Frank. In Roth's fervid imagination—or should we say Zuckerman's?—Frank is less the child innocent than, as he entitles the section of the book comprising a fantasy about her, a "Femme Fatale."

A femme fatale, writes Salecl, has

> a certain ignorance about men, and it is this very ignorance that actually makes her so attractive. Freud pointed out that the ignorance of the *femme fatale*, as well as of young children and wild cats, is related to the fact they have not given up on some part of their libido: since other people have lost this libido, they become extremely attracted to those who still retain some of it.[20]

We can already find in Freud, then, as we can later in *The Ghost Writer*, an association between the young child and the femme fatale (along with the wild beast) as possessing an allure rooted in her own ignorance: we are seduced, that is to say, by what we know about her that she doesn't know about herself. Her ignorance, we feel a little nostalgically, must be a source of self-delight.

Anne Frank

The siren seduces by singing the fatal song of a history that we are unable to remember, but to which, for that reason, we find ourselves compelled to return. The history of which she sings possesses us rather than we it, no matter how many times we repeat or invoke its name. To properly remember the history of the Holocaust, for example, we would need to look not to *The Diary of a Young Girl* but to what came after it: the camps. Yet the *Diary* is the best-known of all published books on the subject—a book that has been outsold only by the Bible.

Along with everything else that, as a young girl, Anne Frank does not yet know about herself when writing her diary, there is what every one of her readers knows, which she, within its pages, can never know: what will bring her diary to an end. It is therefore her ignorance and innocence in a very precise sense that adds an uncanny charm to *The Diary of a Young Girl*, lending a predisposed pathos to our reading of a work whose writing deserves our attention, according to the poet John Berryman, for many more reasons besides the historical conditions that gave birth to it. In 1967 Berryman even wonders whether the *Diary*, despite its fame and popularity, has had any "serious readers" at all.[21]

Like Gilbert and Gubar, Roth sought, in 1979, to revisit and revise our sense of a female writer whose voice comes to us from the confinement of her hiding place in the attic. His use of Anne Frank for fictive purposes was considered by many to be scandalous.

Berryman, though, might well have considered Roth one of the *Diary*'s rare "serious readers," although to understand why that might be the case, Roth too, of course, would require serious readers, and serious readers, when it comes to Frank and (at that time) Roth, turn out to be in terribly short supply.

The Ghost Writer describes itself twice on the first page as a bildungsroman. It is told from the perspective of the older Zuckerman looking back on his younger self, offering, with distinctly Joycean overtones, a portrait of the Jewish-American artist as a young man. We first meet Nathan visiting his literary hero, E. I. Lonoff, with whom he has sought refuge following a recent falling out with his own father. The source of discord is a story he has written and published in a mainstream journal, which has earned him the reputation, among his Newark Jewish community, of a self-hating Jew. The tale features a Jewish family squabbling over an aunt's inheritance—a family divided, not painting pretty pictures of themselves. None of Nathan's own family can understand his "inexplicable betrayal." How could he, why *would* he, represent Jews so scabrously? Nathan's father calls upon Newark's celebrated Judge Wapter to talk sense to his son. The judge writes Nathan a long letter, concluding, "If you have not yet seen the Broadway production of *The Diary of Anne Frank*, I strongly advise that you do so. Mrs. Wapter and I were in the audience on opening night; we wish that Nathan Zuckerman could have been with us to benefit from that unforgettable experience."[22] The name of a young girl, Anne Frank, is thus invoked to censor the zestful Zuckerman, to arrest his pen, to silence him.

Readers of *The Ghost Writer* were quick to draw connections between the novel and its author. Nathan Zuckerman was assumed to be a fictional alter ego for Roth, while the older writer and mentor, E. I. Lonoff, was thought to be based on Bernard Malamud and/or Saul Bellow. It took Claire Bloom, in her memoir, to point out that the character of a reclusive writer shunning the world is based no less on Roth himself, much as the myriad complaints of Lonoff's long-suffering wife Hope (whom Bloom played in the novel's television adaptation) were based, largely verbatim, on Bloom's own complaints to her writing husband about the dissatisfactions of their self-imposed exile, going nowhere, seeing no one.[23] But if Roth is as much Lonoff as he is Zuckerman, can't we make the same claim for Amy Bellette—the young woman in the novel who Zuckerman will fantasize is secretly Anne Frank, who, having survived the Holocaust, is now, as he imagines, living under a pseudonym in America? Like Lonoff, after all, Anne Frank is another figure of the Jewish author, and thus another possible ideal for the young Zuckerman at the start of his own bildungsroman to measure himself against.

There are many problems, says Roth, when attempting to reimagine a figure as untouchable as Anne Frank. At first, "I didn't know where I was going so I began by doing what you're supposed to do when writing the life of a saint. It was a tone appropriate to hagiography. Instead of Anne Frank gaining new meaning within the context of my story, I was trying to draw from the ready store of stock emotions that everybody is supposed to have about her."[24] The novelist's job, however, is to dig deeper into "stock emotions" to access the real feelings running beneath them. For while Anne Frank's idealization is explicable in historical terms—because of the innocent victim she certainly was—her presumed innocence has the effect of desensitizing readers to the personality we meet in her *Diary*. Hence the stock Anne Frank, Anne the hagiographic subject, was, Roth soon realized, no less a fantasy than his own fictional provocation would be.

It is Anne as saintly victim who functions in *The Ghost Writer* as a figure put to rhetorical use in order to censor the critical voices of Jewish writers who come after her. By being canonized, she effectively closes the canon. When the young Zuckerman is encouraged to go and see the Broadway production of her *Diary*, for example, it's in order to discourage him from his own creative ambitions. Used thus, the *Diary* takes over the Bible's traditional role, for here is another book thought capable of turning a wicked son back into a nice Jewish boy. Remember God becomes remember Anne Frank: the invocation of Anne's sacred memory as the new moral law. It's with some irony, then, that, in Judge Wapter's letter, we read that it is the theatrical version rather than Anne's actual *Diary* recommended to Zuckerman as an "unforgettable experience."

The stage play was a Pulitzer Prize–winning adaptation that concluded with a line from the *Diary* taken out of context: "I still believe people are good at heart." So if the figure of Anne Frank is being used to censor Zuckerman, to make him feel that it is she, not he, who has a right to the last word on the Jewish story, the huge success of the Broadway production reminds us that Anne Frank, too, is a censored figure. On Broadway her last word is not her last word. In fact, the oddly upbeat last line of the play juxtaposes somewhat uncomfortably with the truth that the diary ended when Anne was taken to Auschwitz and then Belsen, where she died. More to the point, Anne Frank's *Diary* has itself been severally edited as well as censored. This was a process that began while Anne was still in hiding, as she edited her own diary in the belief that it could be an important artifact if published after the war. It was, in other words, because she could see *herself* as a serious writer, and a writer deserving of serious readers, that she began to think of her diary as a book that needed to keep its possible audiences in mind. It was then edited again after the war by Anne's father, Otto, who sought to erase certain references, especially to her sexuality, but still more to the ambivalent feelings she evidently felt toward both her parents, primarily her mother. And all this came before the

Broadway adaptation, which downplayed Anne's Jewishness in order to tell a more universal and ultimately hopeful story.

Beginning with Anne herself, then, different editors and readers have repeatedly used Anne's life and death to say different things. By the time *The Ghost Writer* was published, there had already been a feature film and at least one TV movie based on the *Diary*, and the claim had been put about that the *Diary* was a fake document ghostwritten by an adult, possibly Otto (an early instance of the perniciousness we have come to recognize as Holocaust denial). Thus the popular sense of Anne Frank as a young girl speaking in her own unmediated voice shows a willful naïveté on the part of its readers. "Facts," as Emily Budick observes, "even about the Holocaust, cannot, it seems, verify their own truthfulness. Why ought we to imagine otherwise? There is no way for ghosts to speak except through the medium of living ghostwriters—whether editors or historians or historical novelists, filmmakers, dramatists."[25]

Heedless of Jewish Feeling

Fantasizing at night in his mentor's study that the attractive young female houseguest upstairs is Anne Frank, Nathan Zuckerman soon imagines how Anne Frank could help to free *him* from his current predicament. Shunned from his community because of his writing, Nathan can conceive of only one way whereby he might be permitted to reenter his community's warm embrace: "Oh, marry me, Anne Frank, exonerate me before my outraged elders of this idiotic indictment! Heedless of Jewish feeling? Indifferent to Jewish survival? . . . Who dares to accuse of such unthinking crimes the husband of Anne Frank!" (170).

"Zuckerman may have invented Anne in his own image," comments Budick, "but so, we are made to realize by the community's demands on him, has the Jewish community constructed her in its own. Anne is an image of the Jews as sacrificial victim and 'saint,' and the Jewish community has as surely wed itself to her as Zuckerman would [marry her] to himself, with similar consequences. She is made to speak for them—a dead teenager forced to assume the role of a responsible adult—and, in the process, her own voice, her own story, are lost."[26] Those who would wed themselves to Anne Frank are thus not pursuing, as Jane Eyre does, a marriage of equals. The closer resemblance here would be to Rochester's first marriage to Bertha (a woman he renamed, in Rhys's retelling, from her original Antoinette). Rochester's first wife was pursued so that she might furnish him with her property, inheritance, and riches. Once she has done so, he prefers to leave her locked up in the attic. And isn't Roth's vision of Amy/Anne in *The Ghost Writer* strikingly similar to Rhys's vision of Bertha/Antoinette as another female figure in the attic exploited and dispossessed of all that belongs to her, including, most important, her own story as told in her own voice?

When, in Zuckerman's fantasy, Amy/Anne goes to see her *Diary* staged, she finds herself in the company of "Carloads of women . . . wearing fur coats, with expensive shoes and handbags. . . . The women cried. . . . I knew then what's been true all along. . . . I have to be dead to everyone" (123). She realizes, that is, that the living Anne—the Anne with hopes, vanities, ambitions, aggressions, desires—must sacrifice herself for the sake of the ideal Jewish girl she has become for everyone else, just as Bertha/Antoinette must sacrifice herself for the spiritual fulfilment of that ideal heroine of English literature, Jane Eyre. If we see this only as a female trajectory, however, we miss the point. For the same, we are given to understand, is true of Zuckerman, who has likewise been advised to go and see the Broadway show in the hope that he too will be persuaded to step back into the shadows, sacrificing his own voice in the interests of preserving this same image of the ideal Jewish child.

Looking back at his 1979 novel, Roth reflects, "The difficulties of telling a Jewish story—How should it be told? In what tone? To whom should it be told? To what end? Should it be told at all?—was finally to become *The Ghost Writer*'s theme."[27] How can one tell a Jewish story after Auschwitz, in other words, when living Jewish writers are continually drowned out by the whispering authority of ghosts? Hence Nathan's fantasy about Anne Frank's survival turns out to be merely a ghost story. The real Anne did not survive. There was no happy ending to her diary on the page or in reality. So it is that, at the end of *The Ghost Writer*, Lonoff's wife, Hope, falls down like a bad pun in the snow.

Hope: A Tragedy

But that was 1979; surely Jewish-American writers are more hopeful today? Not according to Shalom Auslander's 2012 novel, *Hope: A Tragedy*, which tells the story of Solomon Kugel, a man who wishes, to cite the blurb on the dust jacket, "to be nowhere, to be in a place with no past, no history, no wars, no genocides. The rural town of Stockton, New York, is famous for nothing: no one was born there, no one died there, nothing of any import has ever happened there, which is exactly why Kugel decided to move his family there. To begin again. To start anew." Starting anew is the plan. But sadly, things don't go according to plan for Kugel because, guess what, he discovers that none other than Anne Frank is hiding in his attic! Yes, there she is once again, haunting the imagination of the Jewish-American family and the Jewish-American writer, who can't seem to escape her legacy, no matter where he goes.

If Roth's Anne Frank is a femme fatale in the sense of a young, dark, mysterious temptress, beautiful and eroticized, Auslander's Anne Frank is described as "grotesquely old" and a "hideous freak."[28] She is also, quite evidently, a madwoman in the attic, although the reason *she's* going mad is that she's trying to finish that difficult second book—an uncomfortable task for any writer whose debut was a critical success, but even harder if your first book sold more than thirty-two million copies. Selfish, as creatives invariably are, she is, without a doubt, a *difficult woman:* irreverent, antagonistic, manipulative. Auslander's Anne consciously preys on the guilt of Solomon Kugel as someone who cannot face throwing her (an illegal immigrant in America, after all) out of his attic.

It is presumably because he detects its debilitating effects on the Jewish—and not only Jewish—psyche, that Auslander aims at the desecration of Anne Frank's memory. This is a novelist who *wants*—as his Anne wants—to be offensive, and whose book is sometimes capable of inducing the kind of manic laughter one might imagine emitted from the mouth of Bertha Mason. Yet when placed alongside Roth's earlier masterpiece, the later novel suffers by comparison. To be fair to Auslander, when writing his own novel he had not, he admits, been aware of Roth's book, published more than three decades earlier, any more than he was aware of Gilbert and Gubar's excavation of the madwoman in the attic as a recurring literary trope.[29] Because he grew up ultraorthodox, Auslander was not exposed to much secular literature: an ironic condition for the creation of a novel about a character who dreams of starting anew, as if history could be banished, but who, upon finding Anne Frank in his attic, is forced to confront the failure of that project. For it seems that Auslander, postpublication, had a similar lesson to learn: that the supposedly secular world of literary fiction is haunted by just as many ghosts as his disavowed scripture. Even irreverence has a tradition, a history.

But the irony is greater still, for Anne Frank is not the only Jewish writer to haunt Auslander's novel, as we discover when a character passingly claims to have spotted none other than Philip Roth in New York. "I thought he was dead," replies another, though that too is just a forlorn hope.[30] Despite appearances, then, it seems to be less Frank's unassailable authority than Roth's larger-than-life dominion over Jewish-American letters that is really threatening for the contemporary writer. If this is indeed the case, if Roth *has* partly succeeded in usurping Anne Frank's legacy as the sole legitimate spokesperson for postwar Jews, then, to paraphrase Kafka, perhaps there *is* hope, although not, apparently, for Auslander.

You can understand Auslander's frustration: Roth even managed to do a version of the aging Anne ahead of him. In the last of the Zuckerman novels, Roth's 2007 *Exit Ghost*, Nathan reencounters Amy Bellette in New York. She cuts a tragic figure. She is, she tells him, "just a nutty old woman rambling on." Over the course of their conversation Zuckerman remarks, "For most people, to say I've stayed in my childhood my whole life would mean I've stayed innocent and it's all been pretty. For you to say I stayed in my childhood my whole life means I stayed in this terrible story—life remained a terrible story. It means that I had so much pain in my youth that, one way or another, I stayed in it forever."[31]

"We are not the wretched of Belsen!" the young Zuckerman felt compelled to remind his American mother in *The Ghost Writer*. Yet as the series of novels constituting the Zuckerman bildungsroman progress, it does appear that there *is* a kind of Holocaust brain tumor still taking Jewish victims long after the war, even in the United States. This includes Amy Bellette, an actual survivor of the European genocide, and it also includes Nathan's mother. In *The Anatomy Lesson* of 1983, Nathan suffers a terrible writer's block—an inability to express himself that seems connected with what psychoanalysis calls the transgenerational transmission of trauma, as we sense when Zuckerman's mother, Selma, dies of a brain tumor:

> For months she'd been complaining of episodes of dizziness, of headaches, of little memory lapses. Her first time in the

hospital, the doctor diagnoses a minor stroke, nothing to leave her seriously impaired; four months later, when they admitted her again, she was able to recognize her neurologist when he came by the room, but when he asked if she would write her name for him on a piece of paper, she took the pen from his hand and instead of "Selma" wrote the word "Holocaust," perfectly spelled. This was in Miami Beach in 1970, inscribed by a woman whose writings otherwise consisted of recipes on index cards, several thousand thank-you notes, and voluminous files of knitting instructions. Zuckerman was pretty sure that before that morning she'd never even spoken the word aloud.[32]

Zuckerman spends much of the rest of the novel carrying that written word around with him in his wallet as the sole inheritance he has received from his mother. The word "Holocaust" in this passage is "perfectly spelled," and we can catch the double meaning here—the sense in which that word "Holocaust" cast a perfect spell once it entered popular discourse by seeming to capture, in a single term, the incomprehensible history it purports to identify. Hence, despite Nathan's mother's never having uttered the word before, it has now—at this time—become her name, her signature, her identity, *and*, it would seem, the key to her ultimate demise, coinciding with her loss of memory. Thus that which has been silenced is no sooner uttered than it overwhelms, as though the very commemoration of the Holocaust were in some way linked to a kind of Holocaust amnesia, becoming part of the Holocaust disease rather than its cure.

Roth's figuring of the Holocaust as a kind of deadly brain tumor that has taken over American Jewry, obliterating all other aspects of their identity, takes place, in the passage I've just cited, in 1970, for it was really from about the 1970s onward that public memoirs and memorials of the Holocaust accelerated at an unprecedented pace. So perhaps it's no accident that in the last year of that decade we saw the emergence of works—remember the three books published in 1979 mentioned above—interested in what happens to previously silenced voices when we finally start heeding them. *Are* we capable of assimilating their stories into our histories? Or are we still transfixed, like those ancient seamen faced with the singing of the sirens, by a memory without memory, the sound of the nonsymbolizable?

Starting Anew

Along with Auslander's *Hope: A Tragedy* (which dooms the hope that one can ever start anew), another work of fiction by a Jewish-American writer appeared in 2012 dealing with the Anne Frank legacy: Nathan Englander's short story "What We Talk About When We Talk About Anne Frank." Englander's title, recalling Raymond Carver's 1983 story "What We Talk About When We Talk About Love," draws an implicit parallel between the concept of Anne Frank and the concept of love in modern culture.

The Carver story features two couples, each of which has *started anew*—here, by starting on new marriages. The couples spend an evening in each other's company talking ever more freely while getting steadily drunk over a bottle of gin. (The story, incidentally, was written by a newly sober Carver after he had separated from his first wife and moved in with the woman who would become his second.) The subject of which they speak is love.

In the Englander story, by contrast, two couples, both Jewish, spend an evening in each other's company, talking ever more freely while getting steadily stoned. One couple is religiously orthodox and lives in Israel with ten children; the other couple are secular Jews living with their one son in Florida. The subject of *their* talk is the Holocaust and Jewish identity, underlying which is the question of how to *start anew* as a Jew after the Second World War.

Carver's story opens as follows: "My friend Mel McGinnis was talking. Mel McGinnis is a cardiologist, and sometimes that gives him the right."[33] Englander's story begins: "They're in our house maybe ten minutes and already Mark is lecturing us on the Israeli occupation. Mark and Lauren live in Jerusalem, and people from there think it gives them the right."[34]

Mel is a scientist of the heart, but it is his professionalism, his talking, that exposes him by the end of the story as knowing much less about matters of the heart than he's inclined to think. As he confesses later on, when drunk, "What do any of us really know about love? . . . It seems to me we're just beginners at love."[35] "Beginners" was in fact the title Carver originally gave to the story before it was renamed and massively edited by Gordon Lish (a kind of censorship that purportedly made Carver raving and hysterical in the way only a writer can get when he senses that his own voice may be lost). In the Englander story, on the other hand, it is Mark—a Hasid, the son of Holocaust survivors, who has moved to Israel and fathered ten children (it doesn't get more Jewish than that)—who despite his claim to have best understood how to start anew after Auschwitz, is exposed by the end of the story as the least qualified to talk.

In Carver's story, Mel's new wife, Terri, opens the discussion: "Terri said the man she lived with before she lived with Mel loved her so much he tried to kill her." To which Mel responds: "My God, don't be silly. That's not love, and you know it."[36] But as the conversation continues through rounds of greater and greater intoxication, disinhibition, and revelation, Mel finds himself articulating his own murderous feelings toward *his* first wife, whom he professes to hate with such a violent passion that we can't help feeling that it would be even more "silly" to deny that hatred, violence, revenge, obsession, jealousy, madness *are* indeed forms, very often, of love. Nor do we fail to notice how aspects of his first marriage are being covertly reenacted in the dynamics at play between him and his second wife. For what, we might ask, is a beginner, an amateur, a lover, if not someone who is still, in some sense, locked into his childhood: that time of inarticulate, nonsymbolizable infancy when the haze and maze of all those formative relations, attachments, and dependencies were first dreamed of?

Critical for the infant's survival, our first relations are as desperate as they are passionate. A beginner, then (and the implication of Carver's story is that a lover is always in some sense a beginner), begins not just once, but over and over again on account of a past that can only be repeated, never remembered. "The subject forms memory in order to achieve consistency," writes Salecl, "to fashion a story that would enable him to escape the traumatic real." Viewed thus, our memories are as much a means of deceiving ourselves with regard to our history as a way of retrieving it—whereas when our memories cannot quite be formed, when they slip away like dreams, a traumatic relationship to the real will persist in the form of the subject's own drive, "the self-sufficient closed circuit of the deadly compulsion-to-repeat."[37]

In Englander's parallel universe it is hard not to sympathize at least a little with Mark's censure of the diluted strain of Jewishness he detects in his Floridian hosts: "What I'm trying to say, whether you want to take it seriously or not, is that you can't build Judaism on the foundation of one terrible crime. It is about this obsession with the Holocaust as a necessary sign of identity. As your only educational tool. Because for the children there is no connection otherwise. Nothing Jewish that binds" (22). It is, after all, precisely this negative and terrorized form of American Jewish identity that appears as the major blocking agent in Philip Roth's and Shalom Auslander's rebellious fictions, both of which feature neurotic, guilt-ridden postwar children growing up cozy and protected in the suburbs of America but whose families talk as if the Holocaust were still unfolding all around them.

Mark, on the other hand, prefers to defy recent history by asserting a more positive Jewish identity: he's a proudly Hasidic man, residing in Israel with lots of children, and living, as he puts it, "exactly as our parents lived before the war" (23). As the stoned conversation continues, however, the four wind up playing a game in which they take turns speculating whether each of the others would hide them in the attic if things in south Florida ever took a drastic turn for the worse. Mark soon finds himself sheltering with his hosts inside their overstuffed pantry. "So would I hide you?" he asks his wife near the end of the story. "She does not say it. And he does not say it. And from the four of us, no one will say what cannot be said—that this wife believes her husband would not hide her. What to do? What would come of it? And so we stand like that, the four of us trapped in that pantry. Afraid to open the door and let out what we've locked inside" (32).

Paralleling Roth's fictional dissection of the Holocaust brain tumor, Englander's story leaves us with a terrible thought and a terrible image: whether secular or religious, Israeli or American, women or men, these four Jews are *all* Jews in hiding. All insecure subjects shuddering behind high walls stockpiled with food in case of another Holocaust. And it's increasingly unclear whether they're warding off what threatens them from the outside or covering up the inadmissible shame and horror at the terrors lurking within.

Englander's "Anne Frank" is thus, like "love," a term we use liberally, as indeed the very sign of our liberalism. And both are terms that sound, initially, innocent, universal, uniting, even strangely comforting: a modern kind of sacred. But spend some time with them and they turn out to be terms still in hiding, covering a multitude of sins, misrememberings, confusions, uncertainties, tensions, and anxieties. For just as people have been led to do the most cruel, twisted, and violent things in the name of love, and *because* of love, the same may be true of the name of Anne Frank. It is this that truly renders her a femme fatale. Hence while Roth, Auslander, and Englander have all sought to release Anne and her descendants from hiding—from the attic—we are still, I believe, very much beginners when it comes to talking about the Holocaust.

What We've Locked Inside

Carver's Mel dreams of being that most romantic of figures, a knight, but only, he admits, because the knight has armor to shield his face and protect his heart from injury. Englander's Mark, sporting a black hat and a long beard that covers up most of his face like a mask, is likewise revealed by the end of this troubling story to be less a knight for the Jewish faith than a man in hiding. Indeed, Mark resembles Roth's earlier portrait of a religious woman, Ronit, in his novel *Operation Shylock*. Ronit "looked as contented with her lot as any woman could be, her eyes shining with love for a life free of Jewish cringing, deference, diplomacy, apprehension, alienation, self-pity, self-mistrust, depression, clowning, bitterness, nervousness, inward-ness, hypercriticalness, hypertouchiness, social anxiety, social assimilation—a way of life absolved, in short, of all the Jewish 'abnormalities,' those peculiarities of self-division whose traces remained imprinted in just about every engaging Jew I knew." Elsewhere Roth claims that what he most objects to are people who "hide the places where they're split."[38]

Both Englander's Mark and Roth's Ronit are versions of a familiar postwar Jewish type: the type who has sought to *start anew* by re-creating an image of the Jew as whole, undivided, self-contained, and living in that most mythical of ways, "exactly as our parents lived before the war." Is this not fundamentalism in a nutshell? Denial of the past while purporting to be returning to it. Denial of a history in hiding by hiding the places where you're split. The Jews who, in Roth, are the most engaging, on the other hand, preserve their doubleness, a doubleness in which neither side of the self-division is more real than the other, hence the inadequacy of the question so often asked by Roth's readers and also asked repeatedly by Claire Bloom in her memoir of their time together: which is the real Philip Roth?

While the question of who is more real or authentic fails to recognize the peculiarities of self-division that make fantasy an integral part of reality, the unified self, by the same token, appears to Roth as a figure for the definitively unreal and inauthentic. We can see this logic at work, for instance, in *I Married a Communist*, the novel in which Roth (predictably) took revenge on Bloom for her memoir. Bloom's fictional stand-in is the Hollywood actress Eve Frame. The name Eve, of course, belongs to the woman who has stood perennially accused of framing Adam after the collapse of his marriage to the demonic Lilith, and thus takes us right back to the beginning, to the place where we are all beginners, for, despite Adam's wish to start anew with Eve, she proved no less the temptress, no less the femme fatale to the man who would go on to frame her. And yet here, rather tellingly, in his revenge novel on his second wife, Roth refers this age-old battle of the sexes to a different arena altogether, that of Jewishness.

If the ultraorthodox Ronit looking to deny all self-divisions is "over the top" in one direction, Eve Frame is her equivalent in the other. She too denies, or works hard to deny, her splitness. This she does by denying her Jewishness. Eve, we're told, is "a pathologically embarrassed Jew," obsessed with hiding her identity by censoring or silencing every trace of it: "whenever he said the word 'Jew' in public she would try to quiet him down."[39] Whereas in *The Ghost Writer*, none of Nathan's family can understand his "betrayal" in publishing a story that represents his own people as split among themselves, in *I Married a Communist* it is Eve Frame who is charged with "betrayal" for what she has published, and it is Eve Frame who appears as a self-hating Jew. But Eve is accused with evidence quite the opposite to that brought against Zuckerman: Eve Frame is self-hating precisely because she does *not* reveal to the world her Jewish splitness. She ought, as an actress, to know better: "The cheap pleasures of Jew hating aren't necessary. You're convincing as a Gentile without them. That's what a good director would have told her about her performance. . . . He would have told her that the anti-Semitism is over-doing the role. . . . He would have told her, 'As soon as you do that, you're gilding the lily and you're not convincing at all. *It's over the top*, you're doing too much. The performance is logically too complete, too airless.' "[40]

What's "over the top" here is not the spilling over of words and affects, but the vigilance with which one hides one's thoughts and feelings by reining them in and stowing them out of sight, as if in a dark attic. What makes a book Jewish, writes Roth elsewhere, is not what it says or what it's about or what identity it claims to have, but the mere fact that it rambles on, that it won't be silenced: "Jews will go on, you know. It isn't what it's talking *about* that makes a book Jewish—it's that the book won't shut up."[41]

In *The Ghost Writer* Lonoff tells the young Zuckerman that he "has the most compelling voice I've encountered in years": "I don't mean style"—raising a finger to make the distinction. "I mean voice: something that begins at around the back of the knees and reaches well above the head. Don't worry too much about 'wrong.' Just keep going. You'll get there."[42] It's a stirring compliment from a man who confesses to spending most of his writing time turning the same sentences around and around for fear of getting it wrong. But it is ambivalent praise. As Budick observes of a voice said to come from the back of the knees to reach well above the head, what we have is "the odd configuration of a ventriloquist's dummy."[43] Thus while this description of Nathan's voice suggests a potent force in excess of petty concerns with good taste or bad taste, right or wrong, and hence a kind of freedom from the constraints that bedevil the formalist, the stylist, the moralist, the corrector, such a freedom is nonetheless bound to the paradox that, by being liberated from what controls others, the voice as voice turns out to be controlled by something or someone else: some deus ex machina is still pulling its strings. The voice, in other words, comes from elsewhere, from another: a parent or a grandparent, for example, or whoever it was who first put us on his knee to tell us his stories and teach us his language.

The voice is in this sense a transhistorical phenomenon. It belongs to the temporality of traumatic experience: experience that, because it cannot be comprehended *at the time*, is never altogether past. It's in this sense too that the voice that entrances and puts a spell on us is always the voice of the mute, the silenced, the dummy, a voice that belongs not only to Zuckerman or his uncensored author, Roth, but to the siren, the soprano, the hysteric— whoever reverses the rules of civil discourse by singing to others and speaking to herself.

Such a voice does not belong to Nathan's writing hero Lonoff. A recluse he may be, yet the rules he obeys are still the rules of civil discourse and the everyday world. He corrects and revises and frets all the time about getting it right, not wrong. This is something Nathan is disappointed to discover when hidden in his hero's study, a disappointment that might remind us of that which Anne Frank felt toward her own father over their time in hiding— that slow withdrawal of one's idealization of the parent that is perhaps a critical step in any bildungsroman after Freud. Anne Frank, on the other hand, is a different kind of writer entirely. To diarize, after all, is to speak not to the world but primarily to oneself. It is perhaps this quality that Nathan responds to when he later enthuses about the tonality of her voice: "She was a marvelous young writer. . . . Suddenly she's discovering reflection, suddenly there's portraiture, character sketches, suddenly there's a long intricate eventful happening so beautifully recounted it seems to have gone through a dozen drafts. And no poisonous notion of being *interesting* or *serious*. She just *is*."[44]

A Sane Person, in the Twentieth Century

So is Anne Frank's voice the voice of the traumatic past rupturing the present? That, certainly, has been its popular reputation among contemporary readers who encounter the *Diary* after the death of its author, knowing already the name of the history to which she belongs. Yet the *Diary* itself has its own distinct relationship to time. As Rachel Feldhay Brenner clarifies: "As a 'book of time,' the diary presents two kinds of time: the period that it records and the actual duration of the recording. I would argue that in the Annexe situation the time of the diaristic recording counteracts the timelessness of the apocalyptic ending."[45]

The time spent writing the diary counteracts the time the diary is writing. Diary writing in this way enables its author to "keep going," though this is far from easy, and Anne Frank does not deny her sufferings—her death wish is often invoked. Yet as Frank herself puts it, "I can shake off everything if I write; my sorrows disappear, my courage is reborn . . . for I can recapture everything when I write, my thoughts, my ideals and my fantasies." The appalling conditions that gave onto what Nathan sees as the enviable immediacy, liveliness, or "just is-ness" of Anne's writerly voice is the unmitigated terror and reality of a world at war. Like the sirens of Greek mythology, her voice comes to us from a space and time filled with death, the death she knows to threaten her own life at every moment.

For John Berryman, Anne Frank's *Diary* may be the only artifact we have of a real-life bildungsroman—a narration of what it means to pass from childhood into adulthood, or in Anne's preferred term, personhood. As with Zuckerman's later encomium for Frank in *The Ghost Writer*, Berryman's admiration is for the writing itself, accomplished in part because of the author's exceptional moral character and artistic ability, but also because of the strangeness of her situation. It is, writes Berryman, "surprising what it takes to make an adult human being." As he understands it, such a development is surely consequent on the "new idea" for survival that Anne confides to Kitty (the name she gave her diary) on August 10, 1943: "I talk more to myself than to the others." Talking to oneself is, as we've noted, a siren bell for madness in normal circumstances. But these were not normal circumstances. Indeed, in Berryman's view, Anne Frank is, perhaps uniquely, "A sane person, in the twentieth century." He finds evidence of this in her undertaking of silence with others while internalizing her own need for dialogue—a "spectacularly rare" achievement for a naturally garrulous person. By virtue of being her own listener and interlocutor, she begins to change herself in such a way that, says Berryman, renders Anne Frank "more mature than perhaps most persons ever become."[46]

"Let me be myself," Anne tells Kitty, "and then I am satisfied." Her resources for this heroic claim to be able to attain satisfaction even in the most adverse of circumstances are, as she understands them, her courage and her cheerfulness—or what Berryman calls "self-enjoyment," citing the absolute necessity of this characteristic for successful maturation. Self-enjoyment is, as Lacan would have it, precisely what is necessary for the unraveling of history he termed *jouissance*, whose secret is that of the siren or femme fatale as much as the wild beast or young girl. Above all, though, Anne's primary resource for being herself is her diary, which enables the self-conscious splitting of her own subject, creating a kind of private hiding place within her *shared* hiding place.[47] Between her diary's pages Anne can wonder, for example, why it is that for everyone else in the annex she appears clownish—over the top, hysterical—while to Kitty alone she can present a different "voice within" her. Indeed the final words in the diary are not "everyone is good at heart" but a meditation on her own splitness:

> A voice within me is sobbing, "You see, that's what's become of you. You're surrounded by negative opinions, dismayed looks and mocking faces, people who dislike you, all because you don't listen to the advice of your own better half." Believe me, I'd like to listen, but it doesn't work, because if I'm quiet and serious, everyone thinks I'm putting on a new act and I have to save myself with a joke, and then I'm not even talking about my own family, who assume I must be ill, stuff me with aspirins and sedatives, feel my neck and forehead to see if I have a temperature, ask about my bowel movements and berate me for being in a bad mood, until I just can't keep it up anymore, because when everybody starts hovering over me, I get cross, then sad, and finally end up turning my heart inside out, the bad part on the outside and the good part on the inside, and keep trying to find a way to become what I'd like to be and what I could be if . . . if only there were no other people in the world.[48]

We know, from Rhys, from Roth, or from fictional characters such as Lonoff, how common among writers is this reclusive dream of escaping into a world of the imagination with no censoring others in it.[49] Still, no one, surely, in the history of literature, can have lived more intensely or more closely with or alongside others, both those without and those within, than did Anne Frank. It was out of such conditions that she produced her great and only work, surviving a traumatic history for as long as she did by keeping her feelings alive—and feelings, as we've been arguing, when properly felt, are always the feeling of and for others. Thus it is that, as the last eyewitness we have of her reports, Anne was, in Auschwitz, still able to weep with pity for the naked gypsy girls driven past her to the crematory.

Thus it is too that, despite the siren bells warning me against it, I've been unable to resist canonizing her again.

FIVE

Paranoia

Paranoia seems to require to be imitated in order to
be understood.
—EVE KOSOFSKY SEDGWICK, "Paranoid Reading
and Reparative Reading"

Have you ever asked yourself whether the institutions you belong to are really as good as their word? Have you ever found yourself wondering whether the things, people, and ideas you've always trusted might in fact have hidden agendas, maybe even malign motives? Have you ever gotten to the point where you're questioning all you've been taught, or had that discomfiting sense that everything you've been told might need radically rethinking?

When your confidence in those around you begins to wane, and you suspect that even your own thoughts may have been put there by some sort of deliberate propaganda, a kind of mind control or mass hypnosis you've fallen prey to, when it slowly dawns on you that what appears to be real is actually fake, a mirage, and your life is a kind of

Truman Show, then you may decide to withdraw from the world and head for your computer to search the web, to figure out things for yourself, to become self-reliant, an autodidact, a fact checker, a close reader, and actually something of a hero, because while others may be gullible, believing whatever they're told, you're no one's fool, you don't believe everything *they* say, and even seeing, for you, isn't necessarily believing, because now that you've finally understood what's *really* going on you can learn to play them at their own game, hold your cards close to your chest, and communicate your meanings and messages indirectly, elliptically, cryptically, not unlike how *they* do.

So are you paranoid? Possibly. Then again, isn't that also what *all* critical thinking feels like?

Being critically minded makes us "modern."[1] Gullible is what our parents were—or, if you like, it's what *their* parents were. How alarming, then, to discover that a dedicated stance of nongullibility may also have its own gullibilities. And paranoia—which has lately started to garner a reputation for being the most zeitgeisty of modern emotions—seems to be one of them.

Of course, after the revelations of Julian Assange, Chelsea Manning, and Edward Snowden about the surveillance society in which we now live, this might not be deemed surprising. Meditating on the pervasiveness of paranoia in our day, Stephen Frosh notes its cultural expediency: "Just look at the cameras in the street and ask what they are recording, and why, and for whom. The paranoiac is perhaps the one who is perfectly adjusted to such a society."[2] So, as a socially adaptive emotion, paranoia is exactly the type of acculturated or even diasporic feeling that we've been investigating—and, as I'll discuss in the second half of this chapter, few would dispute that paranoia has a distinctly Jewish feel to it too. I mean, who *hasn't* heard of Jewish paranoia? (Isn't that question even an instance of it?) Yet I'm also wondering to what extent paranoia really manifests as a feeling. For while it may be true that there are feelings (guilt, envy) invested in avoiding feeling other, related feelings (anger, admiration), paranoia, as we'll see, has worked harder than most to more or less completely obliterate its status as a feeling at all. It has done so by fleeing into a realm that the paranoiac might like to imagine as free of feeling—the realm of thought—though (spoiler alert!) the notion that there are thoughts that come to mind completely *un*minded by any associated feeling is one with which I cannot, in the end, agree.

Dream Machines

Among the Truthers is journalist Jonathan Kay's book-length "journey though America's growing conspiracist underground."[3] Not untypical of many publications on the popularity of conspiracy theories in America in recent years, Kay's book claims that we are currently living in the "age of conspiracism"—an age he believes to have been inaugurated on September 11, 2001.[4] A "Truther" is someone convinced that he tells the truth about 9/11. Truthers have different theories about what happened that day, but all agree what didn't: the official version of events.

Trutherism is a global phenomenon, but its popularity in North America is what perplexes Kay. Wasn't the "new world" supposed to be the "crown jewel of the Enlightenment" —a land whose hard-won freedoms presuppose the end of fancy, prejudice, and superstition, and the adoption of those superior and uniquely unifying values of reason, rationality, and common sense? Yet even before 9/11 political historian Richard Hofstadter had observed, in the wake of Senator Joe McCarthy's communist witch trials, a "Paranoid Style in American Politics."[5] It was a "style" pertaining, for Hofstadter, to the habits and gestures of a particular political culture or way of thinking, rather than to clinical cases of paranoia. But while Hofstadter located this "style" on the wilder edges of the American Right, Kay believes it has since spread from the fringes to the mainstream, including both right and left wings of the political spectrum. According to one Zogby opinion poll of 2006, an astonishing 42 percent of all Americans claimed not to believe the government's account of how the twin towers of the World Trade Center came down.

America's descent into unreason is analogous, for Kay, to a process taking place in an alternative reality: the virtual space of the internet, whose birth in the mid-1990s was envisaged to "usher in an Enlightenment dreamworld of mutual understanding," but which instead "propelled radicals into their own paranoid echo chambers" (xvii). Wherever there has been a dream of reason, in other words—America, the internet—the "cranks" have been making trouble. And even Kay's own book, which was written, he says, with the aim of recalling America to its rationalist roots, took him at times to "the limits of intellectual discourse" (312). For it turns out that you cannot argue with a Truther. Truthers always come armed with more facts, additional sources of information. When attempting to reason with his subjects, Kay thus consistently found himself forced to give up on argumentation in order to simply insist on what he *knows inside* to be the rightness of his own position and the mad delusion of his interlocutor's: "I sometimes catch myself using forms of logic or turns of phrase that echo the conspiracy theorists whom I'd interviewed" (323).

It is, says Hofstadter, the paranoiac's painstaking research and "extravagant passion for facts" that so often lend conspiracy theories an impressive air of plausibility.[6] The issue, put simply, is one of paranoia's intelligence. Paranoia, on a certain reading, is a pathological form of intelligence. Conspiracy theorists have historically tended to be middle class and well educated—academics, teachers, artists, journalists, civil servants, professionals—although today just about anyone can click through a web of hyperlinking windows to experience those empowering moments of intellectual illumination when patterns emerge, connections are made, historical periods collapse into each other, similarities appear where conflicts had been assumed, and things previously unseen come into the light.

Part of paranoia's glamour is thus its reliable delivery of a hit of grandiosity via an intellectual "high"—a lesson we get no better than from Hollywood when watching, for instance, the mad genius of *A Beautiful Mind*, the lowly but brilliant student uncovering a government plot in *The Pelican Brief*, or the *Truman* sense of a world that's just for *Show*. Indeed, the Truther generally regards himself as just such a type of True-Man: the once regular guy who has seen through the smoke and mirrors to lift the veil of lies. Though the film more often cited by Truthers is another Hollywood blockbuster, *The Matrix*. Unlike *The Truman Show*, which features an elaborate plot to deceive just one true man, in *The Matrix* almost all are victims of a mind-controlling hypnosis that deprives them of their ability to distinguish between appearance and reality. In Truther terminology such people, including most of us, are "Sheeple." *The Matrix*, however, portrays a hero who has found out the truth and come up with an escape route: I can *think* my way out of this!

The Paranoid Style

"A fundamental paradox of the paranoid style," writes Hofstadter, "is the imitation of the enemy": "The enemy, for example, may be the cosmopolitan intellectual [a euphemism for 'Jew,' surely, or am I being paranoid?], but the paranoid will outdo him in the apparatus of scholarship, even of pedantry."[7] This can work in both directions. Freud's best known case study of a paranoiac, for example, was of Judge Schreber, whose intelligence he considered intrinsic to the case. Now, just as Kay finds himself compelled to acknowledge an occasional resemblance between his own turns of phrase and those of his interviewees, so Freud was fascinated to

observe a "striking conformity" between Schreber's paranoid delusions and his own theory for interpreting them.[8] Each man, after
all, saw himself as the enemy of common sense, and each developed
elaborately counterintuitive methods of reading the evidence. It
was on the basis of their alikeness, in fact, that Freud would identify
a similarity between paranoid thinking and philosophical systems
of thinking more generally.

The resemblance is primarily a structural one. Take a theory—
any theory: Freud's theory of the Oedipal Complex, for example—
it's a "theory" because it can never be proven right or wrong, true or
false. You can't *prove* that Douglas has fallen for Rebecca because
Rebecca resembles his mother. Nor can you *prove* that the neoliberal
rhetoric of self-sufficiency isn't intended to shore up the interests of
a powerful few. And you certainly won't be able to prove that you
didn't get that job because, at your age, who knows when you're next
going to have a baby and demand your right to maternity leave. Yet
you can't prove the opposite, either. In the case of all such theories—
Freudianism, Marxism, Feminism—we're in the realm of what Paul
Ricoeur was to term "suspicious hermeneutics."

Now, given the similar gestures of conspiracy theorists and critical theorists—gestures such as close reading, the excavation of
hidden agendas, the ascription of power to a system that operates
best by means of its own obfuscation, and the rendering of such
ideas in a discourse dense with so many impenetrable code words
that one might be tempted to suspect its authors of deliberate
obscurantism—it can sometimes be difficult to spot the difference
between them. So when, in 1991, the postmodern theorist Jean
Baudrillard scandalized common sense with the provocative claim
that "the Gulf War did not take place," he seemed (to those who
did not care for the rhetorical subtleties of critical theory) the
archetypal French intellectual: so out of touch with reality as to be
capable of denying it altogether.[9] Hence the appearance, a decade

later, of a popular movement claiming that 9/11 did *not take place* (at least not in the manner that was presented on television screens around the world) seemed to many to have been partly enabled by an intellectual culture that had so thoroughly discredited rational thought as to have made otherwise intelligent people doubt the evidence of their own eyes. Kay, for example, cites what he decries as Jacques Derrida's "bafflegab": the claim that when we speak about 9/11, "we do not know what we are talking about." This, for Kay, proves that the continental philosopher is indeed "the conspiracy theorist's polite Ivy League cousin" (265).

Yet there remains, for Kay, the problem that even his own unapologetically rationalist approach came to increasingly resemble that of his paranoid subjects. It's an experience that never ceases to unsettle those who write about paranoia, leading Rita Felski to speculate that it is "hard to see how any objections to suspicion, my own included, can entirely escape the snarls of this contradiction."[10] It may be counted as something of an irony, then, if paranoia, or the suspicion that one is serving the interests of a system from which it is difficult if not impossible to escape, may in itself turn out to be another such all-encompassing, inescapable system . . .

Still, the resemblance between paranoid and philosophical thought processes begins with what, at least at first, looks to be an innocuous and even admirable ambition: the pursuit of knowledge. For who, after all, *is* the knowledge-seeking subject if not someone motivated to investigate, research, theorize, contemplate what's really going on, and accept only those answers arrived at not on trust or authority, but independently, by figuring out things for herself? Such people seem heroic if eccentric individuals—individuals who, like the protagonist of many a paranoid thriller, put themselves in danger's way in order to speak truth to power. Though in the era of the internet these idiosyncratic "eccentrics" have become a lot more populous. So if, as Kay suspects, we are living in "the age of conspiracism" (if we are all paranoiacs now), then the expansion of suspicious feelings may be assumed part and parcel of the "information age." For while few can doubt the emancipatory potential of widening access to information, nor can one ignore the rather more paranoid sense that "informing" sometimes takes on, as it did during the McCarthy era, for example. Information, one might even say, is to an extent *always* paranoid: information is the kind of knowledge sought out by those (spies, lovers, conspiracists) for whom the world is not quite as it appears—or worse still, a trap designed to deceive us. Indeed, the dual meaning of the word "intelligence"—its clear-eyed, truth-seeking rationalist sense coupled with its suspicious, shadowy twin from the Intelligence Services—is equally revealing here: intelligence *is* paranoid.

Who Turns Informer?

In seeking to understand why 9/11 caused conspiracism to become no longer just a gesture of the lunatic fringe but a widespread phenomenon respectable even within mainstream opinion, Kay notes that conspiracy theories "are more likely to blossom when great tragedies or national traumas . . . rupture a society's intellectual foundations, and shatter citizens' faith in traditional authority figures" (150). He goes on to compare the impact of 9/11 to that of the Great Lisbon Earthquake of 1755, which features in the philosophical writings of Voltaire, Rousseau, and Kant and has sometimes been viewed as the eruption that brought forth the "Age of Reason." Since Kay's book pitches reason *against* conspiracism, however, his subsequent analysis somewhat occludes a comparison of their respective origins in historical trauma.

The occlusion is a telling one. The shaping influence of trauma on the mind is a Freudian concept, yet Freud, for Kay, is a casebook conspiracist who bends the facts to suit his theories. Nor is Kay the first to suspect as much. It was Freud, after all, who, along with

Marx and Nietzsche, spearheaded the "false consciousness" theories that worked to undermine the achievement of Kay's philosophical hero, René Descartes, by querying what Descartes is supposed to have attained by power of reason alone: a state of consciousness unfettered by radical doubts.[11] While Descartes had famously founded a style of thinking on whose basis the self could rest assured—*cogito ergo sum*/I think therefore I am!—with the advent of these later theorists, the thinking subject or *ego cogito* was again thrown into question. It was Freud's view that the ego "is not even master of its own house." Thus a rationalist like Kay might well agree with Freud's own assessment of what he was bringing, via psychoanalysis, to America's shores: The Plague!

What characterizes the traumatized mind for Freud is an unconscious identification with an aggressive or distressing experience whose representation the mind has not been able to properly assimilate. As such, the mind reenacts or repeats aspects of this experience unconsciously through something akin to hypnotic imitation, despite often imagining itself an opposing idea. Such a conception of the impact of traumatic experience on mental functioning leaves us with a disenchanted image of a mind. The mind, on this view, becomes less and less a reliable instrument of reason, clarity, or self-assurance, but rather, as Adam Phillips puts it, "the trauma itself."[12] The mind, that is to say, always minds something—something it does not wish to know; an ignorance it covers up with more and more knowledge.

Yet the mind does not altogether lack a sense of what it's missing. Thus the paranoid mind, while it does not know what it knows-but-cannot-bear-to-know, becomes ever more interested, even obsessed, in the question of knowledge: how to get it, but also who has it and who controls it. One can note, for instance, how Freud's comparison of trauma to a state of hypnosis bears a striking resemblance to the paranoiac's own suspicion that there may be some malign outside force or influence seeking to invade or control his mind. The paranoiac may have misidentified or misrepresented his persecutor, but he is, as psychoanalysts will often remark of their paranoid patients, *on to something.*

Evil Geniuses

It is René Descartes, not Jacques Derrida, who presents a more likely philosophical precursor for the conspiracy theorist.

Descartes, it's well known, laid the philosophical foundations of rationalist modernity by defeating radical doubt. The thinking subject of his *Meditations* first entertains the possibility—in a postulation as likely heard in an asylum as in a seminar room—that the whole world may be conjured up by an evil genius intent on deceiving him. So in a world where everything looks suspicious, what he must do, he realizes, is rely on the power of his own intellect to reassure himself that he is himself no illusion. I think therefore *I am!* That is, I can trust myself for I alone am beyond the reach of doubt. The mind is thus a fixed point, a safe harbor, upon which basis the Cartesian subject can go on to master his universe and build the world anew.

Now, while Kay's professed wish is that his book will help to save the new world by replenishing its Cartesian roots, he is consistently provoked by the rationalism of those he deems irrational. Consider, for instance, Michael Keefer, a professor of English Literature whom Kay visits in his Toronto home, encountering there the kind of person "most of us imagine when we hear someone described as 'an academic.'" Faced with such a man, Kay finds it especially hard to reconcile the "brilliant scholar" with the Keefer who is also a Truther. How is it that someone who'd once "published an exhaustive article on the philosophy of René Descartes" (10) can be so easily seduced by unreasonable doubts?[13] Yet it's precisely within Keefer's article *on* Descartes that one comes across more than a passing affinity between Cartesianism and Trutherism. Kay, presumably, has not read it.

Descartes's *Meditations* aims to demonstrate how one can be certain whether or not one has been deceived by appearances. How can one be sure, as he puts it in one example, that one is awake rather than dreaming? Although, in what must surely be counted as one of the history of philosophy's most profound ironies, it was in a *dream* that Descartes first experienced the revelation of what he felt certain he could always be sure of: his mind.

This too is the subject of Keefer's article, which looks approvingly at the significance of Descartes's dreams for our understanding of how *cogito ergo sum* enables a form of resistance to systematic doubt—a philosophical breakthrough that occurred "in a dream revelation . . . in a state of divine exaltation" (34). Descartes, in fact, had three such prophetic dreams, wherein he for the first time clearly enunciated the position for which he is best known: "Let [the evil genius] deceive me as much as he will, he can never cause me to be nothing so long as I think I am something" (quoted, 43). To which he added the following caveat regarding the bugbear of false consciousness: "Just as a captive who in sleep enjoys an imaginary liberty, when he begins to suspect that his liberty is but a dream, fears to be awakened, and conspires with these agreeable illusions to prolong his deception, so insensibly of my own accord I fall back on my former opinions, and I am anxious about being roused from this slumber" (quoted, 62).

So false consciousness is akin to that of the dreamer who prefers to remain asleep. And yet Descartes's revelation, as we find it couched here in proto-Trutherist language, is achieved by returning to the moment of awakening that first occurs in his *own* dreams. The Descartes who saves himself from false consciousness was thus at his most awake while asleep, when reality appeared to him as a dream and dream appeared as reality. Likewise, for the archetypal

Truther who views the commonsense world as only a virtual reality (peopled by "Sheeple"), the realm of virtual reality encountered via the worldwide Web is believed much closer to the "Truth."

There's a parallel to be drawn, therefore, between Descartes's reasoning and Freud's case study of Schreber. For just as Descartes withdraws from a suspicious world intent on deceiving him into the privacy and security of his ego (an ego then capable of remastering the world), so Schreber withdraws his "libidinal investment" from "the people around him and from the world outside" by making of that world something "indifferent and unrelated to him." Reality, he realizes, has been "miracled up, fleetingly improvised." So he builds up the world once more in such a way, says Freud, "that he can live in it again. He builds it up through the work of his delusion. *What we take to be the production of the illness, the formation of the delusion, is in reality the attempt at a cure, a reconstruction.*"[14] Paranoia is established, in other words, not on the basis of the subject's radical doubts but on the basis of how these doubts are overcome—with a new certainty. Indeed, for Freud it is precisely this belief that one can create anew a world completely cleansed of the persecutory history that necessitated it that constitutes a classically paranoid delusion.

It is not, however, only the paranoiac who dreams of a new world. Who doesn't? A similar idea, for example, might be said to animate the American dream of a new world. As Thomas Paine wrote in his 1775 best-selling pamphlet *Common Sense*, "We have it in our power to begin the world over again."[15] So the notion of building a new world is common to both the Cartesianism on whose basis Kay believes the new world as "crown jewel of the Enlightenment" was initially founded *and* the Trutherism he suspects of destroying its founding principles. What then, if anything, can we make of this resemblance? For America is, of course, not simply the work of a paranoid delusion. Yet the fact that so many conspiracy theories *do* seem to spring from the new world—What did the government really know about Pearl Harbor? Or 9/11? Who really killed Marilyn? Or JFK? Did the moon landings really happen? Is Bill Clinton a murderer? Or Hillary Clinton? Is Obama really an American? (Birtherism, with Trutherism, is the other major conspiracy theory to have rocked America in the early twenty-first century)—does perhaps suggest that faith in the American dream requires, at least for *some* patriots, just such a disbelief in the American reality.

The New World

Gnosticism, according to self-professed modern Gnostic Harold Bloom, is a quintessentially American religion. Traditionally practitioners of "an esoteric religion of intellectuals," Gnostics have rejected the values enshrined by the "institutional, historical, and dogmatic" Western religions and "opted instead for information above all else." As such, Gnosticism should be distinguished from a "faith" because, says Bloom, "we rely upon an inward knowledge rather than upon an outward belief." Since, moreover, the Gnostics' God is "in exile from a false creation," the revelation granted to the true Gnostic is to "come to see that originally your deepest self was no part of the Creation-Fall, but goes back to an archaic time before time, when that deepest self was part of a fullness that was God."[16] The true American is someone who has arrived at this insight and so freed himself from the determinations of history. He's there, for example, in Ralph Waldo Emerson's injunction to "men drenched in Time to recover themselves and come out of time, and taste their native immortal air," or in Walt Whitman's invocation to "celebrate myself, and sing myself."

Such ecstatic and visionary dreams are world-founding, time-reversing revolutions of the soul, and why not suppose them to be the achievement of true discoveries? I have never been so fortunate, but I cannot deny that others may have ascended to heights that have so far eluded me. Yet if Gnosticism perceives the apparent world a false creation, the invention of a power-hungry inauthentic god, might there not also be a state of false Gnosticism—a false song of myself?

Classical psychoanalytic theory tends to ascribe the paranoiac's solution for doubt (founding a new world) to a megalomaniacal sense of narcissistic self-importance. But there may be an alternative explanation of why the paranoiac dreams of a new world. According to Lacanian analyst Darian Leader, the real purpose of the delusion is "to give the subject the place of an exception": "to survive entails creating a singular, individual space, which is not part of some pre-existing set or group."[17] "Originality" might be another word for this situation of exceptionality, which hints at the temporal as well as the spatial dynamics of a subject imagined to precede history. For, as in the Gnostic imagination of the *Pleroma* (divine plenitude), such a subject belongs forever to an original moment—always before the fall. It's the place, says Melanie Klein, to which the paranoid-schizoid subject flees when unable to accept the reality of a world in which good and bad are inextricably mixed. To recover from this pathology, Klein tells us, the paranoid subject must come to experience the "depressive position" wherein one accepts the messiness of human life, the illusoriness of self-reliance, and the necessity of depending on others for one's own satisfactions.

Lacan, however, sees things slightly differently. While paranoid psychosis still involves a Manichean struggle between good and evil, for Lacan, what underlies the paranoiac's belief in his own exceptionality is a vision of the world experienced as persecutory due to the failure of any third—symbolic—term to mediate between self and other. The "symbolic" takes the infant beyond her imaginary universe. If the "imaginary" in Lacan's schema alludes to the "mirroring phase" with the Mother—that is, the phase when there is no way for the infant to tell the difference between inner and outer worlds—then the "symbolic" generally gets typecast as the intervening figure of the Father: that jealous dad who, incited by the spectacle of blissful unity between his wife and child, demands, "Break it up, you two!"

Of course, developmentally speaking, this symbolic function need not be performed by an actual dad, or by anyone specific at all. The *world out there* can appear in many different guises. But it is important for Lacan that however aggressive this symbolic intervention might be, its benefits should not be downplayed. For without the third term, Lacan indicates, there may be no space between the subject and a (m)other whose nonrepresentation within a "symbolic order" has rendered her presence too close for comfort. As such, the effect on the developing child of a failed symbolic intervention threatens to be a retarding one: the infant unable to see beyond his imaginary universe may, no matter how much he grows, never really mature.

So for paranoiacs, says Leader, it's precisely in order to protect themselves against an outside presence experienced as unbearably invasive that they strive to create a unique place—another world, all of their own. Their move, then, is primarily a defensive one, though it also has implications for how paranoiacs will come to regard themselves. Chief among these may be a sense of their own innocence and the conviction that it's "always someone else's fault." So we can see why paranoid traits appear to have become increasingly normalized: "What old psychiatry took to be the defining features of paranoia—an innocence and a sense of injustice—have now become those of the modern individual."[18]

The modern individual is the victim par excellence: victim of family, friends, school, bank, country . . . you name it, it's always someone else's fault. That the individual may genuinely be persecuted is not what's in dispute. The point, rather, is that *even* the victimized individual may be suffering from paranoia, for while the fact of victimization is one thing, the *meaning* this fact takes on is quite another. If, for example, an individual imagines—even in the case of real experiences of persecution—someone else's guilt as the necessary condition of his own inviolable innocence, then his real experience may well have become the basis of a paranoid consciousness. "One can have been abused as a child," writes Leader provocatively, yet also "have a delusion about being abused."[19] The delusion, in this case, does not pertain to the "fact"—which really did happen—but to the insistence that a particular kind of fact bears witness to its own meaning. So what is it that leads us to imagine that facts, once established, speak for themselves?

The Facts

When the symbolic order traumatically breaks down, as Slavoj Žižek remarked of 9/11, the ability to distinguish between fantasy and reality is obliterated. Žižek's view of the terror attacks was that the outrage lent us the benefit of an enlarged vision: when our Hollywood fantasy becomes our reality, our reality can finally be glimpsed as fantasy. Entitling his essay "Welcome to the Desert of the Real," a line from *The Matrix*, Žižek noted that in the film, "the material reality we all experience and see around us is a virtual one, generated and coordinated by a gigantic mega-computer to which we are all attached; when the hero . . . awakens into the 'real reality,' he sees a desolate landscape" and is greeted ironically by the resistance leader, "Welcome to the desert of the real."[20] And this "real reality"—corresponding to the Lacanian real: the void—is what American citizens encountered on 9/11, when their own virtual reality was punctured. "It is the awareness that we live in an insulated artificial universe," Žižek explains, "which generates the notion that some ominous agent is threatening us all the time with total destruction."

Žižek's article, written shortly after 9/11, is a kind of Trutherism *avant la lettre,* and even shares with Trutherism the use of *The Matrix* as a frame of reference. Truthers, after all, affirm this insight into the fantasmatic components mediating our reception of the terror attacks. However, the comparison between Žižek's conception of 9/11 and Trutherism also helps us to understand what ultimately distinguishes most critical theories from most conspiracy theories. Žižek's critique, focusing on the symbolic—the term that, in Lacanian analysis, the paranoid subject is believed to lack— reflects on the destruction, for so many, of traditional structures of authority on 9/11. The Truther, by contrast, rejects the whole story: who did it, how the towers came to fall, or even, for some, whether they fell at all—it was a hologram.

Another popular Trutherist claim is that the twin towers were brought down by Israeli secret agents and that Jews, having all been briefed beforehand, didn't show up to work there that day. This, as we'll shortly see, is exactly the type of grotesque but widely circulated theory that one continually finds in the history of conspiracism as a phenomenon that has never ceased to obsess itself with "Jewish questions." Indeed, it's not by accident that the importance of distinguishing between critical doubts and conspiracist doubts is also the theme of Robert Eaglestone's short book *Postmodernism and Holocaust Denial.* For Holocaust denial is a questioning of *what really took place* that both precedes and survives debates over the reality or otherwise of 9/11 or the Gulf War. So it's hardly surprising that, as Eaglestone notes, "Many who fight Holocaust denial, and many historians in general, put postmodernism, deconstruction or 'cultural relativism' together and find them threatening." But while Holocaust deniers speak often of their doubts, they're not *really* in doubt. They know what they think. And thus, says Eaglestone, they are "very hard to argue with. . . . Like all conspiracy theorists, they always find new ways of explaining away the consensus of historians."[21]

Hence, while it's true that certain conspiracy theorists have found resources within critical theory with which to support and seemingly validate their own alternative truth claims, the two approaches are, in the most significant ways, completely at odds: conspiracy theorists "doubt" the facts; critical theorists doubt their ideological means of interpretation.

The Truth Within Trutherism

Of course, America is by no means the only country where suspicions about official stories have arisen; nor, necessarily, is it the most susceptible to conspiracism. The Middle East, notes journalist David Aaronovitch, "is awash with conspiracy theories" (especially *about* American power), no doubt because that region in particular has "hosted a great number of actual conspiracies"—the devious and underhand operations of colonial powers intent on deceiving the populations at large.[22] That ex-colonies might be especially prone to conspiracy thinking about malign Western influence is hardly surprising, then, given the real history of malign Western influence under cover of a conspiracy.

Here as elsewhere, and as the Freudian understanding of trauma's impact on cognition suggests, even when a conspiracy is just a delusion, we might still find within it some kernel of truth about the reality that it has distorted but whose official narrative it has been perceptive enough to find wanting. So there is, as we've seen, truth within Trutherism, and that truth concerns less the facts in the air or on the ground than the ideological manipulation of those facts by those in a position of power and influence. Žižek made this point with regard to 9/11 as an event that so closely resembled the fantasy life of America—the Hollywood disaster movie—that it seemed somehow to confirm the perception that the world's most famous metropolis was not rooted in reality. As such, to view paranoid delusions through the lens of a simple binary of true/false, right/wrong, fails to comprehend the reason within the madness in a manner that ironically also mirrors, in its binary thinking, the madness within our reason.

Hurricane Katrina struck the American Gulf of Mexico in 2005, wreaking huge destruction, and most of those worst affected were poor blacks who could justifiably impute institutional racism to the lackluster governmental response. A year later, however, stories also began to circulate that the government's sins were not only those of inaction but of active participation in the catastrophe that had befallen the victims. It was said that the levees had been deliberately destroyed in order to flood black areas. This view is broadcast in Spike Lee's documentary *When the Levees Broke*, in which a number of those interviewed repeat their belief that there was a conspiracy to drown blacks in New Orleans. Lee neither contests nor supports such conspiracy theories in the film, but when asked about them on a TV show, he maintained that it wouldn't be far-fetched to believe the government capable of such a thing.

Aaronovitch understands Lee's reasoning as follows: "The truth or otherwise of conspiracy theories is less important than their existence, because they are, properly analysed, an expression of an underlying reality, representing 'a not entirely unfounded suspicion that the normal order of things itself amounts to a conspiracy.'" Even if the theory is false, in other words, to repudiate it is to dishonor the truth contained within it. Aaronovitch thinks Lee's approach is "entirely wrong," however, given the frequency with which the conspiracy theorist will belong to the opposite end of the political spectrum from the one where you would position yourself.[23] What are we to make of Birthers, for instance, who believe that Barack Obama has no legitimacy as a president because he's not a *real* American? ("Where are his papers to prove it! Just look at him! What kind of a name is that!")

Yet, as deluded as Birthers are in thinking Obama wasn't born where and when he says he was, is there not deep within the unconscious of Birtherism some residue of the repressed memory of the nonwhite *truly* native American whose entire history has indeed been erased from the record books? Birtherism is in this sense, perhaps even more than Trutherism, an archetypal conspiracy theory insofar as it simultaneously invokes and obliterates the memory of the history it raises and erases.[24] If, indeed, this *is* the passion animating Birtherism, then it's a version of the same idea we have already detected variously within ancient Gnosticism, Cartesian rationality, and American Republicanism, as well as paranoia: the Birther is quintessentially someone who believes that the world can be born anew, over and over and over again.

Jewish Paranoia

"Haven't you heard? People have been *saying* that you're paranoid!" is a wicked sort of a joke, though it serves up a serious point. For to deride the paranoiac for her delusions not only fails to uproot those delusions but just as often offers further "proof" of the persecution from which she feels herself to be suffering. To simply judge a delusion as delusional is then not only ineffective, it might even be said to resemble the decontextualizing and dehistoricizing work of paranoia itself. For delusions don't just come out of nowhere. It isn't hard to see the historical inspiration for Jewish paranoia, for example. Why wouldn't a Jewish person after World War II and the countless massacres, pogroms, and persecutions that preceded it, be paranoid? Not only do such fears make sense, but, it could be argued on the back of their historical experiences, Jews would be crazy *not* to feel paranoid.

Still, there's something funny about Jewish paranoia. You can laugh along with it. For one thing, it involves a kind of absurdity of scale, for if what today animates Jewish fears is something as unimaginably large as the history of the Holocaust, then there's a kind of preposterousness to the comfortable, assimilated post-Holocaust Jew who attaches genocidal significance to the least slight, the vaguest discomfort or disagreement. What's more, the inherently indeterminate situation of the diasporic Jew has made paranoia a virtual constant of Jewish modernity. It's there, for instance, in that famous scene from the Woody Allen film *Annie Hall* when Alvy goes to visit Annie's Midwestern WASP family and imagines himself through their eyes seated at the lunch table in a black hat with long side curls and the beard of an old world Hasid. Do they really see him that way? Or maybe it isn't them, maybe it's just Alvy who sees himself that way. *Is* he just being paranoid?

Then there's the scene earlier in the film when Alvy is talking with his good friend Rob:

ROB   Alvy, you're a total paranoid.

ALVY   Wh—How am I a paran—? Well, I pick up on those kind o' things. You know, I was having lunch with some guys from NBC, so I said . . . uh, "Did you eat yet or what?" and Tom Christie said, "No, didchoo?" Not, did you, didchoo eat? Jew? No, not did you eat, but Jew eat? Jew. You get it? Jew eat?

ROB   Ah, Max, you, uh . . .

ALVY   Stop calling me Max.

ROB   Why, Max? It's a good name for you. Max, you see conspiracies in everything.[25]

"Every time some group disagrees with you," says Rob a little later, "it's because of anti-Semitism." Behind every wayward word, behind every difference of opinion, Alvy senses a conspiracy against the Jews. Yet anti-Semitism is also a conspiracy theory *about* the Jews—Jews who, it is believed, are plotting to take over the world. What Alvy is paranoid about, in other words, is that *others might be paranoid about Alvy.* Jewish paranoia suspects not merely a manipulative or false world, but a paranoid world. "Don't you see?" Alvy appeals to Rob, "The rest of the country looks upon New York like we're—we're left-wing Communist, Jewish, homosexual pornographers. *I* think of us that way, sometimes, and I—I live here."

But what does Rob think? He accuses Alvy of paranoia, of conspiracism, of being unduly anxious about anti-Semitism, but what's his personal solution to Alvy's litany of angst?

> ALVY You know, I was in a record store. Listen to this—so I know there's this big tall blond crew-cutted guy and he's lookin' at me in a funny way and smiling and he's saying, "Yes, we have a sale this week on Wagner." Wagner, Max, Wagner—so I know what he's really tryin' to tell me very significantly, Wagner.
>
> ROB Right, Max. California, Max.
>
> ALVY Ah.
>
> ROB Let's get the hell outta this crazy city.
>
> ALVY Forget it, Max.
>
> ROB —we move to sunny L.A. All of show business is out there, Max.

California! Show business! Rob's American Dream of putting on a show and leaving the past—the old world, the East Coast—behind, also merges with another quick-fix to the problem of his dweeby, bespectacled friend: he renames Alvy with an aggrandizing name— Max (which is also, somewhat confusingly, the name that Alvy, perhaps mockingly, calls Rob). This, however, invites the question: who is the real paranoid here? For Rob is all about starting over, making the world anew. Yet surely it doesn't take much imagination to figure out why a showbiz guy in Hollywood with a habit of rebranding his pals, starting with their names, might become a magnet for other people's suspicions . . . what is *he* hiding?

He's hiding his Jewishness. More specifically, we can speculate that what Rob is really hoping to cover up are his self-doubts—*his* Jewish paranoia. Thus Alvy and Rob represent two ways of responding to the distinct and historically ratified suspicion that other people find you suspicious, which is a suspicion you yourself might also have further invited in the attempt to escape their suspicions by means of your own paranoid whisperings (Alvy) or constant changes of appearance/state/name (Rob).

In an essay on "Paranoid Reading" within the humanities, Eve Kosovsky Sedgwick warns that critical approaches that jump too soon to their conclusions end up closing down any future that the critic might not have anticipated beforehand by eliminating the chance of being taken by surprise.[26] The paranoid reading, that is, always risks becoming a self-fulfilling prophecy by somehow never failing to turn up the damning evidence it sets out ready to find. Jewish paranoia precisely encapsulates this dilemma. A healthy survival instinct on the one hand—you'd be mad not to be paranoid, given what you know of the world (even herds of bison in the wild, zoologists tell us, benefit from being paranoid)—entails its own dangers on the other, by creating the very realities it most fears. Thus if you fear anti-Semitism—suspecting others of suspecting you and your nearest of being part of a secret cabal with its own agenda—well, then, suddenly you'll find yourself meeting up with your fellow Jews to figure out how best to change and influence things for the good of your own kind. So suddenly there's AIPAC! And this, of course, cuts in both directions. For if you feel that you're suspected by someone in a minority or marginal position of, say, anti-Semitism or racism or sexism or homophobia, then you may well find yourself feeling hounded or exposed by that suspicion, and thus treating that person differently, more carefully, suspiciously—confirming her prejudice one way or the other.

Such a *mise en abyme* of suspicions mirroring each other reveals how, as the Jewish experience dramatically illustrates, paranoia is a kind of constitutive state of being in the modern world. It is perhaps for this reason that one finds the seemingly inextinguishable "Jewish question" lurking again and again behind a whole range of contemporary conspiracy theories. Indeed, both Kay and Aaronovitch regard the famous anti-Semitic forgery *The Protocols of the Elders of Zion* as a kind of Ur text for most modern conspiracy movements. "Not all conspiracy theorists are anti-Semitic," writes Kay, "but all conspiracy movements—all of them—attract anti-Semites."[27] As such, I found myself, when reading these two journalists' books, continually braced to expect the revelation of anti-Semitic motives behind each and every one of the conspiracy theories they analyze. Yet not every conspiracy theory proved to be an anti-Semitic conspiracy theory. I was surprised, even a little distrustful in such cases. Might I even have been disappointed? If my expectation of anti-Semitism was my own way of pre-empting doubt and uncertainty, you could say my own research into conspiracy theories seems to have prompted my own growing sense of Jewish paranoia: the feeling that anti-Semitism is a global system whose impulses are disguisedly present even when they *appear* to be absent. Uh-oh.

On Being Stalked

It's precisely this form of paranoia as self-fulfilling prophecy that the author James Lasdun narrowly avoids after a prolonged anti-Semitic assault on his person that leads him to wonder if the whole world might not be fundamentally out to get the Jews. While Lasdun steers clear of that conclusion, his painful brush with someone else's extreme paranoia nonetheless causes him "to question and distrust all impressions of other people, my own of them as well as theirs of me."[28]

In New York in 2003 Lasdun was teaching a creative writing class. Nasreen (not her real name), a gifted and attractive Iranian-American student, was in attendance. Lasdun singled out her writing for particular praise, regarding her as the "star" of that class. Unexpectedly, she emailed him two years later to ask whether he would read a first draft of her novel, and before he knew it, grudgingly at first, he was involved in regular email exchanges, putting her in touch with his literary agent. His agent declined to take her on, and her novel has not been published. Not long after that he was being stalked online by Nasreen, with escalating aggression and such terrible consequences for Lasdun's mental health that after five years he lived "in the medium of Nasreen's hatred. I couldn't think about anything except her, and pretty soon I couldn't *talk* about anything except her" (129).

Early in their email correspondence Lasdun, a "happily married man," admits he knew he was being flirted with and rather liked it. It was when the flirtations became more explicit in their intent that he felt compelled to draw a line beneath their relations, and this sexual snub, perhaps, along with his failure to get her writing published, may have provoked Nasreen in her determination to "ruin" him. She started spreading malicious rumors about her "prey" around the internet: he slept with all his female students except her, he set her up to be raped, he stole and sold her unpublished work to other Iranian female novelists who plagiarized, then published it as their own, he is the leading figure in a cabal of Jewish literary racketeers. Anti-Semitism and accusations of his role in a Jewish conspiracy soon became the mainstay of her accusations: "I think the holocaust was fucking funny" (35). "Look, muslims are not like their Jewish counterparts, who quietly got gassed and then cashed in on it" (52). "Your family is dead you ugly JEW" (211). Her strategy, Lasdun at one point surmises, is to elevate her private grievance into something more global and political. So, too, he suspects, is her manner of deploying the gestures of "critical theory and gender studies in her attempt to brand me as a monster" (61).

Admirably, if also out of a paranoid concern lest others will think him culpable, Lasdun's memoir attempts to parse his own complicity in provoking his stalker. Nor, in light of the asymmetry structuring their power relations—teacher/student, man/woman, published/unpublished, married/single, Western Jew/Iranian Muslim—all of which forms part of the campaign she wages against him, does he fail to check his privilege. *"I think,"* she writes at one point, *"this is called verbal terrorism"* (38). It's a phrase that strikes Lasdun as especially enlightening: "I came to appreciate Nasreen's grasp of the dynamics of asymmetric conflict, where she had apparently nothing to lose, and I had everything." A repeated theme of his memoir is thus the way in which weakness can be turned into strength, especially by those online who use the anonymous advantage conferred by so many internet platforms of a space for commentary below the line.

The dramatic difference between Lasdun and Nasreen puts one in mind of Yeats's still resonant lament for an age when "The best lack all conviction, while the worst / Are full of passionate intensity."[29] For it is the passionate intensity of Nasreen's prose that first excites the attention of Lasdun, who also detects, by way of comparison, a relative lack in his own. Indeed, later, when her resentment against him has shown itself, she focuses on his cowardice, his woolly liberal's lack of firm convictions, and "your boring trying-to-be-white style" (57). Lasdun *is*, in appearance, white, but here we have the intimation that, for a Semite, whiteness is put on, fake, not to be trusted. Nasreen's accusation also evokes prewar European anti-Semitism, and most famously the claims made in Wagner's notorious 1850 polemic "Jews in Music":

> The Jew speaks the language of the nation in whose midst he
> dwells from generation to generation, but he speaks it always as

an alien. . . . In the first place, then, the general circumstances that the Jew talks the modern European languages merely as learnt, and not as mother tongues, must necessarily debar him from all capability of therein expressing himself idiomatically, independently, and conformably to his nature in any higher sense. . . . In this Speech, this Art, the Jew can only mimic and mock—not truly make a poem of his words, an artwork of his doings.[30]

Lasdun, as Nasreen portrays him, is just such an unoriginal parasitic Jew debarred from true art and authentic self-expression. Yet her attack comes at him from the left rather than the right, and from someone who has also felt the need to play along with the rules of whiteness so as to advance to what, as she sees it, the Jews have acquired for themselves by just such cowardice—power, influence, connections, publishing deals.

In one sense Nasreen is what every writer wants—a close reader of his work. Yet her closeness to Lasdun's work is so profound that she cannot quite tell the dividing line between his fictions and her reality. "I'm living your short story out," she writes at one point, "and I'm scared" (51). His encounter with Nasreen even causes Lasdun to distrust his *own* sense of the difference between the real and imagined. Over the course of his stalking experience he has the odd impression that he may be living out various scenes from one of his own earlier novels in uncanny ways.[31] This close encounter with paranoia thus shifts all the parameters so that nothing feels sure anymore and nothing seems safe anymore; Lasdun sinks into an abyss of doubt, experiencing, as Nasreen does, almost everything as a source of persecution.

Plagiarism

In Lasdun's portrayal of Nasreen, then, we once again have the figure of an acutely perceptive if delusional state of consciousness, whose impressions, however mistaken, contain a number of enlightening insights. Her claim that Lasdun is a literary racketeer who has sold her unpublished work to other Iranian novelists (writers he has neither met nor heard of) to plagiarize has a special resonance for the paranoid mind wary of those who might wish to control it. For what is plagiarism if not the exploitation of another's thoughts, words, ideas, stories—even experiences?

This has some bearing on how language actually works. Our language is never entirely our own. It may speak through us or for us, but it always predates us—its very appearance within us is proof that some powerful external agent took control of our minds before we had the chance to resist, consent, or say otherwise. Thus our language does not come to us at our own invitation, but has always been put there by another whose influence is then impossible to uproot. Such an insight, albeit in a disavowed form, perhaps underlies the great rage that animates a racist or nationalist discourse such as Wagner's, and the insistence that language, music, and art be kept pure beyond contamination, not bastardized by hybrid forms or pidgin languages spoken by many immigrant groups. The rage of the racist bespeaks a desire to claim as one's own what can never be claimed as one's own, and what, since it will always belong as much to the other as oneself, must remain a locus of uncertainty.

The Gnostics' conception of a true world lying behind the veil of lies is, as we've discussed, a dream of divine plenitude where there is neither time nor law nor any forcible determination that would deprive the individual of her own freedom to sing, unimpeded, the song of herself. If this seductive dream sometimes lends support to those forms of disavowal we find at work within paranoia, it can also yield true insights into how we are able to "know"— via language—anything at all. For such a dream space is also, on a certain understanding, analogous to how we might think of the space of a *text*, which shares with the Gnostics' perception of the true reality an inherent lack of fixity and thus an intractability with regard to every attempt to master, own, appropriate, or reduce it to one authorized meaning. There are as many interpretations of the text as there are interpreters and, as with the Gnostic's *Pleroma*, the text is never past but remains forever present, as infinitely open and playful as the time before time. It is in this sense that our language is shaped by our nonlanguage or infancy, hence perhaps why the experience of language can be, especially for those most powerfully caught up in their formative relations, a way (albeit unconscious) of reversing the laws of chronology and mastery, for in the text those laws don't quite apply. It is, as Phillips observes, "the adult's own currency—words—that reveals to [children] the limits of adult authority."[32] For the very words that are meant to instruct the child are also the means by which the child can learn to subvert the master, play him at his own game. And they can even, as in the case of Nasreen and Lasdun, lead to the claim that what the master has given has in fact been taken.

So feeling plagiarized—that one's own mind has been misappropriated, even when, technically speaking, it hasn't—is often the material of paranoia. For if the paranoiac seeks a place outside of this world, a place safe from another whose presence is felt to be persecuting because too close, then the (fictional) text is the ideal space of such an escape fantasy—truly an alternative reality—yet at the same time, given the unbounded nature of text, the place where the Other's invasive presence cannot but reemerge. This other is thus, like language itself, a boundary-exploding figure in relation to whose terrifying intermingling and proximity the accusation of plagiarism may be deemed, by the one who feels herself persecuted, the best line of defense.

One thing that Lasdun experiences following his own persecution by Nasreen is a new sense of uncertainty about language, about what belongs to whom or who "owns" a text. He used to think he knew what good writing was, he says, but "I don't feel so sure of this anymore (I don't feel so sure of anything anymore)." Lasdun eventually manages to convince himself that the whole world does not sing from the same devilish song sheet. But such is the self-fulfilling mode of paranoia that Nasreen's paranoid fantasies *do* ultimately materialize as versions of the truth. Lasdun *does*, in fact, make contact with the other Iranian novelists she feels are conspiring against her—and precisely because they're also the victims of Nasreen's online vilifications, her victims wind up comparing notes such that the fervid plot of her fantasies in a certain sense takes place. And he *does* eventually use Nasreen's words for personal gain, by quoting them—via many examples of her emails—verbatim in his own book.

Open City

Plagiarism is also a subject of concern in Teju Cole's remarkable novel *Open City*, a work that shines a light on the uncertain space between subjective and objective experiences, revealing how much dream there is in everyday reality. In one striking section of the novel the Nigerian-American protagonist, Julius, meets a bright young Moroccan man, Farouk, during a brief sojourn in Brussels. Farouk is living and working behind the counter in an internet café that Julius frequents during his visit to the European city. The two men strike up a conversation after Julius notices Farouk reading a secondary text on Walter Benjamin's *On the Concept of History*. He is taken aback by Farouk's manner of talking in a "self-certain intel-lectual language" and by Farouk's dismissal of the "big reputation" of a Moroccan writer in exile whom Julius has recently been reading, urging on him instead another Moroccan writer who, he says, is more authentic by virtue of having remained closer to his people and the street: "What I like best about him is that he was an autodidact." Farouk talks to Julius mostly about his personal politics. Occasionally Julius feels he ought to "correct" Farouk's slight factual inaccuracies, but "I was unsure of my ground."[33]

Like Nasreen, Farouk speaks the language of critical theory, and to Julius's ears his terminology—for example, the "victimized Other"—has "a far deeper resonance than it would have in any academic situation" (105). Yet as sympathetic as Julius feels toward Farouk's politics, he is put off by his "rage and rhetoric" and by the way a "cancerous violence had eaten into every political idea" (107). The best, again, lack all convictions, while the worst are full of passionate intensity. And indeed, we start to sense in these passages, although precisely without conviction, that all might not be right or reasonable about Farouk.

Cole's portrait of Farouk is a subtle one. Here is a complex picture of a fascinating young man whose vivid intelligence continually impresses both Julius and the novel's readers, however much we are given reason to distrust his inaccuracies, contradictions, and misrepresentations. And just as Nasreen's milieu for putting the world to rights is the internet, so Farouk's daily scene is an internet café.

The internet café is, for Farouk, the utopian dreamspace where all languages and nationalities can mix and interact, where, despite his focus on the necessary maintenance of cultural differences, "people can live together, and I want to understand how that can happen. It happens here, on this small scale, in this shop, and I want to understand how it can happen on a bigger scale. But as I told you, I'm an autodidact": "I thought about his reference to our previous conversation, when he said he had referred to himself as an autodidact. It was a minor thing, of course, but (and I was sure I wasn't misremembering) he had only used the word in reference to Mohamed Choukri, not himself. This was a small instance, not of unreliability, but of a certain imperfection in Farouq's recall which, because of the absolute sureness of his manner, it was easy to miss"

(113–114). Julius deems these "minor lapses—there were others, and they were irrelevant lapses, actually, not even worthy of the label *mistake*." But while Julius has decided upon the irrelevance of these minor lapses, the vigilant reader remains alert to them, and there are indeed many more such lapses, which, if they aren't mistakes—mistakes can be forgiven—do seem to hint at something not altogether irrelevant for our understanding of Farouk's mental state.

For example, not only did Farouk not previously call himself an autodidact, but he was talking earlier of another man whose life story he now seems to be borrowing (plagiarizing?) as his own. Indeed, as we soon discover, Farouk cannot easily be represented as an autodidact, given the extent of his formal education. His "first degree," he later tells Julius, he took at twenty-one in Morocco, before doing a (failed) master's in Belgium in critical theory; now he is doing another master's, in translation studies, and is considering an eventual Ph.D.

And what are we to make of the contradictory positions Farouk seems to continually but unwittingly take up? He claims to be on the side of Malcolm X over Martin Luther King at one moment, before declaring himself shortly after a "pacifist" (115) who wouldn't even kill a man pointing a gun to his own head. Later, in a bar conversing with Julius and "my best friend" (117) Khalil, a Marxist and a man from his home town, Farouk agrees with Khalil's support for Hamas and Hezbollah ("It's the same for me"), says he is unable to judge Al Qaeda, and calls Saddam Hussein a resistance hero. Julius reflects on these admissions: "I was meant to be the outraged American, though what I felt was more sorrow and less anger" (120). Sorrow, in the Kleinian sense, is the depressive position of the nonextremist: only by accepting the mixing up of good and bad, right and wrong, the infant may overcome the paranoid-schizoid wish to see the world in black and white.

Farouk also, somewhat obsessively, discusses Jewish questions. "As I said before, Julius"—although this is in fact another inaccuracy: it is not something he has said before—"in my opinion, the Palestinian question is the central question of our time" (121). He is, too, a little obtuse about whether or not he believes the official history of the Holocaust: "I'm sorry, the six million are not special. I am always frustrated that this number, this sacred number that cannot be discussed is used, like Khalil said, to put an end to all discussions. The Jews use it to silence the world. I really don't give a damn about the exact figure" (123).

The discomfort is Julius's as well as ours—for here we find what must surely be taken as a serious political critique of the abuse of the memory of the Holocaust in order to silence dissent over Israel's historic and continuing abuses toward the Palestinians, coupled with an abuse of that same memory on the part of a critic who hints that he personally doubts the official history of the Holocaust while insisting that its true facts are not, in any case, what really matters. And then we get this comment: "I am not personally against Jews. There are many Jews in Morocco, even today, and they are welcomed as part of the community. They look just like us, though, of course, they do better in business. I think sometimes that maybe I should become a Jew, just for professional reasons" (124). Nasreen also often reassures Lasdun that she is not, despite appearances, anti-Semitic. In both cases this is an intellectual certainty: since I am a person of principle who does not harbor irrational prejudices—and since I am the underprivileged one, the *victimized Other*—my feelings toward the Jews are to be understood as rational rather than racist.

Farouk's relationship to his best friend Khalil likewise raises certain questions, for Khalil, though a Marxist, is also Farouk's "boss" (123), who owns the shop he works in along with several others across the city. During Julius's time with both men, Khalil continually admits of extremist positions and Farouk, though he often agrees with Khalil, remarks to Julius once Khalil has left: "You just saw me in disagreement with my best friend. We are individuals" (126). But he hasn't disagreed with Khalil, not once. Why? Because he actually agrees with him? Or because he doesn't like to disagree with a best friend who also happens to be his boss? Or because he does not quite have possession of his own mind in the presence of powerful men, hard men—a hard man is how Julius evidently regards Khalil, and a "hard man" is how Farouk will later go on to describe his own father. Aren't we then being invited by Cole's subtle text to draw these associations for ourselves, to wonder whether Farouk is always in possession of his own mind, or whether there might be certain instances, or certain people, who intimidate Farouk, dominate him—hypnotize him?

All of these prior contradictions and inaccuracies mean that we cannot quite trust Farouk's own sense of things when he tells Julius what caused him to fail his M.A. in critical theory. He had submitted a dissertation on Gaston Bachelard's *Poetics of Space*, and the thesis was rejected on the grounds of plagiarism. Farouk, however, believes "that they were punishing me for world events in which I had played no role. My thesis committee had met on September 20, 2001" (128).

Hence we move from critical theory to conspiracy theory—even to quasi-Trutherism. Julius does not tell us whether or not he believes Farouk's account of what went on—he leaves him to speak in his own words, in what we might call an antiplagiarizing gesture. Yet we've been given sufficient hints that Farouk has a habit of revising his own past statements, of slightly rewording the statements of others, and of passing off other people's lives and experiences as his own. We have also noticed that he seems to imagine that he has addressed himself independently, as his own man, when he has merely fallen in with a more powerful person, in spoken and unspoken agreement. And there is also the impression left by having first encountered Farouk reading not the original Walter Benjamin text, but a commentary on it—so, we cannot but wonder, might that be what happened with Gaston Bachelard, too? In this instance Farouk is the one accused of plagiarism, while Nasreen is the one who accuses. But isn't it possible that Nasreen and Farouk are equally oblivious to the chronological precedence of others' texts? In my own experience with students, those accused of plagiarism seem genuinely confused by the charge, as if they honestly didn't imagine they were stealing from another; as if those words and thoughts, once read, seemed so closely to speak their own mind that they actually *were* their own mind.

Farouk has been cast out from Critical Theory and forced instead to do a part-time master's degree in translation studies. Translation, the very language of secondariness, of nonoriginality,[34] is felt by this would-be autodidact as a terrible defeat of his intellectual ambitions. Indeed, for Julius the impression Farouk leaves is of someone whose wound runs too deep to be easily assuaged. Despite his "seething intelligence . . . he was one of the thwarted ones," a man with "a single murderous action in mind" (129).

So both Nasreen and Farouk are highly intelligent, with a lot to say and a lot to teach. Both use critical theory to bolster their conspiracy theories. And both talk obsessively of Jews. It's a disturbing symptom, certainly, but in what way might they be, as we have been suggesting repeatedly of paranoiacs, "on to" something?

Lasdun concludes his memoir of online persecution with a meditation on anti-Semitism: "There is something uncannily adaptive about anti-Semitism: the way it can hide, unsuspected, in the most progressive minds."[35] A sage point. Still, we cannot but notice that this too is a mirror image of how the anti-Semitic imagination regards the Jew: adaptive, uncanny, shapeshifting, hiding unsuspected under apparently progressive guises. The Jew, of course, has learned to be adaptive precisely in order to survive the often treacherous conditions of life in the diaspora. Yet we find, once again, in the paranoid perception of Jews—the anti-Semite's conspiracy theory—a truthful insight about the historical conditions of Jewish existence, albeit one obscured and denied by a malignant, false and ahistorical interpretation.

It's Personal

Ultimately, both Nasreen and Farouk confess to their interlocutors that they have been let down not only by the state institutions and megacorporations of the world but by their own families. It's worth noting this as we return now to *Annie Hall*, to a flashback scene in which Alvy is in bed with his former wife Allison, but something's playing on his mind: "H'm, I'm sorry, I can't go through with this, because it—I can't get it off my mind, Allison . . . it's obsessing me!"

What's obsessing him is who killed JFK. A stereotypical "left-wing Communist, Jewish" New Yorker, he doesn't believe the official story identifying Lee Harvey Oswald as the sole marksman. Allison is "getting tired" of this obsession and questions the logic of a conspiracy that would have to have included just about everyone, "The FBI, and the CIA, and J. Edgar Hoover and oil companies and the Pentagon and the men's-room attendant at the White House?" "I—I—I—I would leave out the men's-room attendant." Here, however, their conversation ends, with Allison expressing a theory of her own: "You're using this conspiracy theory as an excuse to avoid sex with me."[36]

So we have two theories pitched against each other: his conspiracy theory (the government is hiding something) versus her psychoanalytic theory (Alvy is hiding something). Both theories express doubts about the official story. Neither theory can be proved or disproved. You can no more prove that JFK was killed by committee than you can prove that Alvy avoids sexual intimacy with Allison because, say, Allison unconsciously reminds him of his mother. But what suggests that Alvy may not be, despite appearances, a clinical paranoiac, but rather someone with a paranoid *style*, is his response to Allison's theory: "She's right!" He *can* admit doubt. He *can* acknowledge that he might be masking something personal with something global.

Where sex describes our most messy relations with others, a conspiracy theory, as Allison sees it, is a way of *avoiding* intimate relations. Such theories use thoughts to elude feelings. Indeed, while Allison's theory is just as speculative as any conspiracy theory, her *style* is not paranoid, nor is it conspiratorial: she doesn't preclude the possibility of doubting the rightness of her own judgments, and she knows herself to be theorizing. Maybe, too, she's wondering whether she might be being paranoid. Though this raises the question, what kind of paranoia is it that can doubt even itself?

In Defense of Doubt

"Am I being paranoid?" has been and remains a very Jewish question, and the historical predicament of Jews as a diasporic people has made self-doubt a perennial condition of their modern existence. Yet as we've seen, it's for these very reasons that "cosmopolitan intellectuals" have never ceased to awaken doubts, suspicions, and conspiracy theories in others. How, then, is it possible for Jews to avoid that perennial bugbear of the paranoid contagion— "imitation of the enemy"?

The best way to avoid imitation of the enemy is to admit of one's doubts instead of covering up or denying them. Alvy in *Annie Hall* offers a comic example of this idea by contrast with the disavowals of his friend Rob. But another example would be Derrida's remark, cited before, that when speaking of 9/11 "we do not know what we are talking about." As noted, Kay suspects that such "postmodern" jargon helps to legitimate spurious doubts among otherwise intelligent people about what should be considered unarguable realities. Yet while Kay deems 9/11 the inaugurating event of our current propensity to doubt, I would argue differently: that 9/11 in fact signaled the formal *collapse* of our postwar doubts.

Consider, for instance, how many of us who watched the events and reactions of that day unfold intuited—not what the future would *be* exactly, but which camps would form, which battle lines would be drawn, who would say what, who would *explain* things in which terms, what we ourselves would be likely to think, and where we would position ourselves politically, morally, and culturally. When declaring, notoriously, "You're either with us or against us," George Bush may simply have been channeling the zeitgeist. For post-9/11 it is generally—regardless of where you stand—our uncertainties rather than our convictions that have been kept secret, private, unspoken, as if admitting one's doubt about what or how to think betrayed an inexcusable gullibility on our part. Or worse still, implied one might be guilty of something oneself.

Derrida, by contrast, delivering on September 22, 2001, an acceptance speech (on receipt of the Theodor Adorno Award), stated that "with regard to this crime, I do not believe that anyone is politically guiltless."[37] By countering the binary thinking of Bush et al., his remark puts one in mind not only of Adorno but of Klein's depressive. For as we've seen, one cannot elude the repetitive logic of paranoia's imitation of the enemy without first accepting one's own inescapable immersion in this world and its history. Hence Kay's stance that Derrida's 9/11 commentary—*we do not know what we are talking about*—is the sort of "bafflegab" that leads to Trutherism conveniently ignores the fact that Derrida stands virtually *alone* in refusing to come up with a ready-made explanation for what then took place.

A fairer assessment of Derrida's 9/11 response would be to acknowledge his unusualness in choosing to *express* his doubts. And not only "his" doubts. For such doubts, when you look for them, are everywhere, and can even be detected within the rapidly established convention of naming the event by its date. Since, that is, the explicit historicity of the name "9/11" *implicitly* calls into question what it purports to be able to identify—both in terms of its uncertain origins and its unpredictable futures—it's a name that puts the event squarely inside, not outside, time. As such, it belongs to a history whose facts cannot change, but whose meaning is perpetually in motion. These Derridean doubts, in other words, being more than merely rhetorical, cannot, in either the clinical *or* the stylistic sense, be reasonably considered paranoid.

SIX

Mother Love

When I say mother I am not excluding father, but at this stage it
is the maternal aspect of the father that concerns us.
—DONALD WINNICOTT, "Communication Between Infant and Mother"

What is Yiddish in me is inextricable from what is woman in me,
from woman who is mother.
—TILLIE OLSEN

Modern Jews and modern mothers have lots in common. Like
Jews, not only are mothers convenient scapegoats who can find
themselves blamed for pretty much every ill in society, but they
can also wind up feeling terribly bad about this fact—guilty,
paranoid, self-hating, all the various feelings this book has been
associating with modern Jewish experience. And just as postemancipation Jews have constantly sought to prove their worth as
modern citizens, it seems that mothers too, hoping, perhaps, to
show that women's emancipation was no mistake either, have been
acutely susceptible to the demand that they be *practically perfect*

in every way: modern and enlightened on the one hand, virtuous and old-fashioned on the other—both suffragette and Mary Poppins at once.

Yet, like Jews reactively dividing their identities into good and bad versions, neither of which is ultimately trusted by the social order that has imposed this dualism, mothers have just as frequently been viewed as either dangerously bad (and thus a threat to the whole of society) or too good to be true (a no less dangerous threat). Especially the double whammy: the Jewish mother. For it is she who best distils within a single stereotype the contradictory motifs informing both misogynist representations and anti-Semitic ones, not least in the way the feelings said to afflict her are equally the feelings with which she is said to afflict everyone else: guilt, self-hatred, neurosis, paranoia, *and* a feeling we might otherwise have been tempted to suppose benign or beneficial—the feeling of mother love.

In its joking incarnation, a Jewish mother's love is far from harmless. As Dan Greenburg was to summarize her methods in his comic best-seller of 1964, *How to Be a Jewish Mother,* "Let your child hear you sigh every day; if you don't know what he's done to make you suffer, *he* will." And: "Underlying all techniques of Jewish Motherhood is the ability to plant, cultivate and harvest guilt. Control guilt and you control the child."[1]

Thus what, as we'll see, the modern stereotype of the Jewish mother reveals—and reveals, in the view of this book, about *all* mothers—is that a mother's love, however vital it may be for her children's welfare and survival, has become as much a source of anxiety as of assurance, as much a source of sickness as of sustenance, and as much a source of comedy as comfort . . . as if mother love, the very feeling that, if we're lucky, heralds our arrival into the world, is also the feeling that's heralded our queasiness *about* feelings.

Imagining Mothers

If the joke often told about mothers (and especially about Jewish mothers, by their sons) envisages a personality who controls and manipulates via guilt, feminists, unsurprisingly, see things rather differently. Guilt, writes Adrienne Rich, "is one of the most powerful forms of social control *of* women; none of us can be entirely immune to it."[2] Mothers especially. From the moment you get pregnant, or the moment you realize your body isn't altogether your own anymore, you're already in danger of being that ultimate social menace, a *bad mother*.[3] Fortunately, however, family, friends, strangers, and newspaper columnists will always be there to tell you how exactly to mitigate the threat you pose to your own children—usually by cutting back both on work and on leisure. For what makes a mother *truly* a mother is, as King Solomon so long ago divined, her willingness to sacrifice anything and everything—*including* her motherhood—for the sake of her child.

So, the true mother is the loving mother. And a mother's love is self-sacrifice. It isn't hard to see why mothers might feel guilty all the time when maternal worthiness gets measured in terms of such self-abnegation. If this *is* what defines mother love then few mothers can possibly feel, in D. W. Winnicott's memorable phrase, "good-enough"—or even perceive what their own legitimate wishes or rights as mothers might be. "My children cause me the most exquisite suffering of which I have any experience," confesses Rich. "I *love them*. But it's in the enormity and inevitability of this love that the sufferings lie."[4]

Of course, given that most women remain attracted to motherhood, the "enormity and inevitability" of maternal love may well be its own reward.[5] Yet while we may agree that a mother is not simply or even necessarily a biological relation but, rather, someone distinguished by the love she bears for her children, we are not, on that account, compelled to accept the definition of what that love *is*. On whose authority, we might ask, have we defined *for* the mother what her own experiences and passions might mean? Mightn't it be the case that her sufferings are caused less by her love than by the claim that we know exactly what *constitutes* a mother's love?

No Identity Holds Up

The mother defined solely by her capacity for self-sacrifice must be some sort of superhuman: nothing is too much for her. It's precisely this kind of oppressive reasoning that we find, for example, within the right-wing political rhetoric that seeks to withdraw welfare support from mothers by disingenuously celebrating them as natural caregivers. Jacqueline Rose has linked such antidependency ideology to an unconscious wish on the part of its proponents to deny their own vulnerabilities: "As if genuine neediness—being, or having once been, a baby—is what this Conservative rhetoric most hates."[6]

The truth, however, is that mothers in supporting roles are deeply in need of their own support structures. Indeed, they might even be said to *resemble* their babies in their open vulnerability and sense of having been, in some radical way, newly born. Nor, perhaps, should this surprise us, given that women and their babies are literally of a piece. As Rachel Cusk describes in her unusually frank memoir "on becoming a mother," a drama of self-division underwrites the experience of maternity: "Birth is not merely that which divided women from men: it also divided women from themselves, so that a woman's understanding of what it is to exist is profoundly changed. Another person has existed in her, and after their birth they lie within the jurisdiction of her consciousness. When she is with them she is not herself; when she is without them she is not herself."[7] Motherhood, she's saying, tears you apart.

In the artist Louise Bourgeois's various depictions of the moment of *Birth*, one beholds a sort of monstrosity: a dyadic creature with one body and one head pointing in one direction and the other body and head pointing in the other, the only thing now definitely conjoining them an umbilical cord that will soon be cut. In these stark aerial views one glimpses a graphic description of how the maternal experience entails a total negation of the integrity of the human subject. "No identity holds up," writes Julia Kristeva: the mother is "a continuous separation, a division of the very flesh." The mother's own body teaches her that the Other (the alien, the stranger) comes quite literally from within: from her own insides. At the same time, from the mother's divided body we may also infer a "division of language." Maternal experience, that is, makes a mockery of any logic that would presume to stabilize, fix, or know things—especially people. The mother is awakened to the poverty of language, its inability to capture her experience, in which sense, too, her maternity might be said to isolate her by loosening her ties to the common sense world. Her experience, writes Kristeva, "gnaws . . . at the symbolic's almightiness."[8] One need only think here of one's own mother: isn't she somehow *un*thinkable?

Yet if Kristeva makes of motherhood something as destructive as it is generative, it's the very same experience that also allows for the projection of something magical *onto* the mother. The latter view, for example, is evident in Winnicott's description of the "ordinary mother," who devotes herself exclusively to her child's early infancy, "in which to a large extent she is the baby and the baby is her. There is nothing mystical about this."[9] "I disagree that there is nothing mystical about this," responds the graphic memoirist Alison Bechdel. "This seems to me as mystical, as transcendent of the laws of everyday reality, as it gets."[10] For here too we find that, with respect to that shapeshifting experience called maternity, child and mother have no clear boundary or definition with regard to each other. So once again *no identity holds up*, as what the body and experience of the mother tells us is that she has been—as *every*body has been—shared.

The mother, then, whether seen as monstrous or as magical, is a kind of boundary-exploding figure whose sense of alienness, even to herself, reminds us of the way in which the features once said to characterize modern diasporic Jews—transience, secrecy, shapeshifting—saw them faced with a "Jewish Question" which they were unable to adequately answer, rendering them subject to increased levels of scrutiny and surveillance alongside ever tighter systems of social and political control.

A Woman Question

Mothers have probably always provoked such vexatious feelings. "There is much to suggest," writes Rich, "that the male mind has always been haunted by the force of the idea of *dependence on a woman for life itself*."[11] To be "of woman born" is to reckon with this fact that we have all at some point in our lives (in utero in all cases and outside the womb in the majority of cases) been totally dependent on, utterly helpless before, and thus completely subject to a woman—a mother—who has had the power to meet our needs or frustrate them: the power of life and death over us.

It's men, on the whole, who are assumed to be the most ashamed of or enraged by their native dependency. But women are no less ambivalent than men toward their mothers. The cause of *their* ambivalence, says Rich, is the fear of *becoming* their mothers. And specifically, they fear becoming weak and degraded *like* their mothers. So on this account, both men *and* women resent their mothers: the men because they fear female power and priority through maternity, the women because they fear female victimization and *dis*empowerment through maternity.

Of course, many of these mother-resenting women are also mothers themselves—or mothers, one might say, at *war* with themselves. In the fabled antagonism between different mothers huddled together at the school gate, the married moms and the single moms, the stay-at-home moms and the working moms, the lower-class moms and the upper-class moms, all feel themselves the targets, or so they believe, of one another's disapproving gazes . . . who is the better mother? who the truer mother? who the more loving mother? This contemporary "catfight," a sort of recapitulation of the scene of Solomon's justice, was something Rachel Cusk found herself exposed to, for example, when, after publishing a memoir that dared to admit the extent of her maternal ambivalence, she faced vicious levels of opprobrium from a scandalized, mostly conservative, and largely female readership. Yet even an avowed feminist like journalist Daisy Waugh, while aiming to absolve women of the guilt associated with their mothering, can't quite avoid the refractive pitfalls of mother-blaming either. So though, in theory, she lays the ultimate blame at the door of patriarchy, her self-help guide to *Guilt-Free Motherhood* quickly turns into a polemic against the so-called "supermums" who appear as the main source of her own maternal suffering and irritation.[12] Indeed, what are we to make of the fact that so many of the most pronounced disagreements over motherhood today are currently taking place *between* feminists?

Mother Nature

These days, endlessly quoted studies explain the damage done to a child who isn't talked to in utero, who isn't the product of natural childbirth, who isn't breast-fed, who isn't, postpartum, continuously attached to the mother's body kangaroo-style, who isn't played Mozart from the moment of conception, and on and on. The "exponential growth in theories about early childhood is oddly coincident with the rise of feminism," remarks Lisa Appignanesi, with seamless irony. "It is as if educated women needed to be convinced by science of the very real interests of their babies, and as if mother love were not altogether or always that maternal instinct we would also like it to be."[13]

Appignanesi's is a probing observation as well as a funny one, particularly when one contemplates the image thereby evoked of predominantly male scientists advising well-educated women how to love their children with utmost efficiency. But if the scientific discourse of maternity has been partly formulated in reaction to feminism's wish to liberate women from what the institution of motherhood has long since designated their biological destinies, *some* feminists have embraced precisely the same "science" in order to talk up, not down, women's anatomical distinctiveness and positive experiences of childbearing. And even a radical feminist like Rich sought to "convert" woman's physicality—her body, her fertility and, if she so chooses, her maternity—into new sources of specifically female "knowledge and power."[14]

For the influential French feminist historian Elisabeth Badinter, on the other hand, this suggests a reversion to that hoary old notion, *Mother Nature*, and thus amounts to "Feminism's U-Turn."[15] It's one she strongly objects to, hotly contesting, for example, the naturalist feminist's claim that, because of their experience of motherhood, caring is a special aptitude of women. For Badinter, feminism's engagement with motherhood should be less concerned with making a case for its female distinctiveness and more concerned with highlighting maternity's still adverse effects on women's status and identities, both with regard to their career advancement and salaries and with regard to the guilt, anxiety, and self-loathing to which modern mothers are said to be especially prone. It is this, says Badinter, that explains declining birth rates across most of Europe. For while there has never been a noisier lobby of mothers screaming the joys of self-sacrificial parenting from the electronic hilltops, in Badinter's view modern women—working women for the most part—simply don't feel up to doing all that is currently expected of them.

But French women, who are still having as many babies as they used to, appear to have bucked the trend. This, notes Badinter, is curious given that, in the eyes of the rest of Europe, French women (anti-breast-feeding, straight back to work, state subsidies to help them regain their former figures after childbirth) are widely considered to be the "worst" of all Europe's mothers. Badinter cites a long tradition in France wherein women—or rather, privileged women such as those who could once afford wet nurses—rather than being expected to give themselves over entirely to the care of their children once they became mothers, were instead expected to quickly reenter society, to remain sexually alluring for their husbands, and to keep themselves as free as possible from the demeaning duties of childcare. She contends that this French tradition, backed in more recent years by the state, means that, unlike other Europeans, French women have not been put off childbearing because they have not been made to bear their children any more than necessary. Indeed, French women, for Badinter, remain Europe's most modern and emancipated women, for not only are they self- (rather than biologically) determined, but they even appear to have evaded the traditional maternal legacy of weakness, compromise, and self-laceration.

Badinter's trenchant reaffirmation of the core principles of women's liberation is undeniably emboldening. Still, the notion of having been historically liberated from one's duties to one's children in order not to neglect one's duties to one's husband does give one (ahem) pause. As, too, does the thought of those women charged with looking after the wealthier women's offspring. Who, one wonders, is looking after *their* children? Such qualms and questions serve as a reminder that *any* struggle for liberation must take place within a socioeconomic context whose wider responsibility its champions must also come to bear. Though what perhaps threatens to more seriously undermine the philosophy of progress inscribed within Badinter's version of women's lib may be harder to unravel. For doesn't such emancipatory thinking run the risk of turning the traditional figure of the mother back into too much of a bête noire, and thus, implicitly, add succor to those who would ascribe some essential weakness, if not primitivism, to her mind, body, and character?

Bolstering the patriarchal mindset is of course far from the intent of Badinter's polemic. Yet that such a pattern of repetition can be discerned at work *within* liberation does allow us to glimpse what might nonetheless be construed as an inadvertent side effect of the whole *project* of modernity. After all, if being an emancipated modern means, in the first place, gaining autonomy by getting over one's past, then doesn't being modern also mean getting over one's mother as the one place on earth where we're all guaranteed to once have been?

The Jewish Mother

We can see these warring motifs of the traditional versus the modern mother intersecting within the figure of a woman who *could*, conceivably, appear to us as the representative mother figure *of* modernity: Jeanne Proust. For though she was, in many ways, the ideal modern woman who sought, by taking leave of her Jewishness, to assimilate to the bold secular citizenship of postemancipation France, Marcel Proust's mother found that both her Jewishness *and* her maternity seemed continually to pull her back, as if these two aspects of her identity threatened at all times to reclaim her and undermine her hard-won modernity with what one *could* (conceivably) call the incipient signs of her modernism.

For Marcel Proust, as for his near-contemporary Freud, the love between a mother and child bears its imprimatur on all loving relationships. Thus just as, in his masterwork, there are clear lines of resemblance between the adult's romantic entanglements and the child's earlier family ones, so, when Proust once wrote his own amorous letters to a young man with whom he had fallen hopelessly in love, the romantic vision he shared was of himself sitting on the boy's lap as if at the breast of his mother. Then, of course, there's the famous incident described in *À la recherche du temps perdu* concerning the significance of the mother's goodnight kiss. One evening that kiss is dismissed by the narrator's father as an unnecessary foolishness between mother and son, which, when guests are expected, should not be pandered to. The decision on the father's part leads his young son to wait up for as long as it takes for his parents to finish their meal in order to demand the kiss that's rightfully his—a small act of protest that significantly disturbs the order of the family. While his mother endeavors to strictly return her rebellious child to bed, his father tells her she may as well go and sleep in the same room as him. In so relenting, the father also draws a resemblance between mother and son—"I'm not as high-strung as the two of you."[16]

For the boy, on the other hand, though, in his moment of triumph, "I ought to have been happy: I was not. It seemed to me that my mother had just made me a first concession which must be painful to her, that this was a first abdication on her part before the ideal she had conceived for me, and that for the first time she, who was so courageous, was confessing herself defeated." Sensing that he has defeated his mother's efforts to love him in such a way as she would like to see him grow, develop, and become independent of her, he had, he believes, "traced in her soul a first wrinkle and caused a first white hair to appear," effectively killing her with his demand for love.[17]

Mme Proust saw her marriage as a modern one. The Proust family was the prototype of France's new secular bourgeoisie: Proust's father was the son of a Catholic grocer who had become a successful doctor and married a well-to-do Jewish woman from a family who thought her marrying outside the faith (not in a church, but in a civil ceremony) an excellent method of assimilation. One can note too that, in *À la recherche*, the mother (based on Proust's own) who withholds her goodnight kiss, preferring her husband and polite society to her child (whom she tells a maid to put to bed), is doing very well, in the terms laid out by Badinter, to meet the ideal of the modern Frenchwoman. Yet when, at the insistence of her son and exasperated husband, this necessary separation between mother and child breaks down, she ceases to be so ideal, becoming instead too much the mother and not enough the wife or lover.

In the father's grouping his high-strung son and wife against his own type, there seems too to be an intimation that their shared deficiency may be attributable to something else they have in common—their Jewishness. Though their Jewishness, such as it is, is hardly ever mentioned. For both Proust and his mother Jewishness was a source of ambivalence, if not outright shame. The shame was perhaps in not being quite modern enough, or not having altogether let go of that which evidently aroused at least as much affection as it did contempt, as became clear, for example, during the period of the Dreyfus Affair, the event that so profoundly rocked the foundations of modern France. In dividing the bourgeoisie from top to bottom, the Dreyfus Affair saw Jews become much less confident in their Frenchness, as suddenly, it seemed, they were aliens again, not to be trusted. And, indeed, even in his own home it was the case that, while Marcel and his mother instantly sided with Dreyfus, Proust's father sided against him.

So their shared Jewishness seemed to draw Proust and his mother together, particularly during fractious times. It's in this context that one might interpret, for instance, the anecdote about a heated argument that once took place between Proust and his parents that led to the shattering of a pane of household glass. In her response to a note Marcel had sent her, Jeanne suggests they think no more of it and look upon the shattering as akin to the breaking of the glass in a Jewish marriage ceremony—as a token of unity rather than dissolution. To reunite with her son Jeanne draws on not only an explicitly romantic image to reaffirm their unbreakable intimacy but a religious tradition meant to evoke traumatic events of loss and displacement as means of binding the community ever more closely together.[18] It's striking, therefore, that this characteristically diasporic narrative strategy—of remembering the past through the fragments of the present—is one we tend today to think of as distinctly modernist and, even *more* distinctly, Proustian (it's not for nothing that Jeanne's pet name for Marcel was "poor exile").[19]

But Jeanne added a postscript to her note of reconciliation, warning her son not to walk without shoes where the shards of glass still lay on the floor. The postscript, that epistolary afterthought, is perhaps the ideal space of writing for mothers looking to address their rebellious sons with all the necessary wiliness that such communications invariably involve. In Jeanne's case, for example, her postscript could not altogether conceal her ongoing resentment at the pain her son had caused her. Her recourse to the symbolism of shattered glass as both historical trauma and marital covenant seems especially apt, therefore, in that it tells not only of love despite all, but also of love as a state of ambivalence: as that which effectively splits the self traumatically with a sense of its own inassimilable strangeness.

It's this same notion of love as a state of ambivalence that we can find in many a Jewish mother joke—such as the joke about the Jewish mother discussing her son with two other mothers,

> MOTHER 1: My son loves me so much—he constantly buys me gifts.
>
> MOTHER 2: My son loves me so much—he always takes me on holiday.
>
> JEWISH MOTHER: That's nothing. My son loves me so much, he goes to see a special doctor five times a week and talks exclusively about me!

Though the joke seems, at first, to be on a mother who takes her son's obsession *with* her as proof of his love *for* her, isn't the joke really on those other two mothers whose sons are *not* inclined to show their love that way?

Certainly, Proust and his mother seem to have engaged in the obsessive kind of love. Yet the symbolic aptness of Jeanne's take on the shattered glass is not only that it alludes to the ambivalence underscoring their passionate relations with each *other*, but that it also alludes to the ambivalence that marked, for each of them, their sense of Jewishness. It's as if, for both Proust and his mother, their feeling toward their Jewishness and their feeling toward each other were somehow versions of the same feeling, both marking an inescapable tie not to be unraveled by the drumbeat of modernity, nor one that could guarantee them any other form of security.

How ironic, then, that while Jeanne Proust's bid to remodel herself for the brave new world saw her trying and failing to sufficiently separate from both her Jewishness and her motherliness, in the new world of America it was precisely these "old world" virtues that the Jewish mother was envisioned—at least at first—to provide: a sense of continuity, of self-assurance, of roots. Molly Goldberg, for instance, once a household name in the United States via the radio show *The Goldbergs* (1929–1940), was an image of the consummately loving ethnic mother and traditional homemaker. Yet Molly, who would for a while become a kind of national mother figure (not unlike her later incarnation, Oprah Winfrey), was also the product of a distorting nostalgia: for it wasn't in the shtetl that the Jewish mother was domesticated, but in America that she forfeited her role as "woman of business, entrepreneur, manager of the family and its fortunes."[20] As if the Jewish mother's *real* work in America was to pretend, even to herself, to have always and forever been loath to leave her home.

The sentimental figure of Molly Goldberg wasn't, however, to hang around for long. Soon her image was replaced by another stereotype of the (Jewish) mother.

Momism

The mother-cult dubbed "Momism" was to become a national debate in America in the 1940s. The term was originally coined by a male author, Philip Wylie, in a diatribe against American "moms" for their manipulative, overweening, overprotective, meddlesome, and emasculating ways. So the "supermom" was in the first place perceived as a threat to the American male—as well as to an American culture said to be on the slippery slope toward feminization.

But when the concept of "new Momism" arose again more than half a century later, it was the trope of a feminist polemic whose authors, Susan Douglas and Meredith Michaels, explicitly hoped to purify the concept of its misogyny, but whose complaints and vocabulary about the overinvolved mother sound at times nearly identical to Wylie's.[21] The irony that two such opposing agendas should share elements of the same language and, in part, the same critique (of a particular kind of mother figure) does not, of course, make them in any sense political bedfellows, even if their similarity does recall Rich's point that women, no less than men, have sought to resist and arrest the inescapable influence of their mothers. A better explanation, however, as to why Wylie, Douglas, and Michaels should sometimes sound so alike when complaining about the idealization of American mothers is that Momism may be less a gendered phenomenon than a quintessentially American one.

Consider, for instance, the observations of Eva Hoffman, whose memoir of her emigration to North America from Poland as a young woman details her initial fascination at the way "my American friends talk about their mothers":

The oppressive mother, or the distant mother, or the overloving mother, is an accepted conversation trope, like the weather or the stock market or the latest Mideast crisis. My American friends pay their mothers the indirect tribute of incessant and highly subtle scrutiny. They measure the exact weight the mother exercises upon their psyche, and they practice careful equilibriating acts between letting the mother too much in and keeping her too much out.

It's an obsession that baffles her Polish friends, who find the "fuss about something so . . . well, normal" faintly ridiculous: "A mother, for heaven's sake, is a mother" But such mom-talk, Hoffman soon realized, was because America is a land of immigrants, and thus Americans, in particular, "worry about who they are."[22] Momism, then, is the outcome of an insecure feeling commonly found among immigrant populations: the feeling that one's process of "naturalization" has never quite gone far enough.

Momism, in this sense, targets, if not always consciously, the immigrant mother—which is perhaps why the resemblance of the stereotypical Jewish mother to the mother figure inscribed within (old and new) Momist critiques should be so striking. As Joyce Antler summarizes: "Excessive, overprotective, neurotically anxious, and ever present, the Jewish mother became a scapegoat for ambivalent and hostile sentiments regarding assimilation in a new society, changing family dynamics, and shifting gender roles."[23] And certainly, while the sentimental image of the Jewish mother was no less distorting than the stereotype that replaced it, it's hard not to raise an eyebrow at how quickly a love once widely regarded as benevolent and nurturing was so soon to turn into a trope of the monstrous and perverse.

Some aspects of this cultural shift originated from serious sources. In their collaborative study of the American Jewish family, for example, the (protofeminist) anthropologists Ruth Benedict and Margaret Mead include the suggestion that Momism's "mother cult" should, in the case of the Jewish family, be refigured as a "mother plot."[24] So Jewish conspiracy begins at home! For what the Jewish mother is accused of plotting to do to her own family resembles the anti-Semitic theory about what Jews as a people are said to want to do *to the whole world:* render it weak, emasculated, dependent, and incapable of healthy development, both physically and spiritually. As such, the Jewish mother's love, though at first fondly (if falsely) enlisted for its ethnic old-worldliness, was soon enough to be reinterpreted as an atavistic form of aggressive primitivism whose primary aim was purportedly to hold back all progress.[25]

Amid such a broad cultural malaise, there may be little to wonder at in the rather sorry spectacle of Jews likewise seeking to pin their own guilt on their mothers. For not only does the question of one's personal identity always lead back to one's origins—one's mother—but Judaism is also a religion of matrilineal descent, hence mothers are not just biologically but religiously to blame for turning their children into Jews.[26] Thus though the new caricature of the Jewish mother that emerged was to be found in American culture at large, it appeared nowhere more vociferously than in the Jewish, male standup comedy routines of the forties, fifties, and sixties. The Jewish mothers' own sons were the ones to make world-famous the now familiar jokes about a mother so perverse that her love for her children is at once narcissistic and endangering: "Help! Help! My son (he's a doctor) is drowning!'"

The Monster of the Beginning Womb

To read Proust well, argues the critic Michael Wood, you need to deploy a little "readerly craziness" to allow yourself to follow the logic—or illogic—that marks the passionate relation between a son and his mother: a logic—or illogic—that may also be that of the modernist text.[27]

As I've said, certain features associated with literary modernism—instability, fragmentation, quasi-solipsism—may be traced back to the same source that animates Jewish self-hatred: the discovery by the child of assimilating parents that the father's authority is somehow lacking. The same phenomenon also admits of something else: the readmission of the mother's pre-Oedipal influence over the child's imagination before the father established his law as that which, by separating the mother from the child, is meant to draw a firm line between fantasy and reality. If the "fantasy" is the infant's romantic belief that nothing exists outside of his ideal union with his mother, the "reality" is the intervention of the father with news of the world. So the "father" in this rendering of the Oedipal drama, because tasked with moderating the power and influence the "mother" has over her child, occupies the very role that the Jewish experience of modernity saw fraying at the edges and falling apart.

This was perhaps especially true in America, where immigrant Jewish men often saw the waning of their status both inside and outside the home, as one finds in the literature that experience brought forth. In Henry Roth's Depression-era novel *Call It Sleep* (1934), for example, which offers an affecting portrait of a poor, first-generation immigrant family, the mother Genya and her young son David hold on to each other with a passion exceeding any romance. Irving Howe considered the novel the perfect illustration of how and why the Oedipal story should be such an archetypally diasporic one, because of the way in which the migrant family is forever thrown back on itself: thus the child clings desperately to his mother even though this is forbidden by a father whose authority over his wife and child is ruthlessly exploited as the only power left to him. It makes sense that *Call It Sleep* should also be an intensely modernist work: a work in which we can see the same strain on the text that the modern assimilating family was itself undergoing. Indeed, in the generation after Henry Roth, in the literature of the fifties and sixties featuring second and third generations of immigrant Jews, while the mother still remains a central presence, the father either seems to have disappeared from the scene altogether or has no capacity to assert himself even when he's there.

In "Kaddish," for example, Allen Ginsberg's poem of mourning for his mother, Naomi, what should be taboo for the adult son—his mother's sex—is laid bare. Naomi was a paranoiac whose strong medications not only induced hallucinations but caused her body to gain weight and lose control of its regulatory functions. What we have to confront in the poem is a mother's body completely deprived of privacy, its orifices overflowing, and, worse still, a son bearing witness to this mental and physical breakdown,

> One time I thought she was trying to make me come lay her—
> flirting to herself at sink—lay back on huge bed that filled most
>   of the room,
> dress up round her hips, big slash of hair, scars of operations,
>   pancreas, belly
> wounds, abortions, appendix, stitching, of incisions pulling
>   down in the fat
> like hideous thick zippers—ragged long lips between her
>   legs—What,
> even, smell of asshole? I was cold, later revolted a little, not
>   much—
> seemed perhaps a good idea to try—know the Monster of the
>   Beginning
> Womb—Perhaps—that way. Would she care? She needs a
>   lover.[28]

So if the American question par excellence is the question of the mother—what is a mother or what ought a mother to be?—here we have, in a scene rendered all the more scandalous for its casual contemplation of whether or not a son should knowingly commit the ultimate transgression of incest, a curiosity as to whether such a question might be answered "that way": "seemed perhaps a good idea to try—know the Monster of the Beginning Womb."

Roth's Mothers

And then (again) there's Philip Roth.

In an epigraph at the beginning of his notorious 1969 novel *Portnoy's Complaint*, we read a shrink's definition of what the title means: a psychological condition pertaining to guilt and shame feelings about sexual longings, perversions, and dissatisfactions whose "symptoms can be traced to the bonds obtaining in the mother-child relationship." Distinct shades, then, of a barely sublimated Oedipus, after which definition we move on to encounter a specific mother through the eyes of a specific "child": Sophie Portnoy as portrayed by her son Alex.

Sophie Portnoy is, for Alex, "The most unforgettable character I've met."[29] And it's hard not to agree with him. Sophie may well be the most unforgettable mother character *any* reader of literature has met. For who can forget her obsessive knocking on the bathroom door of her adolescent son and demanding to see the contents of the toilet bowl, or her teasing him about "*your* little thing?" (51), or her forcing him to eat her food as she sits nearby holding a bread knife castratingly close? Though she differs in many ways from Naomi Ginsberg, Sophie Portnoy is no less the monster of the beginning womb.

Drawing on extant stereotypes, what Roth's novel imagines is an *adult* son lying on a couch and complaining to his shrink about the effects on his psyche of his middle-class Jewish family—his overweening mother and her overexposed breasts, his correspondingly weak and anally retentive father with his invisible penis—in a hysterical monologue that ingeniously blurs such free associations with that equally taboo-breaking genre, standup comedy. In so doing, Roth, more than anyone, can reasonably be credited with having transformed the stereotype of the perverse Jewish mother into not only a familiar punchline, but something of a global brand: "I am the son in the Jewish joke—*only it ain't no joke!*" (36–37).

For many female readers, however, Roth's caricature wasn't terribly funny. His mocking portrayal of Sophie, they cautioned, stood to damage the reputations of *real* Jewish mothers whose hard work had paved the way for their sons to get on in the world. Certainly Roth himself was quick to deny that his own mother, Bess, was anything like his comic creation. Bess, though, never drew such a firm line between them. In fact it was *her* brilliance: when responding to a journalist asking to what extent she was a Jewish mother like Sophie—"all mothers," she replied, "are Jewish mothers"—she proved, with a semiserious quip of her own, to be the most incisive critic both of the book itself and of the stereotype it made so unforgettable.[30] For, all told, the lasting popularity of *Portnoy's Complaint* suggests a relatability far exceeding a narrowly ethnic point of reference. What Portnoy is really complaining about in the end is a mother "so deeply embedded in my consciousness" that there may be no way of ever escaping her.

Hence, while you feel yourself reaching, almost irresistibly, for the Jewish-mother-joke-in-the-making that saw Roth's own mother take such pride in her novelist son's exaggeration of a stereotype designed to disparage her kind, it would be wrong, I think, to jest away the real insight that Bess's defense offers. And it would be equally wrong to ignore Roth's own claim that his book, however comic, presents a serious investigation into the affections binding mother and child. What Alex complains of, after all, isn't exactly a dearth of mother love. If anything, he frets that his family may have ethnically *over*dosed him in the care stakes. Thus the book's excesses, Roth explains, should not in themselves be considered excessive, but rhetorically justified by the overriding pretext of a patient on the couch: "In psychoanalysis nothing is too petty, nothing is too grand. The place where you're allowed to say anything. Allows for hatred, aggression, pettiness; *nothing censored.* If that's the bargain, that's the bargain. Coarse realism. Any type of exaggeration is permissible. *It* takes the liberties for you."[31] To *really* read what's going on between Alex and Sophie Portnoy, in other words, one needs the sort of readerly craziness that's also demanded of readers of Proust. Indeed, *Portnoy's Complaint* ends with Alex's,

Aaaaaaaaaaaaaaaaaaaaaaaaaaaaaaaaaaaaaaaaaaaaaaaaaaaaaaaaaa
aaaaaaaaaaaaaaaaaaaaaaaaaaaaaaaaaaaaaaaaaaaaaaaaaaaaaaaaaa
aaaaaaaaaaaaaaaaaaaaaaaaaaaaaaaaaaaaaaaaaaaaaaaaaaaaaaaaaa
aaaaaaaaaaaaaaaaaaaaaaaaaaaaaaaaaaaaaaaaaaaaaaaaaaaaaaaaaa
aaaaaaaaaaaaaaaaaaaaaaaaaaaaaaaaaaaaaaaaaaaaaaaaaaaaaaaaaa
aaaaaaaaaaaaaaaaaaaaaaaaaaaaaaaaaaaaaaaaaaaaaaaaaaaaaaaaaa
aaaaaaaaaaaaaaaaaaaaaaaaaaaaaaaaaaaaahhhh!!!!!

And a "Punchline," the first spoken words from his shrink, "Now vee may perhaps to begin. Yes?" (274). The Yiddish inflection of the shrink's words encompasses the joke of the entire novel: the sense that, try as one might, there is no escaping one's background—and in the background is one's ethnicity, and also, of course, one's mother.[32] So while the extreme suffering and desiring of which we hear in the breathless monologue of the adult Portnoy may be an effort to find a language that might fix or settle the relation to the mother and the feelings and behaviors that "the mother-child relationship" invariably arouses, the final word of his monologue, which is not a word at all but a cry of pain—a primal scream—seems to attest to the doomed nature of any such attempt at self-knowledge: for to know oneself is to know one's mother, or who one is in relation to her, and yet no such knowledge, no such language, and no such fixity exists.

Keeping Mum

None of us can "know the Monster of the Beginning Womb." What *can* be assumed, however, is that before we took shape in the "Beginning Womb," someone else's body (or a prosthesis thereof) must have been there first. Someone else has already penetrated the body of our mother. Yet for all its obviousness, the idea that maternity and sexuality coexist within the same body has somehow never ceased to scandalize in a culture that has sought to separate these two things—the Madonna, the Whore. And *even* Freud, it seems, faced with a core culture whose worshipful imagery is that of a Virgin Mother in blissful unity with her divine offspring, couldn't quite evade the problem. Thus while he was perhaps the first to rigorously theorize how a mother caring for her infant "regards him with feelings that are derived from her own sexual life: she strokes him, kisses him, rocks him and quite clearly treats him as a substitute for a complete sexual object," Freud was also a purveyor of the sentimental idea of the mother's unity with a child who was supposed to fulfil all her desires.[33] It's as if, for Freud, there was something taboo about the figure of the mother, for by envisaging the mother and child together as a completed picture, the father of psychoanalysis effectively sidestepped the issue of female perversity to make sexual perversion a matter for men alone.[34]

For psychoanalyst Estela Welldon, on the other hand, female sexual perversions are *primarily* the perversions of motherhood. While male perversion is generally aimed "at an external object, in women it is against themselves: either against their bodies or against objects of their own creation—that is, their babies."[35] By taking out her own frustrations and privations *on* her baby, the perverse mother, rather than being a source of comfort and security, becomes a source of danger and uncertainty for a child who must nonetheless depend on her for its own survival. This perversion is further compounded by the mother's cultural idealization as the fount of all goodness, for it is the very celebration of her role that deprives her not only of outside support structures but of any other outlet for venting her feelings of loss or inadequacy other than on to the child whose care she is charged with. So it's the fact that the child is the one person whom she has real power over that makes the child the inevitable object of her perverse and (psychologically or physically) abusive behaviours.[36]

But if it's relatively uncommon to ascribe, as Welldon does, a sexual motive to maternal transgression, there's certainly no shortage of psychoanalytic *and* nonpsychoanalytic case studies describing the effects on the psyche of a developing child when mothering goes wrong. A broad consensus agrees that when a person isn't quite right, it's probably the mother's fault. This, inevitably, is too much for the mother—a too much that can drive her hysterical as she strives to meet every demand and expectation made of her. Yet while considering the mother responsible for everything is self-evidently to make her life impossible, negating her humanity entirely, it's insufficient to simply reject as unjust the overestimation of her role. That we're all "of woman born" means it's as difficult to defend as it is illegitimate simply to attack the mother when her experiences and our experiences *of* her remain so archaic, unfathomable, indescribable, and shrouded in a kind of darkness or mystery that makes the mother in some senses more or less interchangeable with the notion of the unconscious itself.

Indeed *that*, for psychoanalytic thinker Jean Laplanche, is precisely who the mother turns out to be. For while, in countless postwar writings, the figure of the "Other" has generally alluded to an outsider who arrives from elsewhere to provoke our hatred and paranoia as well as fascination and desire, Laplanche believes that our sense of the Other begins in early infancy and alludes to someone much more intimate and familiar, namely the "adult" who is likely also to be the parent. His primary example of this is the mysterious interaction that takes place for the baby nursing at a breast which is also enigmatically addressing the child. The breast, in this scenario, though ostensibly responding to the child's needs, also has secret wishes of its own. Its "message" is consequently "enigmatic" insofar as the child cannot understand it, nor can the adult know what message she's transmitting. It's a "message unknown to itself, coming from the other and implanted by the other," which gets passed on unconsciously and uninterruptedly down the generations.[37]

While the name of the father can confer a public and social identity on the child, the mother's unmarried name, Darian Leader ingeniously points out, is the archetypal password: the answer to the question that major institutions regularly invoke when wanting to authenticate a subject's true identity, "as if the most secret thing in life is still her."[38] But do we really all secretly identify with our mothers? Winnicott imagines so. Done well, he suggests, mothering is intended to loosen the ties binding the baby to the mother by helping the baby separate and become an autonomous although never entirely independent subject, a developmental process that involves the baby learning from her "ordinary devoted mother" how to be a person, or rather, how to be an ordinary devoted mother. Thus Winnicott puts the mother and her love at the root of *all* persons: not only in that she is, quite literally, their place of origin, but because her love shows the child a model of how to move from being cared for to being capable of caring for itself.[39] So what, then, must she do to achieve this spectacular result?

Survivors

The good-enough mother "has one job when the baby bites and scratches and pulls her hair and kicks, and that is to survive":

The baby will do the rest. If she survives, then the baby will find a new meaning to the word love, and a new thing turns up in the baby's life which is fantasy. It is as if the baby can now say to the mother: "I love you because you have survived my destruction of you. In my *dreams* and in *my fantasy* I destroy you whenever I think of you because I love you." It is this that objectifies the mother, puts her in a world that is not part of the baby, and makes her useful.[40]

The loving mother, in other words—or the mother who shows her child *how* to love—is someone who can allow space for her infant's dreams and fantasies, however perverse, violent, or destructive these might be. She achieves this by herself surviving her baby's bouts of aggression, "not only as a live person, but also as a person who did not change at the critical moment into a vindictive person and did not retaliate."[41] So it's the mother's survival of the baby that ensures the baby's own survival in the long as well as short term.

Winnicott's vision of motherhood as the ability to adapt and survive throughout ever-shifting circumstances has much in common with how we typically describe the historical experiences of immigrating and diasporic peoples. The Jewish mother, for example, as Rich portrays her, "is a survivor-woman, a fighter with tooth and claw and her own nervous system, who, like her Black sisters, has borne the weight of a people on her back."[42] And in Lisa Appignanesi's tribute to her mother, Hena Borenstein, in her remarkable memoir *Losing the Dead*, we can find just such a tale of female heroism, albeit one that also admits of the costs that heroism of any kind involves.

Appignanesi's search for her mother's lost memories in the wake of her subsequent dementia tells the story of her parents' survival in Poland during the Holocaust by means of her mother's fearless passing as a blonde and blowsy Gentile woman while her husband, dark and Semitic-looking, masqueraded less willingly with little bravura and more fear. Her mother's passing as a non-Jew was bound to her ability to seduce and impress using feminine wiles. Like a latter-day Scarlett O'Hara, she "could count on her beauty, her femininity, to achieve her ends"—a manner of remaining perpetually in flux at once quintessentially feminine and quintessentially diasporic in its lack of fixity and facility for moving seamlessly between different states. Yet this was a strategy that, once learned, could not so easily be laid down. Even in Canada, where the family moved after the war, Hena never lost the art of shaping reality differently according to the different people she met. So constant were her fabulations, in fact, that her children were compelled to tirelessly remember her lies in order not to betray her: "Well into my teens, I remember going into a kind of shivering panic when asked my name, but especially when I was asked my place of birth. The question paralysed me. . . . Even when I told what I supposed was the truth, I had a shuddering sense that I was probably lying."[43]

The question of identity that was to become so critical in the modern period was the question of how to account for oneself: who are you? where do you come from? which group do you belong to? what do you stand for? Such a question is invariably tied to the notion of origins, and thus of one's mother, knowledge of whom, as we've seen, is never for granted. In the case of Appignanesi's search for her mother's past, which was partly undertaken in order to better understand her own, she recalls how her mother's survival story and strategies made this difficulty of knowing who one is so acutely tortuous that she couldn't quite believe her own truth. Paradoxically, however, that shuddering sense of "probably lying" even when she believed herself to be speaking honestly carries within it what, all told, may well *be* the truth about human identity: that, as the children of those stranger-survivors we call our mothers, none of us really knows where it is we come from or who it is we are.

She Could Change

In some of the best Jewish women's writing, therefore, we find that the perennial demand on both modern Jews and modern mothers to offer positive accounts of themselves or their own identities is rejected as precisely the wrong kind of question because it leads to the wrong kind of answer. It was with this in mind that American authors such as Tillie Olsen and Grace Paley, for example, were to take the lead in challenging the negative stereotyping that had started to cling to predominantly male-written representations of mothers and Jewish mothers by reinterpreting the very character-istics that were being popularly ridiculed as virtues rather than vices. Their battle, they recognized, was to be an uphill one. In the 1970s, in an essay entitled simply "Mom," Paley even wondered whether the Jewish daughter would ever be able to recover the image of the loving Jewish mother from the cruel lampooning of "her son the doctor and her son the novelist?"[44]

In Paley's short stories, largely populated by lower-class, immigrant single mothers facing a range of challenges, motherhood is, despite its sufferings, a source of strength and positivity for women—a means of overcoming isolation and forging communal bonds between disparate groups. Knowing how little women's lives had been historically imbued with public or political importance, it was not just the unusual content of Paley's stories (housework, childrearing, PTA meetings) but their style and form (digressive-ness, brevity) to which she gave political and social significance. Paley did not, for example, publish a great deal or in long form because, she said, children are interruptive and caring for children is a full-time job. (Tillie Olsen said the same of her own limited output.) Likewise, the way in which her narratives quickly shift mood, meaning, and direction speaks to the experience of her protagonists.

In Paley's short story "A Conversation with My Father," for instance, the daughter is defending to her father a story *she* has written about a mother who decides to support her son, a junkie, by becoming a junkie herself. To her father's insistence that she has written a tragedy, the daughter protests: "It doesn't have to be. She's only about forty. She could be a hundred different things in this world as time goes on. A teacher or a social worker. An ex-junkie!" Her father is not having it: "You don't want to recognise it. Tragedy! Plain tragedy! Historical tragedy! No hope. The end." But his daughter thinks differently, "'Oh, Pa,' I said, 'She could change.'"[45]

A good mother? A bad mother? In Paley's world such configurations seem beside the point as we confront modern mothers—urban mothers, single mothers, multicultural mothers—whose paths have not been determined for them or before them. The mother described in "A Conversation with My Father" is tested in her motherhood, and she certainly makes some unorthodox decisions, but she is also a mother who does not assume that a mother is a fixed entity, any more than does her narrator and any more than does Paley, whose radical and political re-visioning sees the modern mother and the experimental, adaptive modalities of her love as both the principle and the agent of social and political change.

Crazy Feelings

When his mother died, Proust, beside himself, could not quite escape the fear that, by causing her so much anxiety, he might have in some way been her murderer as well her mourner. So perhaps he was seeking to reassure himself when he replied to Barrès, a family friend who had written after his mother's death to assure Marcel that he was always his mother's favorite. Were this really the case,

Proust replied, she would have lived on longer for his sake, whereas it was because of the death of his father that she could not manage to survive.

So why did Proust choose to share his grief-ridden fantasies and magical thinking about his mother's death with Barrès? Barrès was a close family friend, but he was also a well-known anti-Dreyfusard. It "seems strange that Proust should say so much about his feelings for his Jewish mother to this anti-semite," comments Michael Wood, who also suspects—"although I am far from having worked the thought out properly—that Barrès's repellent politics make him the right sort of confessor." I think so too. And one possible explanation may be that Proust tells Barrès that his mother preferred her husband to her son in order to prove that she was not an untrustworthy alien but a properly French woman: a wife rather than a (Jewish) mother. Another explanation, however, more in keeping with the spirit of Wood's speculation, is that, since no one can ever really be the proper addressee for the extent and extremity of the grief that attends the loss of one's mother, perhaps the best one can hope for is to find an addressee with equally crazed feelings about her—even if those feelings are feelings of hatred, which, as Proust's own intense reflections on a passionate affection that might also have been murderous seem to show, is not so far off the craziness of love.

So if our love lives are, as the songs all say, not only passion and pleasure but also suffering and sickness, then it's the love between mother and child that seems to first arouse in us such violent, extreme, and even hateful feelings toward those we cherish most. Hence, just as one needs a little "readerly craziness" to understand the Proust whose text says so much of that formative relation, the same, as we've noted, is true for the Roth whose fictional entry into the mother-child relationship required a free form in which taboos could be broken and any type of exaggeration would be possible.

Roth chose the free associations of psychoanalysis to explore that rocky terrain. Psychoanalysis, Stephen Frosh agrees, "seems the obvious discipline to look to for an exploration of the 'excess,' the ambivalent kind of 'enjoyment' that seems to invest so much urgency and passion in the figure of the other. This is because psychoanalysis deals specifically with the excessive, with what it desires *over and above what is possible*, that is, with what is unconscious, wished for but usually too dangerous to give expression to."[46]

Reflecting, analogously, on the urgency and passion of the hatred we call anti-Semitism, Frosh suggests that the figure of the Jew must stand within the Western unconscious in much the same way as the mother does within Laplanche's configuration of otherness. In scapegoating the Jew, in other words, one is similarly scapegoating the ineradicable and inaccessible generator of oneself. It's an "extreme formulation," he concedes, but he maintains that such a formulation is required to meet and understand "an extreme phenomenon: the recurrent, never-ending, barely even cyclical reiteration of anti-Semitic ideology and practices."[47] Judaism, after all, is both the Other *and* the Mother of a global Christian culture. As such, Jews have historically been, *like* our mothers, not only scapegoated for being unknowable and in doubt, but blamed for being the source of *everyone's* unknowability and *everyone's* doubts in a world where no identity holds up amid the continuous separations.

SEVEN

Affected

To be in one's skin is an extreme way of being exposed.
—EMMANUEL LEVINAS, *Otherwise Than Being, or, Beyond Essence*

As we've seen, in modern times Jews have often been represented as over-the-top personalities—just like everyone else, only more so. Sartre's word for that style of affectation, and for what he considered to be the coerced condition of postemancipation Jews generally, was "inauthenticity"—as if Jews are precisely the kind of modern people to draw attention to their own performances, revealing just how much of life is indebted to a type of art: the art of acting.

What type of art is acting? To reflect properly on the figure of the actor one needs to look not only at the words of the script but at the *body* of the performer. Feelings are not abstract spiritual states: our bodies are alive to them. As such, they move us, and the "us" they move is an embodied one. As our body moves through space and time, it shows itself to be a body that can act. Yet willed action is seldom reducible to a simple cause. Whether or not we've been able to act, or act as we might have wanted to, involves a complex interplay between feeling and expression. And the extent to which we have or haven't been able to *share* our feelings can lead us to feel and thus act very differently.

Every Body

We do not simply "have feelings," Elaine Scarry points out, "but have feelings *for* somebody or something" . . . we love *x*, fear *y*, lust after *z*, and so on. It's because feelings always have an object that they can affirm "the human being's capacity to move out beyond the boundaries of his or her own body into the external, sharable world."[1]

If feelings lay the foundations of a sharable world, then to resist one's feelings—no matter what these feelings might be—is to render the world a colder, less welcoming place. A crucial insight. However, it's not merely that our feelings can be mobilized to *make* the world sharable; our feelings always already *are* shared. Feelings give us away. They attest to our lack of unity and wholeness by telling of a self that can exist only in *relation* to others. This too implies a relation between feeling and expression: insofar as we're capable of perceiving and bringing our feelings to consciousness, we must be dependent on a language learned elsewhere (from family, friends, institutions, states, nations . . .). As such, our feelings can never be fully determined because, as with our words, no one has sole authority or mastery over them. Rather, by continually changing, reverting, rebounding, disappearing, and resurfacing, our feelings, however palpable, require some effort of interpretation, rendering their origin, their meaning, their status, and even their privacy a source of negotiation, uncertainty, doubt.

There is, though, an exception to this rule. Physical pain alone "is not *of* or *for* anything" (5). And since it has no external object, the feeling of physical pain is neither shared nor sharable, opening up the largest possible divide between the one who is and the one who isn't in pain: "To have pain is to have *certainty*; to hear about pain is to have *doubt*" (13).

One consequence of our doubt about the pain of others is that it can make us insensitive, negligent, and cruel. But by the same token, where there's doubt there's also an opening for the imagination. Indeed, the very lack of an object for physical pain to move toward can give *rise* to the imagination, as the one in pain is forced to seek rhetorical forms of expression, such as simile and metaphor, associated with poetry: "It feels *as if* there's a nail sticking into the bottom of my foot." The nail is not identical to the felt experience of the pain, but the actual existence of a nail as a recognizable object in the world allows its image "to externalize, objectify, and make sharable what is originally an interior and unsharable experience" (16). Hence the one in pain achieves some minimal communication of what it is she's going through by finding a sensible correlative in the world of objects and ideas for an altogether different experience.

But how is the imagination working here? Not, I think, by words and images alone. Isn't the appeal being made, rather, *via* language and the imagination, to the *body* of the other? The passage from muteness to meaning can be successful only insofar as it has been able to tap into the sense memory—the memory of physical suffering stored somewhere within the body—of the one listening. To say it "feels as if," then, entails a kind of *theatricalization* of one's pain not so unlike Russian theater director Konstantin Stanislavsky's "magic if"—his formula for actors on stage to practice their craft with an empathic engagement he believed could bring to the theater not so much mime or artifice as an alternative way "in" to the emotional truth of a situation.

So to respond sensitively to physical pain is also to respond creatively. Indeed, what for Scarry "is quite literally at stake in the body in pain is the making and unmaking of the world" (23). The fact that there are chairs, for example, is the sign of an imaginatively adaptive world that has responded to the physical pain afflicting bodies with nowhere comfortable to sit. What unmakes the world, on the other hand, is leaving the body to its own pain—or even adding to its pain by pulling out the seat from under it.

Stupidity

For Scarry the clearest example of unmaking the world is torture. Torture has the exact structure of "stupidity": "a descriptive term for the 'nonsentience' or 'the lack of sentient awareness,' or most precisely, the 'inability to sense the sentience of other persons' that is incontestably present in the act of hurting another person" (294). Stupidity, in other words, as the failure to take others into account.[2] It's all the more extraordinary, then, that torture has so often managed to present itself as a reasonable means of *intelligence* gathering.

Torture can gather no real intelligence from or about the subject it sets about to physically obliterate. By inflicting on the body a pain unfelt and unresponded to by an insentient and hostile world, the torturer returns the body to a state of muteness out of which whatever gets "confessed" is no more than a waste product of the torture itself: the subject will almost certainly say anything to make the thrashing stop. The "confession" that the torturer ostensibly seeks to elicit by violently tearing the truth from its concealment within the body is thus, above all, a confession of "the fact that intense pain is world-destroying," for the consciousness of a tortured body is not only fractured but lies in smithereens (29).

It's the idiom of "betrayal" that helps to justify what is presumed to have been exposed by the tortured subject's confession. Torture is supposed to separate the body from the voice so that the latter may be forced to betray itself and yield up the truth: "The 'it' in 'Get it out of him' refers not just to a piece of information but to the capacity for speech itself. The written or tape-recorded confession that can be carried away on a piece of paper or on a tape is only the most concrete exhibition of the torturer's attempt to induce sounds so that they can then be broken off from their speaker so that they can then be taken off and made the property of the regime" (49). The words confessed to the torturer are framed as a truth obtained by means of a language tamed—though this language has been tamed only after the body has been tamed, for these are words deemed credible precisely on account of their having been wrenched out from the flesh.

"The body," writes Levinas, "is neither an obstacle opposed to the soul, nor the tomb which imprisons it, but that by which the self is susceptibility. The extreme passivity of 'incarnation'—being exposed to illness, suffering, to death, is to be exposed to compassion."[3] Compassion, in other words, requires this recognition that our bodies are endlessly affected by their contact with others, whether they're stroked, kissed, or caressed, bruised, brutalized, or hurt, stimulated or irritated. And even if one shuns all intimacy with others, there is nothing one can do, no actions one can take, to save one's body from its exposure to the elements or its involvement in the world beyond its literally porous borders—nor, indeed, can the body escape its own aging process, that special case of encountering otherness we call time itself.

From the perspective of a power regime, however, it's precisely because bodies are so susceptible to time and change that they are not to be trusted with the truth. As the conceit would have it, the body must be defeated so that the immutable word of the confession can be carried safely away. But if our bodies are so exposed, mightn't it be the case that a similar susceptibility marks our words? For though it may be the fantasy of the torturer to be able to separate the fallible body from the voice—which must be seen to have been prized away without injury *from* the injured body—what the torturer has actually gotten out of the tortured body is only "it"—and "it" is not the voice, it's something else: a neutered, disincarnated, and wholly informational word whose meaning it is to fly in the face of all meaning. To wit, the torturer's stupidity entails insentience toward not only bodies and their affects, but toward words and *their* affects.[4]

Affecting Words

One reason why it's "good to share" is that the failure to communicate feelings that *can* be shared, no matter how distressing this sharing may be, is to draw one's feelings down toward the world-destroying and language-destroying muteness that characterizes physical pain, where they can become a kind of torture.

Needless then, I hope, to say, the compelled confession yielded up to the torturer (or any other "authority" figure) is *not* the type of sharing here being proposed. Rather, the sharing I have in mind suggests a process of *admitting* something to another, even if (*especially* if) that other is oneself. And it's by recognizing the split nature of the subject that such sharing becomes possible. Earlier, for example, we looked at envy as the grievance of the one who feels herself excluded. Her envy is precisely an envy of the ability to share. Hence, as we saw, envy's retaliatory splitting of the subject—an act of aggression that can work, alchemically, to *extend* the space of the shareable. Sharing, in such instances, signifies not only the invitation to participate but the ability to speak a common language, a language in which one can express one's feelings in such a way as to make oneself feel recognized and understood. Without this facility all that is left is violence, whether the violence of self-destruction or the other-directed destruction of a world felt to be permanently at war.

In her memoir of her own period of linguistic dispossession, Eva Hoffman recounts such incendiary incidents:

In my New York apartment, I listen almost nightly to fights that erupt like bushfire on the street below—and in the escalating fury of repetitive phrases ("Don't do this to me, man, you fucking bastard, I'll fucking kill you"), I hear not the pleasures of macho toughness but an infuriated beating against wordlessness, against the incapacity to make oneself understood, seen. Anger can be borne—it can even be satisfying—if it can gather into words and explode in a storm, or a rapier-sharp attack. But without this means of ventilation, it only turns back inward, building and swirling like a head of steam—building to an impotent, murderous rage.[5]

But this impotent, murderous rage can build in not only those whose lives have left them bereft of a vocabulary with which to express or identify themselves but in those without a sensitivity to language such that they cannot seem to experience how language might be made to work for them. More precisely, they cannot sense how words create worlds. What, then, explains the person who hasn't been deprived of a language—indeed, whose vocabulary may even be an impressive and intelligent one—but whose language has nonetheless left him feeling un-spoken for?

In a wide-ranging discussion of early language acquisition, Darian Leader brings together a number of theories pertaining to "crib speech"—the babbling to be heard from babies and infants in their cots at night. Bedtime is that liminal moment on the lip of sleep and consciousness when babies will often practice what they've learned by repeating the fragments of the sounds and words they've encountered during the day. The form of speech that gets most readily internalized and repeated by babies is the imperative—(you) do this, (you) don't do that, and so on. Yet when recited in their cots at night, these imperatives are frequently sounded out as declaratives—(I) do this! (I) don't do that!—as if the word of the Other were being internalized by the baby as its own word *and* its own mastery of words. So it's a repetition, but a repetition with a difference. From the very beginning, the monologue of the baby is fractured, divided between its own subject and another by whom it has been addressed. The baby's monologue is already a kind of dialogue.

Equally fascinating is the form of speech babies hear all day long but tend *not* to imitate: the questioning or interrogative form that makes up most of what mothers will say to their prelinguistic children: Are you hungry? cold? hot? This pattern of nonimitation indicates that the baby is detecting in the voice of the mother something other than the demand to simply parrot and repeat—"Even if they cannot reply with words, infants are being given the *possibility of responding*"—which developmental possibility Leader contrasts to those situations "where the caregiver will not ask any question to a child, but, on the contrary, will *tell* the child that they are hot, cold, hungry or thirsty. The parent knows everything here, and may try to make the child believe that they have no separate subjectivity. This leaves no place for the self to emerge. The infant is simply an object for the Other."[6] In treating the infant as an object, doesn't the "caregiver" come close to the torturer? The torturer, that is, who likewise doesn't regard the voice to emerge from language as being in any way dialogical.

So there's a world of difference between the mother's interrogations of her babbling baby—the form taken by a questioning that works to create a space in which the baby's own voice can be expected to eventually emerge—and the interrogative form of the torturer whose world-destroying and language-destroying methods return the interrogated subject to a powerless infancy. A person's early language acquisition might consequently be envisaged to inform on how that person will go on, in later life, to experience "the question" (being questioned, being *in* question, questioning), whether as an opening for self-development and self-exploration *or* as a tortuous violation of her personhood—the verbal equivalent of grievous bodily harm.

It's likely for similar reasons that, for a great many psychoanalytic patients, the psychoanalytic process is so often felt to be a kind of "torture," whose questions are viewed less as openings than as sadistic interrogations. For these patients the analyst is akin to their first deficient caregiver: someone presumed to already know everything there is to know. Yet by inviting free association as a "talking cure," psychoanalysis may be said to re-create for the patient conditions resembling the babbling moment of crib speech—a speech that was perhaps inadequately or inappropriately responded to in the subject's own infancy, but for which the psychoanalyst, it is to be hoped, has the necessary ear so that the act of listening and responding can help to regain for the subject the possibility of a "dialogical" place within the world of words. For an adult subject especially, the delayed process of breaking through from her monologue into properly dialogical language is liable to be a particularly drawn out, frustrating, and painful one. As a descriptive term, "torture" conveys just how viscerally words can often be experienced in such situations. It's a word that historian and memoirist Barbara Taylor uses, for example, to describe how she felt for many years about the psychoanalysis that she claims ultimately saved her life. "He never touched me physically," she recollects of her psychoanalyst, "not even a hand-shake. But his words tore into me, so that I would sometimes jerk on impact."[7]

Performing Bodies

Since its earliest days, psychoanalysis has been as interested in reading and interpreting the language of the body as of the spoken word. This was the "psychosomatic" or "somatically compliant" body whose pains and symptoms, it was believed, could be relieved by awakening and expressing the repressed feelings thought to be causing them. For Freud and Breuer this was especially true of the body of the hysteric: "We found, to our great surprise at first, that *each individual hysterical symptom immediately and permanently disappeared when we had succeeded in bringing clearly to light the memory of the event by which it was provoked and in arousing its accompanying affect, and when the patient had described that event in the greatest possible detail and had put the affect into words."*[8]

As we've seen, the hysteric has mostly been represented as someone who feels what she feels *too much.* Her feelings aren't fine, they're over the top. And as we've seen too, in modern times Jews have been represented in similar ways—as showy, as performative, as exhibitionist. Cohen of Trinity, the narrator of Amy Levy's short story tells us, is offputtingly "melodramatic, self-conscious." He overshares. He explains himself too much. A "most unattractive lack of simplicity marked his whole personality." Thus he arouses at least as much suspicion as he does fascination, much as the hysteric can never quite be trusted, not only because her feelings render her volatile, but because they make her seem histrionic— theatrical. Hysterical performances raise questions . . . is (s)he for *real?*

Winnicott's oft-cited notion of the "false self" characterizes the human subject that might be expected to develop from a situation of not-good-enough mothering: a situation wherein the mother has turned her child into an object and thus failed to respond to her child's "spontaneous gesture"—the gesture, that is, of a zesty kid beginning to turn an outward face to the world. When the infant gets ignored or rebuffed because its spontaneous gestures haven't been responded to, interpreted, or in any sense "met," an excessively "compliant" self will develop in its place: a self lacking in spontaneity or a sense of its own (bodily) desires or needs—am I hungry? cold? hot?—but all too adept at reading the codes of what is wanted and expected of it as a sort of survival strategy or way of coping in a seemingly insentient world.

The insentience of the world for the child who has been subject to inadequate or unresponsive care resembles in certain ways the insentient world of the immigrant or outsider. Levy's Cohen could serve as a case in point. A constant comedian forever coveting an audience to perform in front of and a round of applause to cheer him on, without these assurances, it would seem, he ceases to exist at all. Cohen, in fact, sounds not unlike Winnicott's example of the "truly split-off compliant False Self"—the "child who grows up to be an actor": "In regard to actors, there are those who can be themselves and who can also act, whereas there are others who can only act, and who are completely at a loss when not in a role, and when not being appreciated or applauded (acknowledged as existing)."[9] So how, then, can we tell when a person is "acting out," or when she's *really* acting? And can one kind of acting ever lead on to the other?

All the Acts

In Tillie Olsen's short story "I Stand Here Ironing" we find another character with a "rare gift for comedy on the stage that rouses a laughter out of the audience so dear they applaud and applaud and do not want to let her go. Where does it come from, that comedy?"[10]

The comic gift belongs to Emily, the eldest daughter of the story's narrator: an impoverished, Depression-era single mother whose work is never done. (Olsen was herself a hard-up single mother born to poor Russian Jewish immigrant parents.) We first encounter our narrator in the oblivion of her domestic servitude, although as she moves her iron repetitively back and forth, she also appears to be undergoing some sort of *interrogation* from someone (a teacher? a social worker? a psychologist?) demanding an explanation for her maternal failings toward Emily. The daughter, we learn, is a young woman in the throes of a physical and mental breakdown traceable back to the narrator's not-good-enough mothering. We never hear the interlocutor's questions directly, however, only the narrator's responses to them, so we cannot be entirely sure whether the address is really the blistering interrogation our narrator feels it to be, or whether she simply interprets it as such.

Either way, our narrator is protesting—and protesting justly—the charges she believes are being leveled against her. She blames the cruel economic and political deprivations of her social world as the true causes of her maternal negligence, and these, there can be no doubt, have played a major role in the domestic drama to which we are bearing witness. Yet what our narrator's stream of consciousness attests to above all is an unassuageable guilt. It's the guilt we've discussed of *generational repetition*, the guilt of someone—a mother—who, though defensively claiming in the face of her interrogator to have shown her daughter "all the acts of love" (16), still feels herself to have been in some essential way *unable* to act. She knows, she says, and may even have known all along—as she acknowledges early on in the story, "even without knowing, I knew" (15), before later attempting a self-justification, "wisdom came too late" (24)—what moves to make, but she has not been moved by what she knows. She took advantage, she concedes also, of the only one of her children to show her "never a direct protest, never rebellion" (16): "What in me demanded that goodness in her?" (16).

What we are privy to in this story is no monolithic consciousness. So fractured and at war with itself is the mind of our narrator that the interrogation purportedly going on from the outside could just as easily be taking place entirely from within. Her point of view shifts continually; sometimes she's on the defensive and at other times she shows a real willingness to open up to the questions being asked of her or even ask questions of her own. Certainly it would be hard to imagine a better presentation of the agitated oscillation between self-defense and self-attack that marks how endlessly tormented a soul in its anguish feels. For here, in this story, we have painfully exposed the innermost mind and heart of a woman who loves her child and can perform "all the acts of love" (she labors on unceasingly throughout the story, ironing her daughter's clothes) but who has not, she senses, despite what she knows and despite what she feels, been able to respond to her daughter's spontaneous gestures.[11] Her guilty self-lacerations are thus all the more discomfiting to read, since these are feelings that have blocked rather than moved her. Though there is no doubt that this mother loves her child, her love has been compliant rather than spontaneous. Her heart has not been able to put on a face and walk into the world.[12]

The story concludes with the narrator's hope that her daughter won't be compressed in the way that both her own life and the ironed dress lying flat in front of her have been. That hope, however, given the crisis currently unfolding, seems unearned. Though if our narrator has failed to always act in the manner she wishes she could have, there *is* within this story the vague potential hinted at by another type of acting—the kind we find on stage. Our narrator's own straitened circumstances mean that Emily's talent is not one her mother has been able to encourage. But the possibility of self-cure through performance is left hanging in this story— signifying, on the one hand, the false self of a daughter reared never to moan or rebel, only to comply and please, and yet, on the other, a possible route for her false self's eventual transcendence.

Theatrics

The history of thought has long since focused on problems like this. Can one *really* go to the source by means of a simulation, or comprehend reality via the imagination, or get to the truth by way of art?

For the eighteenth-century philosopher Jean-Jacques Rousseau, the artifice and artistry of theater was something to disapprove of. Far from doing justice to true sentiments and prestigious passions, theater, he believed, because essentially a spectacle, keeps everything at such a distance that, for the audience, nothing is taking place internally in the moral center of the imagination whence authentic emotion derives. We "daily find at our theatres," he cautioned, "men affected, nay, shedding tears at the sufferings of a wretch who, were he in the tyrant's place, would probably even add to the torments of his enemies."[13] It's a point of view directly at odds with Aristotle's recommendation of theater's power to arouse pity in the audience—a pity that, Rousseau implies, makes men feel for actors on the stage what they fail to feel for those who people their actual lives. Indeed, theater audiences, he suspects, are more likely to resemble tyrants, tormenters, and torturers than to be moral subjects seeking edification.

When it comes to entertainment, Rousseau perhaps has a point. The same, after all, could be said of Rousseau's own highly entertaining *Confessions*. When you read them, Josh Cohen observes, he "brings you up against your voyeurism, your intrusive and sadistic pleasure in the suffering of his naked self."[14] To read Rousseau, in other words, is to be placed in the position of a torturer seeking to elicit maximum humiliation from his confessional victims. But can theater (or reading Rousseau) be so simply drawn down to the level of entertainment? Or mightn't one just as easily draw the opposite lesson from Rousseau's theatrical example, that the man with a dearth of natural pity has *reawakened* pity within himself by means of his exposure not to the suffering of those he meets in life, but to the representation of such sufferings on stage?

Making just this point, Rei Terada proposes that theatricality is "an attribute of all emotion, not pity alone." And she notes that it's precisely Rousseau's *own* stated insistence on the role of the imagination in one's emotional life—"Only imagination is active and one excites *the passions* only by imagination"—that licenses her critique of him.[15] For if I'm required to intervene imaginatively to excite any kind of sorrow, including the sorrow I might be expected to feel at some loss of my own, then theatricality—or the representational "playing" back of experience—must be at least minimally there.

Take, for example, the work of the German Jewish artist Charlotte Salomon, whose epic series of more than seven hundred gouaches painted during the Nazi years and brought to an end by her own removal to Auschwitz she entitled *Life? Or Theatre?* Is there really such a choice as her title implies? Or is what her work shows us that one can never choose between life and theater when there may be no life without the possibility of a theatrical representation of that life in such a way as to enable the kind of emotional distancing and reintegration that makes even a terrible life somehow bearable? (We made a similar observation about the practice of diary writing for Anne Frank.)

As Rousseau put it in his *Confessions*, "the reader does not need to know these things; it is I who need to tell them." So he *was* aware that the representative doubling of himself in a text was his best available means of *moving* himself. This acknowledgment sits uneasily, however, alongside his text's more radical proposal to offer up, by *means* of confession, his "innermost self"—the "portrait of a man, painted exactly according to nature and all its truth"—which, as Cohen infers, is a "self-defeating paradox."[16] Exhibitionism, after all, is a very theatrical (you could even say hysterical) way to act.

The ambivalence we find in Rousseau regarding the role played by the imagination in one's emotional life is not uncommon among people who feel there must be a true, authentic, or natural way of being that they're somehow failing to live up to—a sneaking suspicion about one's own fakery that's surely enough to make *anyone* hysterical (and oh boy, do I empathize). Rousseau was in this sense his own tormenter. For doesn't his representation of the unqualified truthtelling he thought was enabled by confessional language come perilously close to the conceit of the torturer (albeit in structural, *not* moral, terms), given that what he apparently aspires toward is a fully articulable, disincarnated truth?

A century after Rousseau, however, we can find philosophers adopting rather more relativizing stances. According to Nietzsche, for example, for whom to "talk much about oneself may also be a means of concealing oneself," the self is in its *essence* a theatrical construction. "Every profound spirit needs a mask," he admonished.[17] Yet in what could well be the telltale distinction between "thinkers" (no matter *what* they think) and "actors," not even Nietzsche was immune to the type of moral reservations that had troubled Rousseau: "The problem of the actor has disquieted me the longest . . . the inner longing to play a role, to assume a mask, to put on an *appearance;* a surplus of capacity for adaptations of every kind."[18]

Nietzsche's disquiet over the shapeshifting adaptiveness marking the various performances and guises of actors may well have been based as much on personal identification as on aesthetic dispute with the actor's craft. Though what's equally interesting is whom else he perceived to share in these actorial vices: paupers, for instance, forever constrained to "represent themselves as different persons"; and Jews, "the adaptable people *par excellence* . . . what good actor at present is *not* a Jew?"; and finally, women: "If we consider the whole history of women, are they not *obliged* first of all, and above all to be actresses? If we listen to doctors who have hypnotised women, or, finally, if we love them—and let ourselves be 'hypnotised' by them,—what is always divulged thereby? That they 'give themselves airs,' even when they—'give themselves.' . . . Woman is so artistic."[19]

Nietzsche is so sarcastic. Whether or not he secretly identified with them is beside the point: actors, beggars, Jews, and women all blur together here as whorishly hypnotic creatures and natural-born fakers whose art is artifice and whose performances ought never to be trusted.

The Actress

But who, historically, has *really* been doing the acting? Jews and women certainly have things in common in this regard. In Elizabethan England, for example, Jewish characters—most notoriously Shakespeare's Shylock, Marlowe's Barabas—were stage villains never played by Jews themselves (indeed, it's unlikely the playwrights ever met any Jews, England having expelled them three hundred years earlier). And women too were conspicuous only by their absence from the stage, their parts played by boys. It was centuries before women could "act themselves."

No sooner did the actress appear, however, than she achieved cult status and was viewed, increasingly, as an artist of the extremes. On French and English stages in the second half of the nineteenth century, for example, spectacles of feminine suffering became especially popular. And it was on to these stages that there also ventured one Sarah Bernhardt, an actress of whom parts were said, for the first time, to have been written with her in mind. A scandal arose in England, for instance, when Oscar Wilde was (falsely) accused of having penned his play *Salome* to be specifically performed by the "divine Sarah." This controversy may even have contributed to the play's subsequent cancellation by censors made anxious at the thought of the dark, biblical Jewish temptress brought to life by a woman whose contemporary image was being portrayed in analogously seductive terms.

Sander Gilman has compared the frequently misogynistic and anti-Semitic nature of Bernhardt's media coverage with the anthropological studies of Jews later adopted by Nazi Germany. A Weimar anthropologist claimed that "it is the voice of all Jews which marks the Jew as different"—a voice that was also said to "betray" the adaptable Jew's true origins through its distinctive linguistic features bound to an inescapable rootedness in the anatomical difference of the Jew's degenerate body.[20] So a thesis, then, that once again grounds the voice in the body. Yet the linking of language/voice to the *biological* body works in quite a different direction from the link that Freud was to arrive at in wholly different terms. For whereas Freud was developing a thesis whose highly mobile "truth" required an understanding of body and voice/language as being so inextricably bound to each other as to suggest that there could be no deciphering of the one without acknowledging the embeddedness of the other within it, the work of the Weimar anthropologist was not unlike that of the torturer in its aim of locating and identifying, via the body, the underlying nature of his subject by separating from the flesh a voice that would ultimately be shown to index an unchanging and immobile truth: that of the Jew's racial inferiority.

Although it was not just Bernhardt's body image but the hypnotic power of her voice that was gaining her, in some quarters, a psychosexual as well as racial notoriety, Bernhardt made no apology to those accusing her of "betraying" herself. "I am a daughter of the great Jewish race, and my somewhat uncultivated language is the outcome of our enforced wanderings," she declared.[21] The rootlessness in which she dared to take pride was as much personal as it was tribal—her father was unknown to her, while her mother, who supported her family by working as a courtesan, was the daughter of an itinerant Jewish merchant—and Bernhardt not only defended but actively cultivated her reputed lack of cultivation.[22] Thus, unlike the young Emily in Olsen's story, who sickens at her own unfashionably "thin and dark and foreign looking" (that is, Jewish) appearance, these were precisely the physical features that Bernhardt's image would draw its energy and mystique from. And while Emily's self-repugnance led her to starvation and breathlessness (anorexia nervosa, panic attacks), Bernhardt found her powers in precisely those places where others saw only pathologies. Hers, indeed, was an art that not only rejoiced in the enforced wanderings of the Jew, but rejoiced, too, in that period's other prolific wanderings—those of the womb.

It's even said that Bernhardt visited the Salpêtrière hospital to observe Charcot's demonstrations at his Tuesday clinic of his patients' *attitudes passionelles*. Whether that's true or not is unclear, but certainly her famously histrionic performances do seem to have garnered inspiration from the female hysteric. As disorders of the soul go, after all, hysteria is an intriguingly expressive one, and so the hysteric's symptoms have the potential to be extremely theatrical. What better blueprint could there be, one might ask, for a practice so often conceived of as the art of affect . . . of affecting by *being* affected, of moving by *being* moved?

Nervous Power

Bernhardt's style, writes Elaine Aston, had, like that of the hysteric, a kind of "nervous power" that "drew the focus of attention away from the action on the stage to the emotional drama located in the body of the actress, convulsed, contorted and traumatised."[23] It was likewise the "somatic compliance" of just such a body that rendered it, for Freud, so seductively meaningful. But nervous power is a strange sort of power. *Is* it power?

Power, in this conception, is clearly not the logic underpinning torture or war or politics as war by other means. Rather, it's a power grounded in an acknowledgment of its own powerlessness. We might think of nervous power, therefore, as akin to the imperatives that can become declaratives, the passivity that can become passion, the muteness that can become meaning, and the acting "out" that can become acting. For by making of the lifelessly compliant something vivid and compelling, whoever exhibits her nervous power shows herself in such a way as to continually remind her audience that she requires an *effort* of understanding.[24] And what she ultimately gives her audience to understand, I'd venture, is the distinctive power of someone who knows how to let it be *known* that she is, and shall remain, distinctly *unknown*.

The Unknown Woman

There's a genre of early Hollywood movie that Stanley Cavell has identified and called "the melodrama of the unknown woman." It's in these films that we fully experience the compelling mystique of the women in the leading roles—not because of their beauty, but because of something else: "One may doubt whether Bette Davis or Barbara Stanwyck or Katharine Hepburn are beautiful. One cannot doubt that each is distinct. Some people are both."[25]

Reflecting on Bette Davis, for example—specifically her performance in *Now, Voyager* (1942)—Cavell recalls *her* somatic compliance and asks, "How does Bette Davis manage her powers?"[26] And of course when one thinks of Davis, one thinks too of her star turn in *All About Eve* (1950), a movie in which the leading actress *plays* a leading actress: an actress who is being difficult, demanding, hysterical, who feels that she's losing her looks and her power to attract, an actress who fears her star may be dimming, and an actress haunted and obsessed by the presence of a younger actress, Eve, waiting in the wings to take over.[27]

At least, that's the part she *appears* to be playing until we remember that *All About Eve* is not *all* about Eve at all—one easily forgets Eve, but who can forget Davis's Margo Channing, whose power of fascination forces us to feel her pain and pleasure every step of the way? Who can forget her face? A face not fairly described as aged, but neither is it fresh—for there lies the sense of a character, of a life that has suffered and experienced, laughed, loved, lost. This actress knows, and her body shows, something about the others—the boys and girls, women and men, managers and directors—with whom she inter-acts. That this is a performance about performance, an actress showing us what it is to be an actress, is therefore indexed, somehow, by the ever so delicate because ever so *touchy* thematic of her aging.

Something puritanical and stern inhabits the imperative to "act your age." It's a phrase we often first hear as children; its implication is that we must put away childish things, cease to be immature, grow up, take some responsibility for ourselves. Though it's also the kind of judgment one might hear later in life, perhaps as a criticism of those who still appear to be enjoying themselves (their drives) when enjoyment is no longer considered respectable. But as essentializing as the command to "act your age" seems intended to be, the phrase cannot quite escape the sense that another, more interesting meaning is embedded within those same words. Might this then, at however great a distance from our first experiments at crib speech, be yet another imperative that we can learn to internalize in such a way as to make of its law something loose and spontaneous, even declarative?

After all, we're seldom asked, in so many words, to "act" our gender, or our race, or our nationality, even though we're aware by now that these too are roles that require performing. Yet these aspects of our identities have tended to be presupposed: one should *be* a good girl, *be* a good boy, *be* a model citizen, whereas one should *act* one's age. To act your age is thus to acknowledge, as the flesh does, that human identities are forever changing, that we're never the same person twice. So here's an instance where a conservative idiom trips up over some disavowed radicalism within its own discourse, for with the ever-shifting variable of age we are invited, even enjoined, to be actors.[28] It's as if aging—that thing over which we have neither say nor control—were the very basis and possibility of action, of being *able* to act. Is aging, then, another example of the strength that can come out of weakness; another example of nervous power?

Bette Davis, Cavell writes, has "knowledge of this power of her character, this character of her power"; he concludes that "one may take the subject of the genre of the unknown woman as the irony of human identity as such."[29] The irony, he means, that there *is* no human identity as such. It's this irony that empowers the actress as someone who was for far too long forbidden from the world's stage, but who was breathtaking in her mystique as soon as she appeared. Yet, unforgivably, this actress is at risk of getting lost once again as we kid ourselves by telling ourselves we don't *want* to see grown-up women on screen, that we don't *want* faces to wrinkle, emote, or express, but would rather they were rendered immobile, flat and affectless. When one considers what's at stake, that risk, it seems to me, is a genuine and serious one, for without such actresses—without such *faces*—to whom in the future can we turn if we still wish to be shown how to act?

Nerve Endings

While I've just been sunnily summarizing the aging process, it's of course equally possible that I, like that queen of all melodrama Blanche DuBois, am merely romanticizing the shadows. So I should, at the very least, acknowledge that from the same places from which one can derive an abundance of existentially enriching ideas and metaphors (acting, aging, exile: all varieties of radical exposure) there's generally also a story of pain and deprivation, grief and despair. Melodramatists, after all, don't always teach us the art of aging. Some, like Blanche, hide where we can't really see them.[30] Others, like Cohen of Trinity and his author Amy Levy, die young.

Yet affectation does sometimes get a rap it doesn't always deserve, not least because, as we've been suggesting, affectation is a necessary condition of *all* acting, both on and off the stage. And to act "well" an actor must work with her feelings, her nerve endings, her body. Such sensitivities, depending on your state of exposure, don't make for an easy ride. Just look at Tillie Olsen's Emily suffering a nervous breakdown. But we've also considered the example of Sarah Bernhardt, who could spellbind audiences by turning nervousness into nerviness. Bernhardt exposed her spectators to their own exposure, vitalizing their nerves by enervating her own. In so doing, she revealed how what might have rendered her weak—her classlessness, her femaleness, her Jewishness—could become a source of strength. And by strength I mean neither brute force nor imperious authority. I mean ability through expressivity: nervous power.

Conclusion

Intelligence Gathering

Two Jews, Moishe and Itzhik, are walking in the forest in the Ukraine some 150 years ago. In the distance, they see two local guys walking toward them. Moishe turns to Itzhik, panics, and says: "Itzik, what should we do? There's two of them, and we're all alone!"

Feeling Jewish can often sound like a byword for feeling funny: both funny peculiar—strange, odd, out of place—and funny haha: Moishe's exaggerated sense of threat and permanent state of hysteria; talk about over the top, he's hilarious! But how "all alone" is Moishe really? Is it possible that he's only wound up feeling that way because everyone around him keeps insisting they're just "fine"? Everyone, including Itzhik, whose response I can well imagine: "Why are you always so neurotic, Moishe? You see anti-Semites everywhere. Even when there's no proof. You've really got to stop being so insular. *I'm* nothing like you."

It's a dynamic we've encountered before in this book. Like when paranoid Alvy and go-west Rob talk Jewishness on a street in Manhattan (because you can take the Jews out of the Ukrainian forest, but you can't take the Ukrainian forest out of the Jews), or when considering Roth's critique of Jews who "hide the places where they're split." For Roth, that is, every Jew is always both the Jews in the joke. So it's not that Moishe/Alvy is a fantasist and Itzhik/Rob a realist, nor is it the other way round; rather, what we must contend with is the way in which Moishe and Itzhik, or Alvy and Rob, are unassailably implicated *in* each other's feelings.

As someone who sometimes takes the part of Alvy, and at other times the part of Rob, I can identify. I too am the proverbial Jew all alone on a desert island, having built both the synagogue I go to and the one I wouldn't set foot in if you paid me. So what I've sought to do in this book is reveal rather than hide these splits, while also making a case *for* feeling split. And I've done so because it's precisely insofar as my Jewishness *is* something that has split me that it has never ceased to excite a sort of internal questioning—making it not only something I think about, but something I think through, think with, *and* feel with.

Look, don't get me wrong. Some Jews, I'm told, really don't feel Jewish. But even those Jews, I suppose, may find there are situations when they do. In today's warring Ukraine they might, for example. Or in the dis-United States of present day America. Or in a Europe that, forgetful of its history, looks hell-bent on a new era of fragmentation. Or wherever the complex world in which we live has had its problems simplified into one of two options—you're either with us or against us, you're either inward or outward, a leaver or a remainer, a tribalist or a universalist—Jews can find their Jewishness triggered, as it were, as if their own internal splitness had been suddenly roused, like the return of the repressed, causing them to reckon with the, for some, troubling thought that they probably *are* still Jews after all—those original "rootless cosmopolitans" who have so often been scapegoated by an aggrieved nationalist sensibility reacting to feelings of anxiety, loss, insecurity, and displacement under conditions of an ever more globalized and inequitable world.

When it comes to feeling panicky, weak, outnumbered, and existentially threatened, in other words, Jews are by no means all alone. Indeed, the sense of dispossession that might be said to underpin resurgent "nationalist" feelings could hardly have more in common with the feelings of those rootless cosmopolitans accused of aggravating them. So mightn't there be, I can't help wondering, a way of extending the reach of our sympathies on account of such similarities as that? Unless, of course, it is the feelings themselves that are unwanted, mistrusted, and inadmissible.

It's in this context, then, that this book has taken the side of feelings, including the more "difficult" ones (are there any other kind?). Though while wishing to affirm what can be gained from self-hatred, envy, guilt, doubt, love, and nervousness of one kind or another, I don't deny that the passage from feelings that torture and isolate to the imaginative acts that can create a shared and livable world is a terrifying as well as arduous one. What I *do* think, as I hope this book has indicated, is that feelings of *any* kind can sometimes surprise us by becoming their own reward. Thus even Edelshtein, the lunatic, broken-down protagonist of Ozick's short story "Envy," ultimately comes to feel that despite the isolation and the desperation caused by his unrequited passion for Yiddish, what he has never ceased to love, indeed what he has loved all the more for its unspeakable loss, has also rendered him "blessed." This moment of fleeting recognition on Edelshtein's part is not a type of theodicy that would masochistically seek out sufferings with a view to maximizing one's beatific portion. Clearly Edelshtein still wants what most of us want: the easy life, the good life. Yet he can also perceive that his position of social exclusion, with all the hurt and pain and torment that situation has trammeled for him, has *given* him something; something—an insight, a sensibility, a sense of humor, a perspective, a purpose, a passion, a meaning, a mission— that any invitation to a "good life" that failed to capture or incorporate those "blessings" he might very well refuse to take up.

That stated, even when one's feeling isn't encountered as a blessing—and it's only reasonable to suppose that painful feelings are mostly *not* experienced that way—the other gambit of this book has been that greater dangers lurk where one avoids one's feelings. There's the danger, for instance, of those who, in seeking to avoid their own feelings, also avoid acknowledging how (or that) others feel. While in seeking, too, to deny their own powerlessness, such persons are liable to disavow the extreme passivity of their "incarnation," which can frequently lead them toward sadistic, hostile, or manipulative behaviors that treat others (including the others within themselves) as objects in an unending fight to maintain the illusion of personal mastery and control. What's more, it's on this same illusory basis that similar strategies can be detected not only within specific groups or individuals but within the various frameworks (institutional, discursive, technological) by which and in which we now live. Indeed, it's partly as a result of such structures that the particular inflections ascribed to these feelings are acquiring an ever more global reach.

Sadistic intelligence gathering via torture—the "intelligence" imagined to be obtained by being insentient to the sufferings of the one tortured—is not, of course, easily compared to the reassessments this book has attempted with regard to how we have come to view and rely on knowledge in the modern world. So it's with a degree of caution that I nonetheless propose a parallel between the intelligence we deploy defensively and the forms of attack that torturers, also in the name of intelligence, prosecute more literally. Wherever, that is, we can find an idealized notion of knowledge, intelligence, or information whose immutability has been presupposed on the basis of its having been shorn of the unpredictable influence of bodies, words, and affects, then we are not so far from the torturer's conceit that the human voice can be uprooted, with all necessary violence, from the fragile limitations of the flesh.

We have seen this again and again in the case where difficult feelings have been ignored, denied, or dissembled, or have sought strategies for their own resolution. But we've also seen and suggested other ways of encountering these same feelings. And what I've been looking at specifically are various Jewish responses to the difficult feelings with which the turbulences and traumas of modern history have seen Jews stereotypically marked. While in noting how such feelings are always liable to infect others, I've also been tracing the likeness that can be said to have arisen *between* feelings and Jews, both of which, when experienced antipathetically, have been described as unwanted foreign elements invading the personal or political body.

To put this succinctly: feelings are like Jews, Jews are like feelings. It's a strange sort of formulation, admittedly, but one whose mirroring is intended (a) to highlight the inherent splitness that we can find *within* both feelings and Jews, while (b) shedding light on how this splitness is what, at bottom, makes sharing possible. For however putatively "Jewish" they may appear, the feelings I've been analyzing are all, undoubtedly, shared. And as a group of people neither wholly insiders nor outsiders, Jews, as Slezkine puts it, can be considered "model moderns" on account of how their situation of marginality has come to encompass more or less everyone.

So though my aim here has been to include rather than exclude, the Jewish focus should not fall out of focus. Jewishness, even when not dealt with directly, has been animating my analysis throughout. And it has done so not least because feelings themselves, in their uncomfortable, disruptive, unsettling, and wandering nature, *share* in the fantasized characteristics of modern Jews. Thus feelings, on a certain reading, really are Jew-*ish*, much as "just about anyone," regardless of his or her biology, belief, or background, might, in many different ways and within a whole range of cultural and personal identifications, *feel* Jewish. And now, I'd warrant, more than ever.

There are, of course, numerous reasons why the difficult feelings described and discussed in this book remain, for so many, *too* difficult to share. In some cases this is owing to the shame of the emotion itself, as in the case of self-hatred or envy, and at other times the emotion is denied for different reasons. Consider, for example, the misconstruing of one's feeling as a form of instruction: if I admit my anger, am I not then compelled to pick a fight? (No.) Or else one silences one's feelings because one feels that one's feelings are too petty to complain about, for in a *world of pain* what does it really matter how *I* feel? Yet such evasions in themselves inculcate their own set of difficult feelings. When we consider our feelings to be illegitimate, for instance, we're often led to repress them—though it's from just such a repressive mechanism that guilt (still, for me, the trickiest feeling of all) can be expected to result.

In spite of how slight or unsightly or unearned we may think them, then, our feelings *do* matter. And they matter not least because the same feeling that can block us can also move us, depending on our response. But here is not a strong endorsement as to how exactly one *should* respond to one's feelings. Feelings, as I understand them, are not laws or lessons, not knowledge or technique, not treasures or truths, not rights or responsibilities. My aim has not been to propose that we should be following our feelings, performing our feelings, or even trusting our feelings. I certainly don't wish to imply that we should be confessing them. So if I do have a proposition, then it's the somewhat simple if still potentially painful proposal that our feelings ask no more of us than that we strive, as best we can, to feel them.

Notes

Introduction

1. Stephen Frosh, *Feelings* (London: Taylor and Francis, 2011), 10.
2. Classical philosophy since Aristotle has attempted to "fold emotion into unitary accounts of the mind"; Rei Terada, *Feeling in Theory: Emotion after the "Death of the Subject"* (Cambridge: Harvard University Press, 2001), 90.
3. Ibid., 4. Terada analyzes classical theory's sentimental rejection of anyone who questions the integrity of the unified subject on the basis that this could endanger the human capacity for true feeling. Proponents of the classical theory of emotions warn in particular against allowing the disruptive impact of language theory into the realm of affects lest humans be thereby transformed into abstractions: impersonal, cold, and affectless. Terada's book takes the opposing view.
4. Sianne Ngai, *Ugly Feelings* (Cambridge: Harvard University Press, 2005), 1.
5. Ibid., 7. And, by dint of the same excessiveness, overly loquacious. Coming from the Latin *finire*, meaning to end or finish, to feel "fine" perhaps also insinuates that there can be no better form of feeling: fine feelings are feelings so good, so appropriate, that "fine, thanks" suffices—there really is nothing more to say.
6. Although in the case of the black male subject especially, spiraling dangerously out of control is just as often supposed to rupture that subject's quintessential "cool," a state wherein the subject shows nothing of what he may be feeling. The male Jewish subject differs in this respect. Despite the best efforts

251

of Jewish hipsters, seldom do we find Jews, or Jewish men, represented as "cool"; rather, as we'll see, the Jewish man is more often depicted, like the woman, as overemotional, tending toward the hysterical.

7. While rapid change the world over has almost certainly extended the reach of these feelings, times of intense political uncertainty and historical upheaval are liable to bring them on all the stronger. Jews who rarely think of themselves as such, for example, are often pricked into a surprised state of Jewish self-consciousness when external conditions shift suddenly toward the unpredictable and precarious. Alissa Quart has described the economic dimension of this growing sense of precariousness among groups previously believed to dwell in a bubble of comfort and security: "The word Precariat was popularized five or so years ago to describe a rapidly expanding working class with unstable, low-paid jobs. What I call the Middle Precariat, in contrast, are supposed to be properly, comfortably middle class, but it's not quite working out this way"; Alissa Quart, " 'Middle Class' Used to Denote Comfort and Security. Not Anymore," *Guardian*, July 7, 2016, https://www.theguardian.com/commentisfree/2016/jul/07/middle-class-struggle-technology-overtaking-jobs-security-cost-of-living, accessed July 11, 2016.

8. Quoted in Yuri Slezkine, *The Jewish Century* (Princeton: Princeton University Press, 2004), 76.

9. Sylvia Plath, "Daddy" (1962), in *The Collected Poems*, ed. Ted Hughes (London: Faber, 1981), 222.

10. Which isn't to deny the possibility that some radical sense of loss, lack, dispossession, or grief may lie behind all these feelings (or all feelings?).

11. Aharon Appelfeld, *Beyond Despair* (New York: Fromm International, 1994), 6.

12. Quoted in Anna Bernard, "The Last Jewish Intellectual: Borrowing from Edward Said," *Jewish Quarterly* 60, no. 3 (2013): 80–83, 80.

13. Edward Said, "Reflections on Exile," *Reflections on Exile and Other Literary and Cultural Essays* (London: Granta, 2001), 173–186, 178.

14. As Said notes, though the Palestinians have borne, most terribly, the brunt of the "exaggerated sense of group solidarity" and "passionate hostility to outsiders" that so often arises in and characterizes peoples seeking to maintain their existence in exile, the Palestinians' own exile by just such a people has at times allowed "the least attractive aspects of being in exile" to manifest in their own consequent identity formations. "What could be more intransigent than the conflict between Zionist Jews and Arab Palestinians?" Said asks ("Reflections on Exile," 178), and indicates that it's precisely what these two peoples have in common that may have all the more radically opposed them.

15. Epigraph to Zadie Smith's *The Autograph Man* (St. Ives: Hamish Hamilton, 2002).

16. Slezkine, *Jewish Century*, 1; page numbers included parenthetically in text for quotations in subsequent paragraphs.

17. A reaction that seems to be reigniting among significant swaths of populations across a now even more globalized world.

18. For a full discussion of this return of religion to what had begun as a mostly secular form of Zionism see my chapter "The Return of Religion: Secularisation and Its Discontents," in *The Routledge Companion to Literature and Religion*, ed. Mark Knight (Oxford: Routledge, 2016), 80–88.

19. Eva Illouz, *Saving the Modern Soul: Therapy, Emotions, and the Culture of Self-Help* (Berkeley: University of California Press, 2008), 341, 150.

20. Sander Gilman, *Jewish Self-Hatred: Anti-Semitism and the Hidden Language of the Jews* (Baltimore: Johns Hopkins University Press, 1986), 292.

21. Freud also extended the hysterical diagnosis from women to men who he claimed were exhibiting analogous if not always identical symptoms. Richard Appignanesi and Oscar Zarate's graphic book *Hysteria* (London: Self Made Hero, 2015) expands on this theme and also examines the contemporary relevance of the outmoded term as a way of understanding the many plaints of today's world.

22. In defending poststructuralist theories of emotion over and against the classical theory, the goal of Terada's book cannot be, she says, "to construct a model of poststructuralist Freudianism," though she writes "informed by its possibility"; *Feeling in Theory*, 9–10. Approaching its subject from the other direction, the present book is informed primarily by psychoanalytic theories, though its putative "Freudianism," even if not always explicitly, is everywhere informed by the poststructuralist theories that have followed on from it.

23. In what follows, this is something I consider while mindful of the taunt that sought to portray psychoanalysis—qua science of feeling—as a perversely "Jewish science," which charge, since it emanated from Nazi sources, Freud denied in public while occasionally giving it its due in private, a dynamic that possibly underlies why psychoanalysis throughout its history has at times fallen prey to the very forms of prejudice and hatred—racism, anti-Semitism, misogyny, homophobia—that it can also help to work against. For a full examination of this fraught history see Stephen Frosh, *Hate and the "Jewish Science": Anti-Semitism, Nazism, and Psychoanalysis* (Basingstoke: Palgrave, 2005).

24. Adam Phillips, *Becoming Freud: The Making of a Psychoanalyst* (New Haven: Yale University Press, 2014), 39.

25. Matthew Garrahan, "Lunch with the FT: Larry David," *Financial Times*, April 7, 2012, http://www.ft.com/cms/s/2/f9b4936c-7a53-11e1-9c77-00144feab49a.html, accessed February 2, 2016.

26. See in particular "Respecting the Ineradicable: Religion's Realism," *Textual Practice* 26, no. 3 (2012): 519–540; and "The Return of Religion."

27. Philip Roth, *Deception* (1990; London: Vintage, 2006), 78.

28. One thing I feel might be shameful about writing this book is that it could be construed as a sort of weakness on my part: psychological, but also moral or political. Why, for example, have I chosen to shut myself up in the ghetto? Aren't I being unnecessarily narrow? Why can't I simply address myself in a universal tongue or speak from a position of total neutrality that excludes nobody? (As if.)

29. Roth, *Deception*, 198.

30. In *Portnoy's Complaint* (1969; London: Vintage, 1995), the self-hating Jew is also described as "the best kind" (265).

31. Henry Bean, "Introduction," to *The Believer: Confronting Jewish Self-Hatred* (New York: Thunder's Mouth, 2002), 1–24, 5.

32. "The claim that hysteria ceased to exist can hardly be taken seriously for a simple reason. For both Charcot and Freud, the symptoms of hysteria were fabulously changeable"; Darian Leader, "Hysteria Today," in *Hysteria Today*, ed. Anouchka Grose (London: Karnac, 2016).

33. Slezkine, *Jewish Century*, 322.

34. This phenomenon is cogently analyzed in Dean J. Franco, *Race, Rights, and Recognition: Jewish American Literature since 1969* (Ithaca: Cornell University Press, 2012).

35. David Bradley, "A Eulogy for Nigger," in *A Eulogy for Nigger and Other Essays* (London: Notting Hill, 2015), 1–21, 1, 2.

36. Ibid., 13.

37. Frosh, *Feelings*, 2.

38. Other feelings not given specific chapters but touched on throughout are melancholy, anxiety, and nostalgia. I address anxiety and nostalgia more directly in "Circumcision Anxiety," *Textual Practice* 27, no. 4 (2013); and "Life-Writing and the East End," in *The Edinburgh Companion to Modern Jewish Fiction* (Edinburgh: Edinburgh University Press, 2015), 221–236.

39. These have their associated Yiddish terms—for example "kvelling" and "schlepping naches"—whose self-consciously mocking tone (these specific terms refer to the pleasure to be gotten out of reflected glory) shows awareness of the cultural propensity to overcompensate by taking positive feelings to excess. The same might be said of the term "schmaltz," which describes the sentimental and usually nostalgic aesthetic that can commonly be found in certain folkish forms of Jewish cultural production—it's a word that perhaps recognizes that there can be too much of a good thing and that such sickly sweet sentiment risks clogging the heart's arteries as might goose fat. Though surely the most ironic usage in traditional Jewish diction is the term uttered in

celebratory praise: "mazel tov," usually translated as "congratulations" but meaning, literally, "good luck!"

40. One could go on and on about the less lovely sides to pleasure-seeking, piety, pride, and so forth, and, as Frosh points out, even happiness has its more destructive aspects: "It is not for nothing that a common phrase used when someone has wrecked everything around them, hurt those who need them and ruined things of value . . . is, 'Are you happy now?' 'Happy' here means, 'Have you finally spent your wrath?' But also, 'Does the destruction you have wreaked now match the nastiness inside you?' " (49), from a chapter in Frosh's *Feelings* taking direct aim at the happiness industry.

41. Ngai, *Ugly Feelings*, 10.

ONE
Self-Hatred

1. Sander Gilman, *Jewish Self-Hatred: Anti-Semitism and the Hidden Language of the Jews* (Baltimore: Johns Hopkins University Press, 1986), 2.

2. See also Josh Cohen, *The Private Life: Why We Remain in the Dark* (London: Granta, 2013).

3. Jean-Paul Sartre, *Being and Nothingness*, trans. Hazel Barnes (1943; Oxford: Routledge, 2003), 78.

4. Adrienne Rich, *Of Woman Born: Motherhood as Experience and Institution* (New York: Norton, 1986), 235.

5. Henry Bean, "Introduction," to *The Believer: Confronting Jewish Self-Hatred* (New York: Thunder's Mouth, 2002), 1–24, 15.

6. Gideon Lewis-Krauss, *A Sense of Direction* (London: Pushkin, 2012), 312–313.

7. Sigmund Freud, *Jokes and Their Relation to the Unconscious*, trans. James Strachey (1905; St. Ives: Penguin, 1991), 157.

8. Haggadah is the book that tells the Exodus narrative via various liturgical sources and is read communally ahead of the Passover meal.

9. David Mamet, *The Wicked Son: Anti-Semitism, Self-Hatred, and the Jews* (New York: Schocken, 2006).

10. Friedrich Nietzsche, *The Will to Power*, trans. Walter Kaufmann and R. J. Hollingdale (1901; New York: Vintage, 2000), §277. For a recent rendering of the unrelenting demand to "express your inner nature by clear and constant signs," see Dave Eggers's chillingly dystopian Google-era novel, *The Circle* (St. Ives: Hamish Hamilton, 2013).

11. Paul Reitter, "Misreading Kafka," *Jewish Review of Books*, fall 2010, https://jewishreviewofbooks.com/articles/172/misreading-kafka/, accessed February 2, 2016.

12. Paul Reitter, *On the Origins of Jewish Self-Hatred* (Princeton: Princeton University Press, 2012), 24, 66.

13. "Those are my principles, and if you don't like them . . . well, I have others" (Groucho Marx).

14. Jean-Paul Sartre, *Anti-Semite and Jew*, trans. George Becker (1945; New York: Schocken, 1995).

15. Gilman, *Jewish Self-Hatred*, 3.

16. Reitter, *Origins of Jewish Self-Hatred*, 30.

17. Stephen Frosh, *Hate and the "Jewish Science": Anti-Semitism, Nazism, and Psychoanalysis* (Basingstoke: Palgrave, 2005), 26.

18. Quoted in Stanley Tsigounis and Jill Savege Scharff, "Introduction to the Persecutory Object," in *Self-Hatred in Psychoanalysis* (East Sussex: Taylor and Francis, 2003), 3–22, 5.

19. As he spells out in his case study of "Little Hans," for example, in which he eschews the popular prejudice regarding circumcision as a mark of the Jew's weakness, emasculation, and castration—a prejudice to which Hans himself seems to have fallen prey—to invest the same rite with a kind of bravery, resilience, and implicit machismo.

20. Adam Phillips, "The Art of Nonfiction No. 7," *Paris Review*, spring 2014, no. 208, http://www.theparisreview.org/interviews/6286/the-art-of-nonfiction-no-7-adam-phillips, accessed February 2, 2016.

21. Amy Levy, "Cohen of Trinity," in *The Complete Novels and Selected Writings of Amy Levy, 1861–1889* (Gainesville: University Press of Florida, 1993), 478–485, 478; page numbers included parenthetically in text for quotations in subsequent paragraphs.

22. Bernard Malamud, *Conversations with Bernard Malamud*, ed. Lawrence Lasher (Jackson: University Press of Mississippi, 1991), 39.

23. Philip Roth, *Reading Myself and Others* (London: Vintage, 2007), 279.

24. Gilman, *Jewish Self-Hatred*, 210.

25. James Wood, "My Hero: Philip Roth," *Guardian*, March 22, 2013, http://www.theguardian.com/books/2013/mar/22/my-hero-philip-roth-james-wood, accessed February 2, 2016.

26. Stanley Tsigounis, "Detoxification Possible and Impossible," in Tsigounis and Scharff, *Self-Hatred in Psychoanalysis*, 225–232, 226.

27. Gary Shteyngart, *Little Failure: A Memoir* (St. Ives: Hamish Hamilton, 2014), 33.

28. Wayne Koestenbaum, *Humiliation* (London: Notting Hill, 2011), 54.

29. Zadie Smith, *NW* (St. Ives: Hamish Hamilton, 2012), 225–226.

30. Quoted in Zadie Smith, "F. Kafka Everyman," in *Changing My Mind: Occasional Essays* (London: Penguin, 2009), 57–70, 70.

31. Ibid., 70.
32. Sarah Kofman, "Scorning Jews: Nietzsche, the Jews, Anti-Semitism," in *Selected Writings* (Stanford: Stanford University Press, 2007), 123–158.
33. Prefacing her study of cultural representations of the Jew in modernity, Juliet Steyn admits that the "most painful" criticism her work has received "is that which has sought to classify me as a Self-Hating Jew." But it's an accusation she risks "in my attempt to grasp, to decipher and to describe the conflicting emotions which the idea of the *Jew* arouses." *The Jew: Assumptions of Identity* (London: Cassell, 1999), vii.
34. Reitter, *Origins of Jewish Self-Hatred*, 2.

TWO
Envy

1. Quoted in Melanie Klein, "Envy and Gratitude" (1957), in *Envy and Gratitude and Other Works* (London: Vintage, 1997), 176–235, 189; page numbers included parenthetically in text for quotations in subsequent paragraphs.
2. Though when a critic has confidence in her own creative ability, a constructive criticism—one that genuinely aims at helping others—becomes possible.
3. Quoted in Helmut Schoeck, *Envy: A Theory of Social Behaviour* (Indianapolis: Liberty Fund, 1966), 208.
4. Ibid., 201.
5. Max Scheler, *Ressentiment*, trans. Lewis Coser (Milwaukee: Marquette University Press, 2010), 39.
6. Schoeck, *Envy*, 179.
7. Sianne Ngai, *Ugly Feelings* (Cambridge: Harvard University Press, 2005), 128.
8. Moreover, the slaves' invention of a metaphysical future world where justice would be served seems to attest to their own creative ability as a potentially mitigating factor within their antagonism.
9. Scheler, *Ressentiment*, 86. Scheler finds evidence in the "dialectical method" "which wants to produce not only *non*-A, but even B through the negation of A" (41). That a method of violent reversal should have taken such a firm hold over the intellect proves for Scheler that we moderns are actually the ones to have turned resentment into a golden rule.
10. Quoted in John Forrester, *Dispatches from the Freud Wars: Psychoanalysis and Its Passions* (Cambridge: Harvard University Press, 1997), 15; page numbers included parenthetically in text for quotations in subsequent paragraphs.
11. Frantz Fanon, *The Wretched of the Earth*, trans. Constance Farrington (St. Ives: Penguin, 1963), 30.
12. Scheler, *Ressentiment*, 36.

13. Quoted in Forrester, *Dispatches from the Freud Wars*, 20.
14. Forrester, *Dispatches from the Freud Wars*, 22.
15. Ngai, *Ugly Feelings*, 149.
16. It's "the emulated subject's life and not the emulator's that most radically changes as result of the latter's actions. Defined throughout by an ability to shapeshift, Hedy maintains a comparatively consistent identity. In contrast, by being 'copied,' the single Allie is transformed by Hedy's mimetic behavior into something she previously was not: a duplicate"; ibid., 152.
17. Ibid., 161.
18. Ibid., 168.
19. It is by no means an art film either, but a genre or "B-movie," that type of aesthetic that seems to poorly emulate the Platonic ideal of singular and true art by being a pale imitator (a hybrid, parasitic, and thus potentially threatening form). Thus while Ngai excuses herself for her "poor taste" in choosing a "lurid thriller" (130), and uses, incidentally, a clothes metaphor to make her apology (for "hanging a large coat on a small peg"), the film's own aesthetic is in fact critically related to the interpretation of emulation she draws from it.

    A not dissimilar debate has arisen among critics of Elena Ferrante's Neapolitan novels (surely the greatest exponent we have of how this characteristic borderlessness between female friends can so quickly mutate from admiration to aggression, from love to hate, and from a united front to an enraged and ultimately futile attempt at separation). Ferrante's critics have been perplexed as to how such a singular and original achievement in modern literature should share so many properties with what usually and derisively gets called chick-lit.
20. Scheler, *Ressentiment*, 28–29.
21. Sigmund Freud, *Moses and Monotheism* (1939), trans. Katherine Jones (New York: Random House, 1967), 135.
22. Forrester, *Dispatches from the Freud Wars*, 31–32.
23. Klein had been Winnicott's mentor, but relations between them later seem to have soured, possibly on account of the envy Klein may have felt after reading a paper by her former mentee, which she commended but then went on to eviscerate.
24. Eva Hoffman, *Lost in Translation: Life in a New Language* (London: Minerva, 1989), 124; page numbers included parenthetically in text for quotations in subsequent paragraphs.
25. Quoted in Schoeck, *Envy*, 213.
26. Ruth Leys, *Trauma: A Genealogy* (Chicago: University of Chicago Press, 2000), 8–9.
27. John Mowitt, "Trauma Envy," *Cultural Critique* 46 (2000): 272–297.

28. Scheler, *Ressentiment*, 20.

29. Cited in Schoeck, *Envy*, 211.

30. Mowitt also argues that "trauma envy" can explain the theoretical attempts of various thinkers to universalize the experience of trauma for the sake of political and moral legitimacy, a trend he critiques especially in the work of such post-Lacanian thinkers as Slavoj Žižek. If the "angry white men" have felt alienated and excluded by the identity politics of recent years, many now clearly feel that they are *finally* being represented—in the presidential election of Donald Trump in the United States, for example, or in the various populist movements that have been gaining traction across Europe. The toxic tone of much of this discourse has been dismaying, to say the least, for the liberal mindset, though if recognition of one's wound is the name of the game, then what else should "we" have expected?

31. Eva Hoffman, *After Such Knowledge: Memory, History, and the Legacy of the Holocaust* (New York: PublicAffairs, 2004), 68.

32. Cynthia Ozick, "Envy; or Yiddish in America" (1969), in *A Cynthia Ozick Reader*, ed. Elaine Kauvar (Bloomington: Indiana University Press, 1996), 20–63.

33. Ibid., 21.

34. Cynthia Ozick, "America: Toward Yavneh" (1970), in *What Is Jewish Literature?*, ed. Hana-Wirth Nesher (Philadelphia: Jewish Publication Society, 1994), 20–35.

35. Nor is she alone. "I ought to say a little something about my vocabulary," remarks Lenny Bruce in his autobiographical *How to Talk Dirty and Influence People* (1965). "My conversation, spoken and written, is usually flavored with the jargon of the hipster, the argot of the underworld, and Yiddish"; quoted in Frank Kofsky, *Lenny Bruce: The Comedian as Social Critic and Secular Moralist* (New York: Monad, 1974), 72.

THREE

Guilt

1. Emmanuel Levinas, "Cities of Refuge," in *Beyond the Verse: Talmudic Readings and Lectures*, trans. Gary Mole (London: Athlone, 1994), 34–52, 40.

2. Denise Duffield-Thomas, *Get Rich, Lucky Bitch! Release Your Money Blocks and Live a First Class Life* (CreateSpace Independent Publishing Platform, 2013), passim.

3. Adam Phillips, "Against Self-Criticism," *London Review of Books* 37, no. 5 (2015): 13–16.

4. Samuel Beckett, incidentally, was one of the few writers whom Adorno considered up to the task of "interrupting Auschwitz," to cite the title of Josh Cohen's masterly booklength investigation of thought and art responding to Adorno's figuring of the postwar state of aporia. See Josh Cohen, *Interrupting Auschwitz: Art, Religion, Philosophy* (London: Continuum, 2003).

5. Theodor Adorno, *Negative Dialectics* (1966), trans. E. B. Ashton (London: Routledge and Kegan Paul, 1990), 362–363.

6. Ruth Leys, *From Guilt to Shame: Auschwitz and After* (Princeton: Princeton University Press, 2007), 30; page numbers included parenthetically in text for quotations in subsequent paragraphs.

7. This type of thinking could also explain certain applications of the policy of "trigger warnings" currently taking over university campuses in the United States and elsewhere. A trigger warning is generally issued on the premise that students may find their traumas triggered by unprepared exposure to certain expressions or ideas.

8. Adorno, *Negative Dialectics*, 365.

9. The most powerful registration of this idea may be expressed by the fact that Adorno was not alone in making this shift. Especially among Jewish thinkers/ survivors, one can find the same moral turn: it's there, for instance, in the philosopher Emil Fackenheim's decree not to hand Hitler posthumous victories, in the historian Yehuda Bauer's commandment not to be a bystander, and in the ethical thinker Emmanuel Levinas's reiteration of the commandment not to murder.

10. Saul Bellow, *Mr. Sammler's Planet* (St. Ives: Penguin Classics, 2007), 1; page numbers included parenthetically in text for quotations in subsequent paragraphs.

11. Rebecca Solnit, "Men Explain Things to Me," *Guernica*, August 20, 2012, https://www.guernicamag.com/daily/rebecca-solnit-men-explain-things-to-me/, accessed February 3, 2016.

12. Both are the case, of course, and while theory can sometimes be used by those seeking to allay their own guilt to retain certain privileges, it can also, even when employed subversively, become a source of destructive criticism (see "Envy") and an animating factor in certain forms of conspiracy thinking (see "Paranoia"), all of which motivations tend to be both unconscious and bound to the individual rather than amounting to any kind of argument against critical theory per se.

13. Evidently Eisen's war experiences have likewise taught him how to be a man of action, yet his understanding of intervention differs from Sammler's. In his view, when you hit a man you must really hit him, otherwise he will kill you: "We both fought in the war. You were a Partisan. You had a gun. So don't you know?" (242). Given Eisen's nationality, it is hard not also to read his

character as a sideswipe on Bellow's part regarding the logic underpinning Israel's excessive use of force.

14. Stanley Crouch, Introduction, to Bellow, *Mr. Sammler's Planet*, vii–xxiv, xxiii–xxiv.

15. Julie Ellison, "A Short History of Liberal Guilt," *Critical Inquiry* 22, no. 2 (1996): 344–371.

16. Ellison also suspects her guilt to be the hither side of the hysteria more commonly found among her conservative political opponents whose "moral panic" (wherein some *other* is the guilty one threatening the moral fabric of society) is coupled with a view of the liberal as engaging in a self-defeating ethos lacking in moral backbone.

17. Jon Ronson, *So You've Been Publicly Shamed* (London: Picador, 2015), 184.

18. Michel Laub, *Diary of the Fall*, trans. Margaret Jull Costa (London: Harvill Secker, 2014), n.p.

19. And mightn't this too, at least in *certain* circumstances, render one's personal hatred a passion potentially more suited to the difficult work of (re)building a social contract and social justice than exhortations to act always on the basis of an abstract humanitarian love?

20. Though a very contemporary reappraisal of shame, this move also has its roots in early-twentieth-century existentialism. For Sartre, for example, "shame" is an authenticating emotion: "not a feeling of being this or that guilty object but in general of being *an* object; that is, of *recognizing myself* in this degraded, fixed, and dependent being which I am for the Other. Shame is the feeling of an *original fall*, not because of the fact that I may have committed this or that particular fault but simply that I have 'fallen' into the world . . . and . . . I need the mediation of the Other in order to be what I am"; Ellison, "Short History of Liberal Guilt," 357. To be reduced to an object—a thing—is the price we must pay to gain entry into the social world. Indeed, since, as social creatures, we thereby depend on others for not only our identities but our *subjectivities,* our shame reflects the unremitting condition of our powerlessness. While guilt confers on the subject a sense of agency, then, even if only within their fantasies, shame implies a complete lack of it. In shame we feel ourselves entirely determined by the gaze of a disapproving world. It's for this reason that Sartre believes shame has greater existential authenticity than guilt. Thus while he elsewhere makes of the modern assimilating Jew an exemplar of bad faith (it's the "perpetual obligation to prove that he is French that puts the Jew in [this inauthentic] situation of guilt"), the inauthentic Jew *can* become authentic, for Sartre, if he accepts, rather than hides, the mandatory nature of his shame. Unlike the inauthentic Jew continually striving to meet an ideal he has not set for himself and can never achieve, the "authentic Jew" derives a

certain pride from his existential humiliation. Jean-Paul Sartre, *Anti-Semite and Jew*, trans. George Becker (1945; New York: Schocken, 1995), 87.

21. Giorgio Agamben, *Remnants of Auschwitz: The Witness and the Archive*, trans. Daniel Heller-Roazen (New York: Zone, 1999), 96–99.

22. Lisa Appignanesi, *Losing the Dead: A Family Memoir* (London: Vintage, 2000), 21.

23. Bellow, *Mr. Sammler's Planet*, 260.

FOUR
Over the Top

1. Renata Salecl, *(Per)versions of Love and Hate* (London: Verso, 2000), 63.

2. Stanley Cavell, *A Pitch of Philosophy: Autobiographical Exercises* (Cambridge: Harvard University Press, 1994), 132.

3. Sandra Gilbert and Susan Gubar, *The Madwoman in the Attic: The Woman Writer and the Nineteenth-Century Literary Imagination* (1979; New Haven: Yale University Press, 1984), xi.

4. Ibid., 360.

5. Gayatri Chakravorty Spivak, "Three Women's Texts and a Critique of Imperialism," *Critical Inquiry* 12, no. 1 (1985): 243–261, 251.

6. Ibid., 249.

7. Cavell, *Pitch of Philosophy*, 132.

8. Quoted ibid., 169.

9. Salecl, *(Per)versions of Love and Hate*, 63.

10. Ibid.

11. Cavell, *Pitch of Philosophy*, 136.

12. The same may be suggested of Freud with regard to his female hysterics. For while hysteria, in turn-of-the-century Vienna, was a diagnosis that referred primarily to a patient's doubt about herself and the questioning of her own sexual identity, this sexual anxiety was associated not only with those anatomically in possession of the hysteric's notoriously "wandering womb" but with those "wandering Jews," such as circumcised Jewish men, the other reputed hysterics of the age.

13. Debra Shostak, "Roth and Gender," in *The Cambridge Companion to Philip Roth*, ed. Timothy Parrish (Cambridge: Cambridge University Press, 2007), 111–126, 113, 115. And what is masturbation if not the semiconscious splitting of the subject into self and other and the erotic compulsion to overcome that split through the achievement of blissful self-satisfaction/unity? And what is a compulsion if not evidence that any such "achievement" can be only momentary, never lasting?

14. Josh Cohen, "Roth's Doubles," ibid., 82–93, 88.
15. Philip Roth, *The Facts: A Novelist's Autobiography* (New York: Penguin, 1988), 112; Hana Wirth-Nesher, "Roth's Autobiographical Writings," in Parrish, *Cambridge Companion*, 158–172, 162.
16. Claire Bloom, *Leaving a Doll's House: A Memoir* (St. Ives: Virago, 1996), 158.
17. David Plante, *Difficult Women: A Memoir of Three: Jean Rhys, Sonia Orwell, Germaine Greer* (Aylesbury: Futura, 1984), 49.
18. David Plante, "Conversations with Philip," *New York Times*, January 1, 1984, https://www.nytimes.com/books/98/10/11/specials/roth-conversations.html, accessed February 2, 2016.
19. Philip Roth, *The Ghost Writer* (London: Jonathan Cape, 1979), 180.
20. Salecl, *(Per)versions of Love and Hate*, 71–72.
21. John Berryman, "The Development of Anne Frank," in *Freedom of the Poet* (New York: Farrar, Straus and Giroux, 1976), Kindle edition. My citations from Anne Frank's *Diary* are borrowed from this source, except where otherwise indicated.
22. Roth, *Ghost Writer*, 102; page numbers included parenthetically in text for quotations in subsequent paragraphs.
23. Notably, Roth's depiction of the writer as a stubborn egoist and recluse appeared in this novel before his adaptation of Plante's Rhys account.
24. Philip Roth, *Reading Myself and Others* (London: Vintage, 2007), 143.
25. Emily Budick, "The Haunted House of Fiction: Ghost Writing the Holocaust," *Common Knowledge* 5, no. 2 (1996): 120–135, 129.
26. Ibid., 129.
27. Roth, *Reading Myself and Others*, 144.
28. Shalom Auslander, *Hope: A Tragedy* (London: Picador, 2012), 88.
29. Shalom Auslander in conversation with Bidisha about *Hope: A Tragedy*, London, *Jewish Book Week*, February 26, 2012, http://www.jewishbookweek.com/past-events/1068/video.
30. Auslander, *Hope*, 113.
31. Philip Roth, *Exit Ghost* (London: Vintage, 2007), 181, 193.
32. Philip Roth, *The Anatomy Lesson* (New York: Farrar, Straus and Giroux, 1983), 41.
33. Raymond Carver, "What We Talk About When We Talk About Love," in *What We Talk About When We Talk About Love* (London: Vintage, 2009), 114–129, 114.
34. Nathan Englander, "What We Talk About When We Talk About Anne Frank," in *What We Talk About When We Talk About Anne Frank* (London: Weidenfeld and Nicolson, 2012), 1–32, 3; page numbers included parenthetically in text for quotations in subsequent paragraphs.

35. Carver, "What We Talk About," 120.
36. Ibid., 115.
37. Salecl, *(Per)versions of Love and Hate*, 62, 63.
38. Philip Roth, *Operation Shylock: A Confession* (New York: Simon and Schuster, 1993), 124; Roth, *Reading Myself and Others*, 46.
39. Philip Roth, *I Married a Communist* (London: Vintage, 2005), 152.
40. Ibid., 157–158; italics mine.
41. Roth, *Reading Myself and Others*, 140.
42. Roth, *Ghost Writer*, 72.
43. Budick, "The Haunted House of Fiction," 126–127.
44. Roth, *Ghost Writer*, 169.
45. Rachel Feldhay Brenner, "Writing Herself Against History: Anne Frank's Self-Portrait as Young Artist," *Modern Judaism* 16, no. 2 (1996): 105–134, 119.
46. Berryman, "The Development of Anne Frank." "On Robben Island," Nelson Mandela recalled, "some of us read Anne Frank's Diary. We derived much encouragement from it. It kept our spirits high and reinforced our confidence in the invincibility of the cause of freedom and justice."
47. Berryman notes that Anne also effectively becomes her own psychoanalyst once she has split herself in two, which has the effect of unblocking previously repressed traumatic memories and dreams and freeing up their associated affects. These are experiences in the annexe that Anne confides only to Kitty.
48. Anne Frank, *The Diary of a Young Girl*, ed. Otto Frank and Mirjam Pressler (St. Ives: Puffin, 2002), 336.
49. Think too of a figure such as Emily Dickinson, retiring in the last part of her life to a reclusive existence in her own version of the attic. Not that you necessarily need to be a writer to identify with the figuring of hell as other people.

FIVE

Paranoia

1. E.g., Thomas Docherty's thesis *On Modern Authority* (Sussex: Harvester, 1987) characterizes "the modern critic" as one whose stance is always oppositional (244).
2. Stephen Frosh, "Relationality in a Time of Surveillance: Narcissism, Melancholia, Paranoia," *Subjectivity*, December 2015, 1–16, 13.
3. Jonathan Kay, *Among the Truthers: A Journey Through America's Growing Conspiracist Underground* (London: HarperCollins, 2011); page numbers included parenthetically in text for quotations in subsequent paragraphs.
4. See also, e.g., David Aaronovitch's *Voodoo Histories*, Mark Fenster's *Conspiracy Theories: Secrecy and Power in American Culture*, Peter Knight's *Conspiracy*

Culture: From Kennedy to the X Files, and Chip Berlet's *Right-Wing Populism in America*, among others.

5. Richard Hofstadter, "The Paranoid Style in American Politics," in *The Paranoid Style in American Politics* (London: Vintage, 2008), 3–40.
6. Ibid., 37.
7. Ibid., 32.
8. Sigmund Freud, *The Schreber Case*, trans. Andrew Webber (St. Ives: Penguin, 2002), 66.
9. Jean Baudrillard, *The Gulf War Did Not Take Place* (1991), trans. Paul Patton (Bloomington: Indiana University Press, 1995).
10. Rita Felski, "Suspicious Minds," *Poetics Today* 32, no. 2 (2011): 215–334.
11. Paul Ricoeur, *Freud and Interpretation: An Essay on Philosophy*, trans. Denis Savage (New Haven: Yale University Press, 1970), 33.
12. Adam Phillips, *Terrors and Experts* (London: Faber, 1995), 102.
13. Michael Keefer, "The Dreamer's Path: Descartes and the Sixteenth Century," *Renaissance Quarterly* 49, no. 1 (1996): 30–76, 30; page numbers included parenthetically in text for quotations in subsequent paragraphs.
14. Freud, *The Schreber Case*, 59, 60; italics in original.
15. In his 1979 speech announcing his candidacy for the American presidency, Ronald Reagan quoted this statement, to which he appended the addendum "We still have that power." A beginner, as we said in the previous chapter, is someone who, having repressed his (nonsymbolizable) past, begins over and over and over again. And one can find countless other examples, from Trump's promise to "make America great again" to certain (though not all) formulations of the Brexit promise to "take back power" and thus reestablish national independence by withdrawing the United Kingdom's membership from the European Union.
16. Harold Bloom, *Omens of the Millennium: The Gnosis of Angels, Dreams, and Resurrection* (New York: Riverhead, 1996), 27, 235, 183.
17. Darian Leader, *What Is Madness?* (London: Penguin, 2011), 92.
18. Ibid., 80.
19. Ibid., 81.
20. Slavoj Žižek, "Welcome to the Desert of the Real," *The Symptom*, online journal for lacan.com, issue 2 (2002), http://www.lacan.com/desertsymf.htm, accessed November, 5, 2013.
21. Robert Eaglestone, *Postmodernism and Holocaust Denial* (London: Icon, 2001), 6, 10.
22. David Aaronovitch, *Voodoo Histories: How Conspiracy Theory Has Shaped Modern History* (London: Vintage, 2010), 8.
23. Ibid., 331, 335.

24. One can conjecture too that Birthers may well have personal stories that in some ways shadow the national amnesia their ideology is enacting. This would seem to be the case for Birther in Chief Donald Trump, for instance, whose father's family came to America as immigrants from Germany, but who falsely claims in his book *The Art of the Deal* that his father was of Swedish origin.

25. Woody Allen and Marshall Brickman, *Annie Hall* (1979) (Kent: Faber and Faber, 2000), 9–10.

26. Eve Kosofsky Sedgwick, "Paranoid Reading and Reparative Reading; or You're So Paranoid, Your Probably Think This Introduction Is About You," in *Novel Gazing: Queer Readings in Fiction* (Durham, N.C.: Duke University Press, 1997), 1–40.

27. Kay, *Among the Truthers*, 289.

28. James Lasdun, *Give Me Everything You Have: On Being Stalked* (London: Jonathan Cape, 2013), 124; page numbers included parenthetically in text for quotations in subsequent paragraphs.

29. W. B. Yeats, "The Second Coming" (1921), in *W. B. Yeats* (St. Ives: Everyman, 1997), 39–40, 39.

30. Quoted in Sander Gilman, *Jewish Self-Hatred: Anti-Semitism and the Hidden Language of the Jews* (Baltimore: Johns Hopkins University Press, 1986), 209–210.

31. *The Horned Man* (2002), a satire of the paranoid managerial culture regarding sexual relations on campus.

32. Phillips, *Terrors and Experts*, 1.

33. Teju Cole, *Open City* (London: Faber, 2011), 103–105; page numbers included parenthetically in text for quotations in subsequent paragraphs.

34. Ironically, were Farouk to read Walter Benjamin's great essay "The Task of the Translator," he'd discover that, for Benjamin, the language of translation can be even more refined and original than its source material.

35. Lasdun, *Give Me Everything You Have*, 196.

36. Allen and Brickman, *Annie Hall*, 21, 22.

37. Quoted in Žižek, "Welcome to the Desert of the Real."

SIX

Mother Love

1. Dan Greenburg, *How to Be a Jewish Mother* (Los Angeles: Price/Stern/Sloan, 1964), 13.

2. Adrienne Rich, *Of Woman Born: Motherhood as Experience and Institution* (New York: Norton, 1986), 206.

3. Though often more guilty still are those women who, whether by choice or circumstance, do not have children and thus find themselves subject to an unwritten law that deems socially acceptable an open questioning of the childless. In such cases the suspicion lurks that a woman without children must be either a pitiable victim of something or cold-heartedly guilty of something— for what kind of woman *wouldn't* be a mother?

4. Rich, *Of Woman Born*, 21, 22.

5. Though Rich acknowledges the pleasures as well as pains of motherhood, the radical feminist critique may have made the choice to have children an even harder one for certain women. "I don't think people have to have children" remarks American feminist author Grace Paley in one interview, before wryly adding, "My daughter has no children. I wanted to. It was easy for me because there was no political opposition to it"; *Conversations with Grace Paley*, ed. Gerard Bach and Blaine Hall (Jackson: University Press of Mississippi, 1997), 266.

6. Jacqueline Rose, "Mothers," *London Review of Books* 36, no. 12 (2014): 17–22, http://www.lrb.co.uk/v36/n12/jacqueline-rose/mothers, accessed February, 2, 2016.

7. Rachel Cusk, *A Life's Work: On Becoming A Mother* (London: Faber, 2001), 13.

8. Julia Kristeva, "Stabat Mater," in *The Kristeva Reader*, ed. Toril Moi (New York: Columbia University Press, 1986), 160–186, 179, 178, 185.

9. D. W. Winnicott, *Babies and Their Mothers* (London: Merloyd Lawrence, 1987), 6.

10. Alison Bechdel, *Are You My Mother? A Comic Drama* (London: Jonathan Cape, 2012), 35–36.

11. Rich, *Of Woman Born*, 11.

12. Daisy Waugh, *I Don't Know Why She Bothers: Guilt-Free Motherhood for Thoroughly Modern Women* (London: Phoenix, 2013).

13. Lisa Appignanesi, *All About Love: Anatomy of an Unruly Emotion* (London: Virago, 2011), 277.

14. Rich, *Of Woman Born*, 284.

15. Elisabeth Badinter, *The Conflict: How Modern Motherhood Undermines the Status of Women* (New York: Metropolitan, 2010), 55.

16. Marcel Proust, *The Way by Swann's* (1913), trans. Lydia Davis (London: Penguin, 2002), 39.

17. Ibid., 41.

18. Breaking the glass in the Jewish marriage ceremony recalls the destruction of the temple in Jerusalem and the exile that followed.

19. Evelyne Bloch-Dano, *Madame Proust: A Biography*, trans. Alice Kaplan (Chicago: University of Chicago Press, 2007), 198.

20. Rich, *Of Woman Born*, 202.

21. Susan Douglas and Meredith Michaels, *The Mommy Myth: The Idealization of Motherhood and How It Has Undermined All Women* (New York: Simon and Schuster, 2004). Douglas and Michaels take specific aim at the political manipulation of American "moms" into the good and the bad. The bad mother—the welfare mom, the single mom, the black mom—is a figure whose media appearances are so scandalous that she thereby also helps to demarcate what a good mom is: white, middle-class, married, concerned with nothing but her children. Yet Douglas and Michaels also acknowledge the extent to which public scrutiny of *any* mother will ultimately find its way to *all* mothers, such that the "good mom" may likewise find herself, in the wake of increased surveillance, a figure not to be trusted because never really *good-enough*.

22. Eva Hoffman, *Lost in Translation: Life in a New Language* (London: Minerva, 1989), 265, 264.

23. Joyce Antler, *You Never Call! You Never Write! A History of the Jewish Mother* (Oxford: Oxford University Press, 2007), 2.

24. Quoted ibid., 84.

25. The psychologist Erik Erikson once free-associated about the Jewish mother as someone who keeps her children deliberately needy by manipulating them through food, reminding them of their weakness and poor chances of survival without her care, and always showing too much of her overabundant breasts while simultaneously complaining that her children have destroyed her body, leaving her in ruins, like the Jewish temple. Erikson's own interpretation of his free association was that the mother's unconscious communication to her child was that (s)he should understand the Jews' diasporic history as a lesson in why the proper home for Jews is the body of their mothers, a place from which it would be unwise and unsafe to stray too far.

26. Sociological studies have also shown that even Jews with no religious affiliation or learning tend to associate their identities with their mothers, as opposed to their fathers.

27. Michael Wood, "Proust and His Mother," *London Review of Books* 34, no. 6 (2012), 5–10, http://www.lrb.co.uk/v34/n06/michael-wood/proust-and-his-mother, accessed February 3, 2016.

28. Allen Ginsberg, "Kaddish" (1959), in *Selected Poems, 1947–1995* (St. Ives: Penguin, 1996), 93–111, 104.

29. Philip Roth, *Portnoy's Complaint* (1969; London: Vintage, 1995), 2; page numbers included parenthetically in text for quotations in subsequent paragraphs.

30. Quoted in Antler, *You Never Call!* 233.

31. Quoted in Bernard Avishai, *Promiscuous:* Portnoy's Complaint *and Our Doomed Pursuit of Happiness* (New Haven: Yale University Press, 2012), 14–15.

32. Thus for me the most poignant joke in the book is the "family joke" that "when I was a tiny child I turned from the window out of which I was watching a snowstorm, and hopefully asked, 'Momma, do we believe in winter?'" (34). There she is again, lurking like a deity behind everything. Notably, Freud interpreted jokes as simultaneously revealing and disguising forbidden thoughts/feelings that can usually be traced back to the incest taboo (a point I introduce somewhat hesitantly, given that Roth's novel is clearly also a joke *on* psychoanalysis and a send-up of its interpretative orthodoxies).

33. Sigmund Freud, "Three Essays on the Theory of Sexuality" (1905), in *The Essentials of Psycho-Analysis,* trans. James Strachey (St. Ives: Penguin, 1991), 277–375, 358.

34. Which may be why many prominent psychoanalysts after Freud (Klein, Winnicott, Lacan, Bowlby, Laplanche) turned attention to both the mother's neuroses and those of the child in relation to her.

35. Estela Welldon, *Mother, Madonna, Whore: The Idealization and Denigration of Motherhood* (London: Karnac, 1988), 72.

36. The mother thus parallels Henry Roth's immigrant father "acting out" his thwarted ambitions and aggressions at home. Though Welldon's book was at first banned by feminist bookstores for its putative mother-blaming, by acknowledging the mother's victimization as someone who has been disempowered and isolated by her maternal status, the book has a strongly feminist point to make while also reaffirming the basic insight that the victimized will often go on to victimize.

37. Jean Laplanche, *Essays on Otherness,* trans. John Fletcher (Oxford: Routledge, 1999), 79–80, 259.

38. Darian Leader, *What Is Madness?* (London: Penguin, 2011), 62.

39. A related but complicating idea we get from Winnicott (which Welldon echoes) pertains to what happens when mothering goes wrong. In such cases the child has been turned into the mother and the mother the child, but now it's because the child has been unconsciously *required* by the mother to be the mother's own carer to make up for a deficiency in care in the mother's own childhood.

40. Winnicott, *Babies and Their Mothers,* 31–32.

41. Ibid., 32.

42. Rich, *Of Woman Born,* 203.

43. Appignanesi, *Losing the Dead,* 51, 33.

44. Quoted in Rich, *Of Woman Born,* 235.

45. Grace Paley, "A Conversation with My Father" (1974), in *The Collected Stories* (London: Virago, 1999), 237–243, 242.
46. Stephen Frosh, *Hate and the "Jewish Science": Anti-Semitism, Nazism, and Psychoanalysis* (Basingstoke: Palgrave, 2005), 201.
47. Ibid., 215.

SEVEN

Affected

1. Elaine Scarry, *The Body in Pain: The Making and Unmaking of the World* (Oxford: Oxford University Press, 1985), 5; page numbers included parenthetically in text for quotations in subsequent paragraphs.
2. Intellectuals caught up in the enthusiasm of a particular idea, theory, or system of thinking are by no means immune to this structure of stupidity. I never feel more stupid than when I come away from company and, in a sort of opposite but analogous movement to *l'esprit de l'escalier*, rather than admonishing myself because "I might have said *that*," I admonish myself because "*they* might have had something to say!"
3. Emmanuel Levinas, *Otherwise Than Being or Beyond Essence*, trans. Alphonso Lingis (The Hague: Martinus Nijhoff, 1981), 195.
4. There can be no more sublime example of the true import of art and the imagination when it comes to (re)making an unmade world than Hisham Matar's *The Return: Fathers, Sons, and the Land in Between* (London: Viking, 2016). In what must surely count as one of the most extraordinary repudiations of stupidity and insentience of the kind we've been describing, Matar's searingly compassionate memoir works to undo the logic underpinning a regime of power (Gaddafi's Libya) whose literal use of torture against specific bodies also incites the psychic torture afflicting all others.
5. Eva Hoffman, *Lost in Translation: Life in a New Language* (London: Minerva, 1989), 124.
6. Darian Leader, *What Is Madness?* (London: Penguin, 2011), 158–159.
7. Barbara Taylor, *The Last Asylum: A Memoir of Madness in Our Times* (St. Ives: Hamish Hamilton, 2014), 92.
8. Josef Breuer and Sigmund Freud, *Studies in Hysteria* (1895), trans. and ed. James Strachey (London: Hogarth, 1957), 255; italics in original.
9. D. W. Winnicott, *The Maturational Processes and the Facilitating Environment* (London: Hogarth, 1979), 150.
10. Tillie Olsen, "I Stand Here Ironing" (1954), in *Tell Me a Riddle and Yonnondio* (London: Virago, 1980), 13–25, 16; page numbers included parenthetically in text for quotations in subsequent paragraphs.

11. While generally for Winnicott it's the mother's fault when a false self develops, he allows that often that's because the father has failed to assume his parental role. In Olsen's story, though, the false self afflicts only the child subject to the most deprivation. The same narrator, we hear, has since had four more psychologically robust children; changing circumstances along with the changing nature of the person can make of the same woman a completely different mother to each of her progeny.

12. I am alluding to one of Sylvia Plath's mothers on a maternity ward in "Three Women: A Poem for Three Voices," (1962), in *The Collected Poems*, ed. Ted Hughes (London: Faber, 1981), 176–187: "It is a terrible thing / To be so open: it is as if my heart / Put on a face and walked into the world" (185).

13. Quoted in Rei Terada, *Feeling in Theory: Emotion after the "Death of the Subject"* (Cambridge: Harvard University Press, 2001), 37.

14. Josh Cohen, *The Private Life: Why We Remain in the Dark* (London: Granta, 2013), 143.

15. Terada, *Feeling in Theory*, 37, 38.

16. Quoted in Cohen, *The Private Life*, 143, 142.

17. Friedrich Nietzsche, *Beyond Good and Evil: Prelude to a Philosophy of the Future* (1886), trans. Judith Norman (New York: Cambridge University Press, 2002), §§169, 40.

18. Friedrich Nietzsche, *The Gay Science* (1882), trans. Thomas Common (New York: Dover, 2006), 178.

19. Ibid., 179.

20. Sander Gilman, "Salome, Syphilis, Sarah Bernhardt, and the Modern Jewess," in *The Jew in the Text: Modernity and the Construction of Identity* (London: Thames and Hudson, 1995), 97–120, 102. Gilman cites the Weimar anthropologist Hans F. K. Günther's citation of the seventeenth-century orientalist Johann Jakob Shudt: the Jew's language "betrays a Jew the moment he opens his mouth" (101).

21. Quoted by Elana Shapiro, "Sarah Bernhardt," *Jewish Women's Archive*, http://jwa.org/encyclopedia/article/bernhardt-sarah, accessed February 4, 2016.

22. When Marilyn Monroe (whose "illegitimate" origins, unknown father, and extraordinary glamour and self-mythologizing somewhat resemble Bernhardt's) converted to Judaism for the sake of her marriage to Arthur Miller, she claimed to already feel an affinity to Jews as "the orphans of the world." As Jacqueline Rose notes (*Women in Dark Times* [London: Bloomsbury, 2014]), "the Hollywood moguls were predominantly East European Jews trying to escape their past," hence the irony that, while they adored Marilyn for appearing "as un-Jewish as she could possibly be" (106), she would seek to affirm the darker sides animating her bottle blonde and would continually rage at her

reputation—largely based on the scripts men had written for her, whose parts she played to perfection—as a hapless, innocent ingénue. But while many of the men in her life seemed to have been unable to tell the difference between the actress and the roles she performed, Lisa Appignanesi fascinatingly describes (*Mad, Bad, and Sad: A History of Women and the Mind Doctors from 1800 to the Present* [London: Virago, 2008]) how Marilyn's psychoanalyst, recognizing the link between her ego deficiency and her craft, sought to draw on her acting talents as a source of ego empowerment: "He tried to keep her working. She tried, too. It needed time. But time ran out" (388).

23. Elaine Aston, "Studies in Hysteria: Actress and Courtesan, Sarah Bernhardt and Mrs Patrick Campbell," in *The Cambridge Companion to the Actress*, ed. Maggie Gale and John Stokes (Cambridge: Cambridge University Press, 2007), 253–371, 258.

24. The concept of "difficulty" is worth thinking about in this context, both in terms of the intellectual difficulty that has arisen in response to such subjects (hermeneutic approaches like psychoanalysis), and with regard to the highly gendered stereotype of the prima donna, the "difficult actress."

25. Stanley Cavell, *Contesting Tears: The Hollywood Melodrama of the Unknown Woman* (Chicago: University of Chicago Press, 1996), 123.

26. Ibid., 127.

27. Davis's performance is the precedent for Gena Rowlands's equally compelling performance in John Cassavetes's *Opening Night* (1977).

28. Another example of a brilliantly camp inversion of a normative cliché—"They don't make women like that anymore"—occurs when a conservative father is impressed by the performance of old-fashioned femininity he meets in someone who he does not realize is a drag queen toward the end of *The Birdcage* (1996). The script's invitation to the film audience to notice what gets both admitted and denied in his use of the word "make" (a neat demonstration of Judith Butler's theory of sex and gender) is another instance, like drag itself, of the way in which repetition not only confirms but subverts that which it repeats—here by drawing attention to the role of repetition at the origin of *all* identity formations and not simply those that recognize themselves as performative.

29. Cavell, *Contesting Tears*, 129, 134.

30. Cf. Norma Desmond, Gloria Swanson's aging actress dreaming of a comeback predicated on a time-reversing beauty regime in *Sunset Boulevard*.

Acknowledgments

Many thanks to my superb editor at Yale University Press, Jennifer Banks, for her brilliant notes, and for making the editing process such a warm as well as enlightening one. Thanks too to Heather Gold at Yale for her patience and assistance, and to Dan Heaton at Yale for his diligence, intelligence, and welcome humor.

Thanks to my family and Josh's family for their unstinting support, and for invaluable guidance, encouragement, and inspiration, thanks in particular to Adam Andrusier, Lisa Appignanesi, Chloe Aridjis, Toni B, Josh Baum, Josh Cohen, Yehoshua Engelman, Andrew Franklin, Stephen Frosh, David Glover, Clare Hanson, Nikita Lalwani, Nicky Marsh, Diana Matar, Hisham Matar, Peter Middleton, Chris Oakley, Renata Salecl, Poppy Sebag-Montefiore, Zadie Smith, John Stokes, Nicole Taylor, and Ruti Teitel. Thanks also to the University of Southampton's School of Humanities for granting me leave to complete this work.

I have no idea what John Forrester, of blessed memory, would have felt about this book, although I'm quite sure he'd have found plenty to disagree with in it—it's another reason why I miss him.

As for you, Josh, I shook my fist at each of your notes before I saw that you were (nearly) always right. There would have been no book without you, but more important, no life outside the book without you, Manny, Isaiah . . . our lovely shared world.

Index

Index

Index